DELIVERANCE DAY

DELIVERANCE DAY

The Last Hours at Dachau

MICHAEL SELZER

J. B. LIPPINCOTT COMPANY

PHILADELPHIA AND NEW YORK

Printed in the United States of America

The photograph on page 85 was taken by Max Koot; the photograph on page 93, by the author. All the others are U.S. Army photographs.

U.S. Library of Congress Cataloging in Publication Data

Selzer, Michael.
  Deliverance day.

  Bibliography: p.
  1. Dachau (Concentration camp)   2. Holocaust,
Jewish (1939–1945)   I. Title.
D805.G3S446   940.54'72'43   78-17099
ISBN-0-397-01230-6

Dedicated to
Gertrud Mainzer and to
Walter J. Fellenz
and Carel Steensma
and the tens of thousands
who were with them
on the final day

Contents

Illustrations

Author's Note and Acknowledgments

Philosophers tell us that facts are ambiguous, and historians, that they are elusive. Dachau concentration camp was liberated by units of the United States Army on April 29, 1945. For the thirty thousand prisoners who were liberated, this event was obviously of enormous significance. But it was also highly ambiguous in the sense that they—and indeed humanity for generations to come—must remain scarred by the terrible reality that Dachau represents.

The facts connected with the liberation of Dachau are unusually elusive. Heinrich Himmler, Hitler's crony and the chief of the SS, had issued orders a week or so earlier for the murder of the entire prison population of Dachau. Although the first steps in this diabolical scheme were taken, in the end Himmler's orders were not carried out. Why? We do not really know.

Two units from different divisions of the United States Army claim—independently of one another—to have liberated the concentration camp. It seems impossible to determine what the actual facts are in this connection.

Other uncertainties remain. The history of the camp published by the Comité International de Dachau includes the minutes of the meeting of the International Prisoners' Committee held in the *Jourhaus* on the evening of April 29, the first meeting to take place after the liberation. According to these minutes, the commander of the American forces in the camp gave orders for the execution of two of the most notorious *Kapos,* or trusties. The officer has denied to me that he ever issued such an order. Two further reports were repeated to me by a number of prisoners and have found their way into numerous books about Dachau. One is that the United States Army was notified of the desperate plight of the camp by three prisoners who managed to escape from one of the deportees' columns and found their way to American headquarters. The other is that in

11

the night after the liberation of the camp, the Waffen-SS mounted a counteroffensive aimed at regaining control of Dachau. My judgment is that neither of these reports is correct, and that their reiteration by survivors of the camp only points to the extent to which rumors were rife at the time and later were transformed into legend.

The events of this day still arouse extraordinarily deep feelings in most of the people whom I interviewed for this book. In some instances individuals acted during the course of the day in ways that were uncharacteristic of them—a circumstance which I think can quite legitimately be attributed to the gruesome sights that greeted the American liberators and to the uncontrollable outpouring of feelings that their arrival caused among the prisoners. Almost without exception, the men and women whom I interviewed spoke to me with what I believe was great (but in many instances, unwitting) candor. I was, and remain, deeply touched, not only by what they told me but by their willingness to share their intimate experiences (many of which they had never recounted before) with a total stranger. I felt honored by their openness, but also burdened by a great responsibility toward them.

In consequence, I have experienced a conflict between the obligation to report what I learned and the obligation to respect the trust that so many people, American veterans and Dachau survivors alike, placed in me. This conflict has been exacerbated by the impossibility of ascertaining the facts connected with many important episodes during that day. But the confidences I feel particularly concerned about relate not so much to facts as to my perception of what those facts meant to—and said about—the people who reported them to me.

I have tried to reconcile these difficulties by offering what is essentially a reconstruction of the liberation of Dachau. Out of concern for the people whose story this is, quite a few of whom wish to remain anonymous, I have disguised names and certain facts that could help to disclose the identities of all principal characters except for the two German officers in Niederdorf and Rabbi Eichhorn. In two further respects the personalities depicted here are not, in conventional terms, historically authentic. I not only paid attention to the facts reported to me during the interviews but, as indicated above, to the personalities of the men and women whom I was questioning, and to their impressions (not all of which seemed to me unbiased) of other people connected with the day's drama. These impressions gave me some insight, I believe, into how these individuals responded to the events of the day, and that insight has strongly colored my telling of their reports.

Furthermore, largely for technical reasons, which include a desire not to introduce too many people into this account, and to incorporate anecdotes that are of interest in themselves but do not justify the inclusion of their authors as separate characters, I have conflated a number of accounts given to me. That is to say, while much of an individual's story, as told in this book, belongs to the (pseudonymous) person in connection with whom it is told, there are in almost every instance additional episodes, experiences, and insights that do not belong to that individual but to another, who makes no independent appearance in this book. An additional justification for this somewhat unorthodox procedure is that it further helps to protect the anonymity of the subjects. And so, even where his friends may know the real identity of, for example, Colonel James Frazer or Lieutenant William Jackson, or of Joachim Berenson or Ernst Kroll, they should not assume that every aspect depicted pertains to the real-life person.

I have not interviewed all the individuals who appear in this book. The German officers at Niederdorf are an obvious instance where I have tried, as best I could, to reconstruct an entire episode. To my great regret, I was unable to find the opportunity to interview one of the most remarkable men connected with the story of Dachau, the ingenious and heroic figure who appears here under the name of Commander James Connally. For some of the episodes connected with his depiction I have relied on Vincent Brome's *The Way Back;* for the others, I have attempted a reconstruction that is based in part on testimony of people I interviewed, and in part on my own attempts at filling in the gaps. For reports of the fate of the Hungarian marquis George Pallavicini, and for certain other data, I have found highly informative the memoirs of a former inmate, Nerin Gun, *The Day of the Americans*. Much invaluable background material about the camp and its liberation is contained in Paul Berben's *Dachau 1933–45,* published by the Comité International de Dachau.

Numerous people have contributed in important ways to research for this book. First and foremost, of course, were the dozens of men and women, former inmates of Dachau and United States Army veterans, who shared their recollections with me. As mentioned above, a number of these have asked not to be mentioned by name, and rather than distinguish between these and others, I hope all will consider themselves included in the dedication of this book. In addition to allowing themselves to be interviewed, several of these people gave me written accounts of their experiences, on which I have drawn extensively here, photographs, and other mementos.

The Institute for Holocaust Studies was of great assistance in the initial stages of this project, and I would particularly like to thank Mrs. Stella Wieseltier, of its staff, and its director, my colleague Professor Yaffa Eliach, of Brooklyn College. Invaluable help also came from officials of the General Archives Division of the United States National Archives; from the Still Photo Record Center of the U.S. Department of Defense; from the New York Public Library; from Barbara Distel, director of the library at the Dachau Concentration Camp Memorial Site; and from Dr. Horst of the Deutscher Wetterdienst in Offenbach.

This book was written during a time of personal crisis for the author—a consequence of human foibles not totally unlike those which ultimately created the Third Reich (cf. *New York Times,* January 9, 1977; *New Republic,* March 12, 1977). This circumstance shaped the writing of this book in a number of ways, among them by delaying its completion by a year. The friendship and support of many people have enabled me to surmount this crisis. This is not the place to thank by name those people who proved particularly staunch and steadfast supporters. In direct connection with the completion of this book, however, I would like to acknowledge the patient encouragement of Gene Young and Beatrice Rosenfeld, my editors at Lippincott. And among the many contributions of my wife, Miriam, *eshet chayil,* have been hours spent in research and translation connected with this book—and the infinite delight of our first child, Sarah Esther, born shortly after I began the first draft of the manuscript.

New York City
February 1978

Attienti ben, che per cotali scale
conviensi dipartir da tanto male.

—*Inferno,* XXXIV, 83–85

1. Clara's Story

If you passed Clara Greenbaum on the street, you would at once guess the setting of her life today—that she lives on New York's Upper East Side; earns her living as a professional (she's a gynecologist); spends her weekends, whenever she can get away, in a cottage overlooking Long Island Sound; subscribes to good causes; and is much sought after, on account of her vivacity and intelligence, as a guest at dinner parties. You might well sense, even on first getting to know her, an area of impenetrable inner reserve—tension, even—which you would probably attribute to the conflict between her onerous professional obligations, which she takes seriously, and her impulse to lead a vigorous and diversified life. It is unlikely that you would guess the real source of her reserve lies in experiences she underwent thirty-five years ago when, as an active member of the Maquis, the French underground, she was arrested by the Nazis. Her husband, on an assignment for the Maquis at the time of her arrest, escaped a German dragnet. But Clara and her two small children were sent to a satellite camp of Bergen-Belsen, the infamous concentration camp in Germany, and were incarcerated there for twenty-seven months.

Clara told me her story while I was finishing work on a book about the personalities of the Nazi leaders. I had fascinating materials to work with, but at times my encounter with the vicious and sordid minds of these men aroused almost unbearably intense feelings of horror and depression in me. By chance, it was at one such time that I spoke with Clara. Far from giving me the sympathy I sought, she

17

said, "I don't know why anyone would want to write such a book. I can tell you for sure, I wouldn't want to read it."

Her hostility and dogmatism stunned me, and all I could say by way of reply was a sarcastic "Gee, thanks, Clara."

She was not at all apologetic. "Look," she persisted firmly. "That's all over with. Thirty years or more. Enough's enough. Everyone and his uncle is writing books about the Nazis, and I think the whole interest in that is sick. Let's just bury the past and get on with our lives."

Her voice was quite shrill now, and was making me curious rather than angry. "That's not at all like you, Clara," I said slowly. "I know you don't believe that we should simply forget history."

"We shouldn't be obsessed by it, either," she replied.

"I agree. But I don't think that's relevant in this instance."

We argued back and forth for a few minutes. Finally I came out and asked her directly. "What's bothering you about this book, Clara, *really?*"

"If you have time someday, I'll tell you."

"No, Clara. Tell me now."

"Why not?" She shrugged her shoulders. "I often get depressed, you know, and all sorts of images from the camp come back to me. And when that happens, I try to force myself to remember the last day."

"The last day?" I asked.

"Yes, the day we were liberated." It was then she told me the following story:

The last day began just like all the others had. From the very beginning, I had made a point of inventing all sorts of little rituals and procedures for myself—to give me something to hang on to, if you know what I mean. So each morning I would wake up by myself a few minutes before the *Block Kapo* [the trusty prisoner in charge of the barrack] came in. The first thing I would do was to check that my children were all right. I was the *de facto* nanny of our *Block*. If a child's mother died, or if there were too many women to allow a mother and child to share a bunk, the children would be moved to the bunk behind me, where my own children slept. Sometimes—it depended on how long a child stayed alive—there would be as many as five in that bunk.

Ordinarily I would wake them up so that they wouldn't be frightened out of their sleep by the *Kapo*'s shouts and curses when she came in. But sometimes they looked so angelic in their sleep that I just couldn't bear to wake them up and force them back into this terrible world in which we were living. It was selfish of me, I know, and I would feel guilty about this afterward, when they were woken up so brutally by the *Kapo* and I would have to comfort them.

But today was such a day. I let them sleep. Anyway, the next thing I would do every morning was to see whether the two women in my bunk were alive. If they were, good for them. But if they were dead, I wanted to be the first to know it. Every prisoner had some little treasures hidden away in her clothes—a small scrap of food, or something—and so I would try always to be the first to search a corpse for that. Also, if you needed an extra pair of socks, or a scarf, or whatever, just about your only chance of getting it was from a dead body.

This day, both women were alive. Having made this little inspection, I lay back again and updated my calendar. It wasn't a written calendar, or anything like that, and I never really knew what day of the week it was for sure, or the date. What I counted was the number of days I had been in the camp. I just kept the figure in my head, and would update it every morning, first thing. During the course of the day I would repeat the number to myself so that I wouldn't get it wrong. I'm amazed that this system was entirely accurate. When I got out of the camp, one of the first things I did was to check my number against a calendar. It was right on the nose: eight hundred and eighteen days!

Then I always had another few moments before the *Kapo* came. Those were the best moments of the day for me. I was awake, almost no one else was, it was quiet and peaceful, and I felt that I had some semblance of privacy. Oddly enough, that was one of the things I missed most in the camp. Not food or anything like that, though of course I missed those, but privacy. You could never be by yourself.

So I lay back, my head resting on my hands, and enjoyed the luxury of the moment—the luxury of being oblivious to other people, sounds, thoughts, feelings. . . .

The next thing I knew, I was waking up again! I had fallen asleep! This had never happened to me before, and I was in a terrible panic. For a second I thought I must be dead, because there seemed no other way of accounting for the fact that I hadn't been woken by the *Kapo*. And then an even worse panic. I must have missed the morning *Appell,* the roll call. The punishments for that were terrible. In fact, in our camp you could be hanged for less. I looked for my children. They were still sleeping. I thought, Oh, my God. They, too, are going to be punished. . . .

And then I realized that I was not alone. In fact, no one had left the room, even though, as I could soon tell, most people were awake. Some women were standing in the aisle between the bunks; just standing there, not walking. Some were sitting on the edges of the lowest tier of bunks. A few were whispering to each other. Everything I saw and felt told me that something terrible had happened. The *Kapo* had not come in to wake us up!

You must understand. In that world, when something went wrong, it was something which had gone wrong for the prisoners and would bring some new torture, some new indignity, to us. Not to the guards, of course. Their destiny was infinitely above us, so much so that they were like gods. Really, they *were* our gods, since everything in our lives, just about, and certainly our lives, seemed to be at their whim.

And so when we weren't woken up, there could be only one explanation. They were playing some fiendish new game with us, like a cat does with a mouse that is in its power. What kind of game? Who could tell. Perhaps they did not wake us up so that we would all miss the *Appell,* and then all of us would be punished for having missed it.

We stayed in the *Block* for a long time. I've no idea how long, perhaps it was two or three hours. Certainly they were the longest hours in my life. No, I didn't think of anything. My mind was completely blank; you see, I was so utterly frightened. Every second might be the one in which the doors would suddenly be kicked open, with guards and dogs and guns firing. I was quite rigid with fear; my fists were clenched. Goodness only knows how fast my heart was beating. And you couldn't hear a sound.

Suddenly there was a horrible scream, which almost made me die with fright. This is it, I told myself, and I turned around for my children. Can you imagine: the poor babies, they were also awake and were lying petrified like the rest of us!

But it wasn't the guards. One of the women had gone crazy and was running toward the door, stumbling over other women, colliding with the posts that held up the roof. For a short moment, as she opened the door, the room was filled with light, and then she slammed it behind her and was gone, though we could still hear her screams, growing fainter every moment.

We all knew that in the next second a shot would ring out: a guard would have had his morning target practice. In fact, there was no sound, and in a while we could no longer hear the woman. But that didn't mean anything, of course.

Now the silence in the barracks was, if anything, even more complete. If you can imagine being even more frightened than utterly and totally frightened, that's how I was feeling now.

After some time—again I can't tell you how long it was—there was again a sudden flood of light, but this time without any noise. I came to my senses sufficiently to realize that one of the women had crept out of the building to see what was going on.

But she, too, did not come back. And once again the complete terror, the complete silence.

And a third time the door opened. Another woman, as silently as the one before, had gone out to see what was happening.

This one, though, left the door open behind her, and it was as if the light that now filled the room also cleared my head a little. I was still horribly frightened, but I noticed that I was also very thirsty. From my childhood—oh, God, how far away that was!—I remembered the doves Noah sent out. The first two did not return, but the third did. But I put that out of my head as quickly as I could. In the concentration camp you cannot have hope. Only determination.

Presently I could hear some soft noises, as if there was some movement going on near the door. I lifted myself up on one elbow, and because we were on the third tier, I had a good view, even though we were at the far end of the room. I could see that a lot of women had gathered by the door and that some of them were taking that brave, dangerous step into the outside.

Hannah and Adam, my two children, climbed over and lay next to me, their faces buried into my body. I could feel how heavily they were breathing. You know, this was the first time in two years that they had come to me in my bunk. Once, at the very beginning, they had tried to, but the women in my bunk screamed at them that there was no room, and they never tried that again. I'll never forget how, that time, after she finished screaming at the children, one of the women muttered to herself, but audibly, "What the hell are kids doing in this place, anyway?"

But now the women didn't object. They knew, as everyone did by now, that something special was going on. Soon, most of the bunks between us and the door had been emptied. I climbed down, and the children did the same. It wasn't a question of *deciding* to climb down. You did what everyone else did in the camp as a matter of course. There were hardly any matters on which you decided yourself.

Hannah and Adam each held one of my hands; the other children were close behind. We walked to the door. I should say that my mind was still quite blank, that I was still horribly frightened. But I remember that all the bunks we passed were empty. This was unusual. Ordinarily, when we got up in the morning for *Appell,* there were always at least eight or nine people who didn't get up. They were dead, or just about dead. Or else, even if they still had strength in their bones, they had lost their will to live, and just would not get up. Sometimes we talked to them, tried to revive some desire in them to live, but at other times we had no help to give them, and they would be shot.

We were outside. It was a pleasant day, slightly overcast, but bright. Again I felt an awful thirst, and I thought that I would stop at a certain place near the *Appellplatz,* the assembly ground, where there was a ditch, and see if I could get some water there, since it had rained the previous night.

I was in luck. Not too many people knew of this place since it was just underneath the overhang of a building—between the piers on which the building stood, I should say—and although the water was muddy, it was fresh.

We moved to the *Appellplatz.* For the first time, I became aware of hundreds, thousands of other people. From all sides they were converging on the *Appellplatz.* Many were walking by themselves, but there were also some who were leaning on friends or relatives, and others who were crawling on all fours, too weak to walk. Some of these had collapsed before reaching the *Appellplatz* and just lay on the ground, dying. You didn't stop to pick them up—what was the use?—and it was a common enough sight in the camp to see people die, so I didn't think too much about it then. But I often think about them now, the people who died on that last day, and I wish that I had stopped at least once to help one of them, if only by saying a few comforting words to them.

The first thing that struck me when we were on the *Appellplatz* was that prisoners were standing or sitting or lying all over the square in an entirely disorderly way. I had never seen that before. Ordinarily, the *Appellplatz* was a place to avoid, since it was completely open, and just that fact made you feel insecure—you felt exposed there. But it wasn't only that. It was, objectively, a dangerous place because it was where the particularly sadistic guards would hang around when they were bored. They would wait there until a prisoner who for some reason had to cross the *Appellplatz*—perhaps someone who did not have the strength to walk around it, or who simply didn't know better—appeared, and then they would find some way of amusing themselves with her. So the only times one would go to the *Appellplatz* was for the morning or evening roll calls, or when they made us all turn out to watch a hanging, which wasn't always during the regular *Appell*. Of all places in the camp, I hated that spot the most.

This was the first time I had seen the *Appellplatz* looking so *untidy,* and that bothered me. It's almost as if I wanted there to be carefully drawn up lines of prisoners, rather than people just scattered all over the place. I can't tell you how disorienting that was, and of course it only increased my anxiety.

I had already noticed by this time that there were no guards around. I'd even looked up at the guard towers and seen that they were empty. You might think that this would have astonished me and delighted me. But it didn't. I'd noticed that the guards had disappeared and thought no more about it.

How can I explain this? Somehow, deep inside me, I had always known that I was going to survive, and that one day I would be liberated. You can put this down to wishful thinking, but the fact is that I always, *always* was completely certain of this. Which is not to say that I didn't also have many moments when I thought I was about to be killed. Nowadays I tend to think that the main thing that gave me this confidence was that I knew my children would not survive without me. Hannah was seven, and Adam just under four. There was no way I was going to let them die.

But today didn't seem like the day of liberation, because I was much too frightened. The fact that the guards had disappeared did not seem to me to mean anything more than that they had disappeared. It was almost incidental to the entire situation. One reason for this, I'm sure, is that we were very much less organized than most camps, where prisoners had ways of learning about what was going on in the outside world and so on. We had none of that, no real way of knowing how the war was going, or that the Allies were close at hand.

But apart from that, there was never a moment in the camp

when you weren't aware of the guards. During the day, you saw
them everywhere, but even if there were periods when there were no
guards in sight, you had their image printed on your retina, and you
could not escape them. At night you dreamed about them. They
were, in that horrible sense I described earlier, our gods, and we
were like primitive savages who are votaries of a fearsome and evil
deity. So the fact that the guards weren't visible today did not mean
that they were not there. They were. In our minds. And believe me,
for many people they still are there to this day.

Perhaps this will help you understand what I'm saying. We were
on the *Appellplatz* for a very long time. I'm sure it must have been at
least four hours. During that time, so far as I'm aware, all of us
stayed *on* the *Appellplatz*. No one approached the gates, or even the
firing line—the line near the fence where any prisoner would be shot
on sight. Isn't that odd? Today we could have walked to the firing
line without danger, for there were no guards on the towers. In fact,
we could have walked to the gates, opened them, and simply left the
camp. Physically, a number of us had sufficient strength to manage
all that. But the fact is that we didn't, because the guards were *inside*
us. To such an extent, we had become slaves.

What were my thoughts during this time? I hardly had any, to
tell you the truth. The main thing is that I was overwhelmingly anxious. And that also has to do with being a slave. You see, we were
now in a sense free, because the guards weren't there. Part of me
thought that they might return at any moment, doing horrible things
to us; but another part of me slowly began to realize that they had
left, that this was all over—one way or another.

Can you imagine, in any way, how terrifying this freedom was
to us? There was so little in our lives. Almost everything we had, the
structure of our lives, came from the guards. In some ways it was irrelevant to us how brutal they were. In fact, their very brutality
pointed up their power, their command of the situation, and in a per-
verted way reassured us, who had absolutely no power, no control
over our lives, that the world had not disintegrated *completely*. Think
of the savages with their evil god. They hate their god and are desperately frightened of him. But what happens when that god van-
ishes, taking with him every last semblance of structure that is left in
their lives? Taking away the purpose of their lives, almost, which has
up to now been primarily to confirm the god's divine nature?

I know this sounds sick to you. But did you suppose for a

moment that it was only our bodies that were imprisoned—and tortured?

So I stood there on the *Appellplatz* for hour after hour. I was like a zombie, mentally and physically immobile. Adam stood with me, holding my hand still. Hannah and the two orphans sat close by me. They were too weak to stand, though none of them was seriously ill.

Just beyond the wire fence, on the north side, there were some fields, which were plowed and cultivated all the time we were there. An old farmer, I remember, and a horse which looked even older than he. Quite often, I used to take the children to where we could look at those fields. I wanted them to see crops grow, and to see an animal other than the big dogs that the guards had. And sometimes I used to point toward the fields and the world outside, and I would say *"Freiheit,"* freedom. It was one of the first words Adam learned; I planned it that way.

Just behind the fields there were some hills. They were low hills, with scrub growing on them and one or two trees. Today, when we were standing on the *Appellplatz,* we faced in the direction of these fields and hills.

Hours went by in more or less complete silence. But then I heard a noise. It was a metallic, clanking noise—not at all unpleasant, though at first it wasn't very loud—and it seemed to be coming from behind the hilltop.

Just about everyone else heard the sound, too, and people began perking up. In a moment I saw something move. At first I could not make out what it was. All I could see was a long, thin rod, as it seemed to be, pointing up to the sky; and I remember wondering how that rod fitted the sound we were hearing.

Then the rod tilted down a bit, and I could see that it was in fact the gun barrel of a tank. For a few moments I could not see or hear anything more because of the commotion on the *Appellplatz*.

So, then, this really was the end. They were going to mow us down with their machine guns. Or perhaps they were going to drive over us, crushing our bodies under the tracks of their tanks.

As people do in such situations, we all huddled close together. I gave Hannah my hand, pulled her to her feet. The two orphans managed to get to their feet, too, and then the five of us joined in the rush—well, it was hardly a rush, no one had the strength for that, but you know what I mean—to the center of the *Appellplatz*.

We might all have gotten ourselves killed in the crush if the panic had lasted for more than a few moments. But then, at the same instant almost, people throughout the crowd noticed that the second tank, immediately behind the first one, was flying a Union Jack—the British flag—from its turret.

We moved back a step or two. Those who had been sitting down before the first tank appeared sat down again. Motionless, once more, and in complete silence, we watched.

More and more tanks followed. I don't remember how many there were, but there were a lot of them. And behind them were trucks, military trucks, with their canvas tops down so that we could see the soldiers sitting on benches.

The first tank came up to the main gate and then stopped. The rest of the convoy halted behind it. Then the hatch on top of the front tank opened and a man stuck his head out of it. He did not move and seemed just to stare in our direction.

Then the tank began moving off to the side, stopped for a moment, and then started up again, creeping slowly past the fence of the camp. The other vehicles followed. None of the other tanks opened their hatches, but in the trucks all the soldiers had got to their feet, holding onto the rails above their heads, and were looking in our direction.

The entire convoy began circling the camp. A while later—it may have been about twenty minutes, because they weren't moving very fast—the first tank reached the main gate again. It stopped. The man was still looking out of the turret hatch. The entire convoy stopped behind the front tank. And then, a moment later, the front tank began moving again.

All this time I had been feeling completely blank, but now I was seized by the fear that the British were going to leave us. A moment later, though, I saw that that wasn't the case, and I felt relieved. The British were not leaving. They were circling the camp for a second time! It was one of the strangest things I've ever seen. Certainly it was one of the strangest things of that day.

So they went around a second time, and when they had done that, they drew up in a neat formation in front of the gates. First the tanks, then the trucks turned off their motors. It was again completely quiet.

All this was taking place perhaps thirty or forty yards away from me, so I could see quite well. The troops climbed down from their trucks; all the tank hatches were opened, and more soldiers, wearing funny helmets, climbed down from the tanks.

There were no orders given—I know that because I could have heard. As a group, but a rather disorderly one—they weren't in any kind of military formation—the soldiers came up to the wire. One of them threw something at the fence—I suppose to see whether it was electrified—and when they saw it wasn't, they came up closer still. I would say that there were as many as four or five hundred men. I remember noticing that they didn't appear particularly different from Germans. I don't know what I expected them to look like.

They came up to the fence, as I say, and just stood there looking at us. I couldn't understand their behavior at all. I thought about that; in fact, it had suddenly become very important to me to try to figure out why they were just standing there and staring at us. But I couldn't make any sense of that. I wish I could tell you how eerie that was, watching them staring at us in that inexplicable way.

But then I saw one of the soldiers double over and throw up. Soon another was doing the same, and then another. And then I understood. They were looking at us in disgust. We repelled them. We made them feel like vomiting!

A deep despair came over me. I felt like Adam when he first knew he was naked: horribly and irremediably ashamed. I looked around me and saw myself and the other prisoners for the first time through the eyes of those British soldiers. We *were* disgusting to look at, no doubt about it. It's odd, isn't it, that I had never really realized that before?

A moment after that first soldier threw up, a strange thing happened among the prisoners. We began turning away from them. We turned our backs to them. We didn't want them to see us. And if, a short while before, we had in some dim kind of way wanted them to come into the camp, now, very strongly, we wanted them to stay where they were—or else to go away. We were so ashamed of ourselves.

Our movement triggered off something among the soldiers. Some of them, at one end of the crowd, began throwing things over the fence, and from the scrambling among the prisoners I assumed that it was food. The soldiers nearest the gate, however, formed into some kind of rank and stood at attention. I saw that one of the soldiers in the strange helmets had climbed into a tank. He started up its engine and then rammed through the camp gate. When it was down, he backed over it, crushing it into little fragments, and then parked the tank in its former spot.

By now all the other soldiers had formed into ranks and, at an officer's command, marched into the camp. We were liberated.

Do you think that that really meant very much to me? Sure, in some distant way it did, but only in a very distant way. I took my children by the hand and walked away from the soldiers, who suddenly had become very busy and purposeful. I had no idea what they were going to do—what does one do when one liberates a concentration camp?—and all I knew was that I didn't want to have any of them look at me in that way again. I wanted to walk off and hide behind one of the barracks.

It was Hannah who wouldn't let me. I took a few steps away from the soldiers when I heard a sound that was terrible, but which I could not at first identify, even though in some strange and remote way it seemed familiar to me. Then I understood. My daughter was crying. She was crying! Do you understand? For the first time in three years this little child was crying! She was crying so hard that I thought her thin little body would collapse under the force of its convulsions.

She had known that you cannot allow your feelings in the concentration camp. But she also knew, now, that she could cry, that it was safe to cry.

And she was crying for her father, the father she had last seen when she was four years old and could scarcely remember. I tell you, I have never in my life heard any cry of pain like that child's. Adam, too, was crying, but he was crying like a small child, as he had done a few times before in the camp, and I don't think he really had a sense of what was going on. But Hannah's cry was different. It was the most tragic wail I have known. If it was like anything, it was like the mourning of an old woman.

And I? I followed my daughter's example; I learned from her. I sat down with her, and for several minutes I screamed. Oh, I screamed so loudly. I can't tell you exactly why I did it, but I had to so badly, and while I screamed I pounded my fists into the ground, and finally I collapsed sobbing, lying on the ground with my face down.

I felt strong hands lift up my shoulders and bring me to my feet. I was hardly aware of it, I was still sobbing so much. But the touch of those hands opened up something else in me, and I knew that what

I wanted more than anything else in the world was for someone to put his arms around me, and hold me, and rock me slightly while I cried on his chest. And that's what he did, and what I did, and after a while I realized that like little Hannah I, too, was screaming for my father.

All this time the soldier was holding me, and my head was buried in his chest, not only because I wanted it to be there but also because I couldn't bear the thought of him looking at me with that look of disgust. And when I stopped crying I turned away from him so that he couldn't see me, and took my children, and walked off. I've often wondered who that soldier was, what he looked like.

The British were slowly getting the camp organized. There was a huge table set up, and soldiers were dishing out soup for us. But when we got to the table I realized that the soup was too rich, and I asked for some water, with which I diluted it. But even then it was more than our stomachs could bear, and it made us feel a bit sick. But other prisoners, who had gulped the soup down without diluting it, were in much worse shape, and I think that some even died from it.

The rest of the day passed by quickly enough. I was exhausted, the children even more so, but the British would not let us go to sleep until after a short interrogation in which they asked for our names, names of relatives, that kind of thing, for a Red Cross list. That night I slept in a bunk alone with my two children. And that was the end of my last day as a prisoner.

It was nearly a month before Clara left the camp. The other women chafed at the delay, restless, even though the war was not yet over, to return to their homes, and to their families if they were still alive. But that sense of shame persisted in Clara and made the outside world seem frightening. Perhaps, as she now thinks, it was only her vanity. The days passed, however, and gradually her fear of returning to the world, and to her husband (who, she now learned, had managed to find his way to Canada), began to dissipate. One day word came through that passage had been arranged for her and the children to Montreal. A bus arrived to carry them, and others who were headed for North America, to Cherbourg.

Not many miles from the camp, little Adam suddenly began to jump up and down excitedly in his seat, shouting with joy—for the first time in his life, Clara realized—and pointing at a horse grazing in its paddock. "Look, look!" he exclaimed. "Look, there's a *Freiheit!*"

Clara's story was the inspiration for this book. How had other people experienced their liberation from the concentration camps, I wanted to know, and what does the memory of that mean to them now? And the soldiers who liberated them: what had it felt like for them?

Clara, I believe, intended her story of the last day at Bergen-Belsen as an object lesson. Study the Nazis, she seemed to say, but don't forget that we have been freed from them. And that is also why I have wanted to write this book. It is a necessary reminder that scars are, after all, healed wounds. The memory of the pain lingers, of course, and the wound itself flares up from time to time; but these facts are not necessarily more real than the equally unassailable fact that there has been a healing.

I selected Dachau rather than Bergen-Belsen as the camp whose liberation I would write about for a number of reasons. It was the first Nazi concentration camp, and its existence coincides almost exactly with that of the Third Reich. We tend to think of concentration camps as places where Jews were murdered. Thousands of Jews indeed were murdered at Dachau and its satellite camps, but except for short periods of time, Dachau's Jewish population was always only a small proportion of the prisoners there. The tragedy of the concentration camps has a distinctively Jewish element, but I think it important to counteract the notion that the camps, as such, were a distinctively Jewish tragedy. Dachau, with its heterogeneous population, seemed an obvious choice for this reason, too. Moreover, unlike most of the other camps, Dachau was in an American zone of combat, and thus was liberated by the United States Army. In the aftermath of the Vietnamese War, it seems important to me to recall, both for American soldiers and for well-intentioned critics of America's military might, the role of the United States armed forces as the world's principal defense against tyranny and inhumanity. Many of the people I interviewed for this book, former inmates of Dachau, know full well that it was the United States Army that saved their lives. They acknowledge that fact with abiding gratitude; and we would, perhaps, do well to ponder it for ourselves.

On March 21, 1933, the police commissioner of Munich—a certain Heinrich Himmler—announced the establishment of a "concentration camp," the first such institution of the kind under the new regime. This camp for enemies of National Socialism, Himmler warned, would be run *ohne jede Rücksicht auf kleinliche Bedenken,* "without any concern for petty scruples."

The phrase must have sounded ominous, but it is unlikely whether even Himmler and his associates could have imagined, at the outset, the bestialities that would be perpetrated in this camp as a matter of course during the next twelve years. Statistics about the camp are incomplete—many of the records were destroyed in the closing days of the war by SS officials trying to cover their tracks—and no one can any longer say with confidence how many men and women were imprisoned there. The most authoritative guesses place the number at about a quarter of a million persons. Of these, perhaps between forty and fifty thousand met their deaths at Dachau.

For all its infamy, then, Dachau was a relatively small camp. (By contrast, over ten times as many people were *killed* at Auschwitz as passed through Dachau. The gas chambers and crematoria at Auschwitz could "process" in a little over forty-eight hours the number of people murdered in Dachau over twelve years.) Nor, in many respects, was Dachau a typical concentration camp. Despite its high mortality rate, it was not regarded as an extermination center. A small gas chamber was constructed late in 1942; and although it certainly was put to use (despite some reports), its full capacity seems never to have been utilized. The crematorium, too, was relatively small. Working at full speed, it could dispose of, at the most, 350 bodies a day. Dachau's population, moreover, appears to have been far more heterogeneous than in most camps. Except in the days following the *Kristallnacht* on November 9, 1938, when over 13,000 German Jews were brought there, and during the last months of the war when prisoners were shipped to Dachau from other concentration camps that were close to the lines of the advancing Allied armies, the Jewish population of Dachau was never large. During the prewar

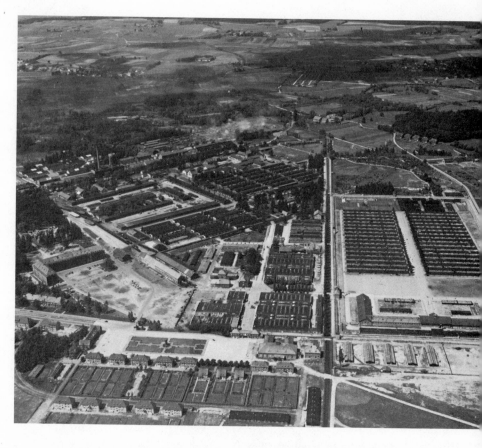

Aerial view of Dachau concentration camp, taken by a U.S. Army Signal Corps photographer on May 27, 1945.

At right, the Lagerstrasse (*prison street*), *running from north to south, divides the two rows of prison barracks. To the south is the* Appellplatz (*assembly place*), *flanked by the huge U-shaped storage facility. Straddling the fence along the prison compound's perimeter are guard towers and the* Jourhaus, *entrance to the camp east of the* Appellplatz.

At center, in the cluster of trees outside the northwestern corner of the prison compound, is the camp's gas chamber and crematorium. Most of the buildings nearby are workshops and laboratories that were run by slave labor.

At bottom can be seen the large courtyards and buildings that housed SS officers and enlisted men.

years, the inmates were mainly political prisoners (most of whom were either Social Democrats or Communists); professional criminals who had served out their prison terms but were considered "too dangerous" to be permitted to return to civilian society; Jehovah's Witnesses; homosexuals; and "antisocials"—beggars, vagrants, hawkers, and others who were offensive to those in power. Once the war began, their numbers were swelled by resistance fighters from the countries occupied by Nazi forces; hostages picked at random from the populations of those countries in reprisal for acts of resistance; anti-Nazi Germans who had emigrated before the war to countries that were subjugated after 1940 by Hitler; veterans of the Republican forces in the Spanish Civil War; Gypsies; and certain other special categories, such as Polish Catholic priests, Wehrmacht officers and men suspected of political and other offenses, and a small group of distinguished prisoners, among them Pastor Martin Niemöller, former Austrian chancellor Kurt von Schuschnigg, former French premier Léon Blum, and Italian general Sante Garibaldi.

To a greater degree than any other concentration camp, therefore, Dachau's population mirrored the diversity of elements against whom Hitler and his movement felt an implacable hatred. In a number of other respects, too, Dachau has a special place in the history of Nazism. Situated only ten miles away from Munich—the birthplace of Nazism—Dachau was the first concentration camp and thus the prototype of organized Nazi terror. It served as a training academy for concentration camp administrators, the most infamous of whom was Rudolf Hoess, the commandant of Auschwitz.

Perhaps it was the affection due to Dachau, in the minds of the SS, as their alma mater, that explains the odd practice of sending to the camp, even from very far away, men and women destined for execution. On several occasions groups of Russian officers—prisoners of war—were brought to Dachau for execution; early in the war, fifty-five "suspect" Polish intellectuals were taken there for the same purpose. Enzo Sereni, the heroic Palestinian who had been parachuted into Italy to assist the resistance there, was also brought to Dachau for execution; as were four women, captured British agents, one of whom was the exotic spy Noorunisa Inayat Khan. Most of these victims were executed in Dachau's famous shooting pit, adjoining the crematorium. Others were hanged from nooses conveniently placed next to the ovens in the crematorium. And there is irrefutable evidence that others were thrown alive and conscious into the ovens. . . .

The little town of Dachau, dominated by an ancient castle, is a picture of traditional Bavarian rural charm. The camp itself was built around the remains of an explosives factory, erected during World War I and then dismantled in accordance with the disarmament program forced on Germany under the terms of the Versailles Treaty by her conquerors. In this sense the sordid effect that Dachau represents is linked, literally in concrete, to the factors that in substantial measure were its cause—the self-righteous revanchism, and the greed, of the World War I Allies.

So much began, therefore, at Dachau. And that makes it appropriate for us to watch it come to an end there, too.

2. April 29: Before Dawn

Lieutenant Bill Jackson, the I Company commander, woke up feeling cold and damp. He cursed, realizing that the trench he had dug around his small pup tent had not been deep enough to protect him from the rain that had been falling through the night. But his first concern was to ensure that his carbine, tucked under the blanket with him, had remained dry. The condom he kept around its muzzle was still securely in place. The rest of the weapon felt dry to the touch, though he would have to check it out completely by daylight. This done, he now could permit himself the satisfaction of remembering that he had a pair of dry socks in his knapsack. He would put them on when he got up. He checked the time. It was not quite four o'clock, about an hour before the company would have to be roused.

Slowly, he recognized that it was not only the cold and damp that was making him uncomfortable. There was something else, and at first he could not figure out what it was. Abruptly, he realized it was a dream that had awakened him. But try as he might, he could not remember it. He felt—uneasy.

Jackson was a Cheyenne Indian who relied unhesitatingly on his gut reactions in combat, while his men made sense of new situations by comparing them to what was already familiar. He knew that the only way they were going to end this war was by killing every Kraut who stood in their way. His men, on the other hand, half believed Smitty, the company philosopher, when he said, "Hell, all you gotta do is show up at the peace table with a coupla dozen cartons of Chesterfields and you can walk off with half of Europe."

35

Jackson attributed this to their arrogance as white men rather than to their provincialism, for the small towns and even the farms from which they came seemed to him quite sophisticated when measured against life on the reservation in Oklahoma on which he had grown up. Jackson did not think that his men were any the less effective soldiers because of their way of looking at the strange world in which they found themselves. True, there was not very much in common between Main Street in Ames, Iowa, or a ranch in Colorado, and the battlefields on which Jackson and his men had been fighting their way across Europe for the past twenty-one months. But Jackson did not believe that a soldier who failed to recognize this difference was a poor soldier as a result. He knew full well the extent to which a mighty army imposes its own reality on an environment. It was quite understandable to him, therefore, that his men should look at the world around them through their hometown eyes. Their carbines could eliminate many a discrepancy. For himself, however, it was no less natural that he should perceive situations in terms of the messages—good, bad; fast, slow; dangerous, safe; and so on—that mysteriously arrived from somewhere inside himself to resolve his uncertainties. His men could insist, and in fact they did insist, that Coke tasted better than French wine. That made Coke better than French wine—or, certainly, more valuable. What mattered for Jackson, on the other hand, was whether he was thirsty or not, and, if so, whether there was any liquid around to slake his thirst.

The feeling of uneasiness with which he had awakened persisted. Jackson tried to reassure himself by thinking back on the exhilarating events of the past two weeks. Nine days ago—it was April 20, Hitler's birthday—Nuremberg had fallen after bitter fighting. The parade down the streets of the shattered city, with massed formations from the two divisions, had been one of the proudest moments in his life. And the next day had begun that incredible race toward the Danube, in which they rushed through town after town at a speed exceeded only by the retreating Heinies. "Hell, you wouldn't know there was a war on," the GIs joked to each other, "if there weren't so many damned men in uniform around." The end of the war seemed only days away. On the twenty-fifth, the battalion reached the Danube at a place called Marxheim. The men agreed that if this spot was Karl Marx's home he deserved nothing better, because the Danube seemed like a muddy little river, and anything but blue and beautiful.

And now here they were, scarcely twenty miles from Munich. They would get there today. Or, at the very latest, tomorrow. It was obvious that, except for scattered pockets of resistance, the Krauts had no more fight left in them. The war was as good as over.

Why, then, was he so scared? It came as a shock to him to realize that *that* was what his uneasiness was all about. He was scared. But why? Why *now?* Was this the day that a bullet with his name on it would come tearing into him from a sniper's rifle? In these last days of the war nothing terrified Jackson and the other men in his outfit more than the thought that with victory so close at hand they would not be alive to see it. The fear—and the sadness—that each of them felt now when one of their number was killed reminded him of the company's first days in combat, way back in Sicily.

But Jackson knew that he would live to see Munich, and the end of the war. Last year the men had had as their slogan "Win the war in '44." Jackson had been skeptical. This year their slogan had become "Stay alive in '45." In his guts, Jackson was certain that he would.

All the same, he was scared. He did not know what the day held in store for him. But he would be more careful today than he had ever been before in his life. He tried to fall asleep again, and was just dozing off when a GI opened the tent flap and said that Colonel Wiley wanted to see him right away.

"C'mon in, Bill," Colonel Robert Wiley said genially in response to Jackson's salute. As always, Wiley looked vigorous and poised for action, an impression he conveyed even after hours of grueling combat. Burly, taciturn, and enormously efficient, Wiley enjoyed the trust and respect of his men despite the fact that he was not ten years older than the youngest of them. They knew he would never try to win glory at their expense and they thought of him as a soldier's soldier.

Wiley, on the other hand, did not consider himself a fighter but as someone responsible for looking after his men and getting the job done. An engineering student with an outstanding record, he had excelled brilliantly in the officers' training program he had entered two days after Pearl Harbor. His precision and thoroughness as an officer led to a succession of rapid promotions that was unusual even in wartime. And it was these qualities, too, that spurred him on to the heroism that had already brought him the Distinguished Service Cross and the Silver Star. What others might consider acts of bravery were for him primarily instances in which he did what had to be done. Not that he was callous, for he felt every casualty in his battalion as deeply as any man, but the wider purposes of the war seemed to him distant and unreal. He was not fighting to rid the world of the Nazi specter so much as to overcome the enemy who stood in the way of the objectives he, Wiley, had been assigned.

"Orders came from General Payne an hour back," he explained to Jackson. "Delivered by messenger, no less. Here, read them."

At that moment Henry Stock, the colonel's German interpreter, arrived.

"I was just telling Lieutenant Jackson about our orders for today, Stock. Let me read them out loud. Save time that way."

He cleared his throat, lit up a Camel, and began reading: " 'Tomorrow the notorious concentration camp at Dachau will be in our zone of action. You will assign elements of the Third Battalion to seize it. When the camp is captured, nothing is to be disturbed. International commissions will move in to investigate conditions when fighting ceases.' That's what it says. There's other stuff about moving on to Munich, but that's not what interests me right now, except that I'm going to have to keep K and L companies on the front, the advance to Munich, which means that you're going to be taking your boys to this camp here, Bill," Wiley said, pointing at the map.

Jackson went over to study it closely. After a few moments he looked up. "Heck, Colonel, the perimeter here is about three miles. I'm going to secure that with *one* company?"

"That's one thing has me worried, Bill, but there's just no alternative. I guess they know what they're doing up at division headquarters. So that's what it's going to have to be. I'm moving in there with you, so if the situation becomes too much, we'll be able to get reinforcements in as quick as possible. The other thing is that I didn't get any intelligence about the camp. I don't know how many prisoners there are. I don't know how many Krauts are there. I don't even have a map of the camp. There's got to be a lot of buildings, walls—the works. It's a big prison camp. But all I've got is the map you're looking at, and it shows the place as a large empty area, which it obviously is not. So we're going to be playing it very much one step at a time."

Wiley paused and turned to Stock.

"I asked you to come here figuring you'd know a bit more about this place than I do. All I've heard is that concentration camps are where Hitler locks away his enemies and that they're run by the SS. But I wouldn't swear to that because from our skirmishes with the SS in the Vosges I'd say it doesn't make too much sense to have such tough soldiers guarding a prison camp. Can you add anything to that, Stock?"

The two officers looked up at the interpreter, who seemed quite upset. "Dachau, sir? Did you say Dachau?" he asked.

"However you pronounce it, yeah," Wiley replied, slightly embarrassed that he had called it Dat-chaw.

" *'Dass ich nicht nach Dachau komm,'* " Stock said, almost in a whisper. "When I was a kid, sir, we had a poem, but I only remember that last line now. It was a kind of prayer that God should make us good so that we don't get sent to Dachau." The fear in his voice, so thin and quiet, was almost tangible.

"What else can you tell me about this place, son?" Wiley asked.

Jackson was astonished to hear the colonel, who was only a few years older than Stock, address him as "son," and he had never seen the colonel behave so gently. He himself did not care much for Stock. The son of Jewish refugees from Germany, Stock seemed to Jackson to have a Krautlike aura about him; and he wasn't very sociable, preferring instead to spend his free time reading books. Still, Jackson figured, it must be tough on Stock to be invading his own country, even if his family had been forced into exile.

"I remember once, I was probably about twelve then, sir," Stock said quietly, "so that must have been about 1934 or 1935, we went to visit an aunt of mine in Munich. It was a lovely summer's day, and everyone in the train seemed very happy. People were singing, the way Germans do when they're on vacation, and some were eating out of picnic baskets. Anyway, before every stop the conductor would come into the car and announce the name of the next station. Shortly before we were to arrive in Munich, he came in and called out 'Dachau!' I was only a kid then, sir, but I can still remember how, suddenly, everyone stopped laughing and singing and talking, and an awful hush came over everyone. And that's the way we were sometime later, when we finally got into Munich.''

"But can you tell me something about the camp. . . ?'' Wiley asked.

His question trailed away even as a quizzical expression formed itself on Stock's face.

"No, I guess you can't,'' Wiley said.

Less than ten miles away, but behind enemy lines, a long freight train stood, silent and immobile—a dark and incongruous monolith on the flat farmland that stretched away into the fog on either side. A ragged hole disrupted the sleek lines of the locomotive where a Typhoon's rocket had passed through the boiler. A neat row of bullet holes ran along the roof for the entire length of the train.

In one of the boxcars, Yaakov Kovner regained consciousness. He remained fully stretched out on his back, taking in first the condition of his own body, which appeared not to have worsened, and then of the world around him.

It seemed only seconds ago that the train had ground to a halt, the screaming of its brakes giving way to a muffled explosion and a long burst of machine-gun fire as an airplane streaked over the cars. But looking through the skylight that was almost directly above him, Yaakov could see that it was dark outside. That meant that hours must have passed since the attack—hours he blessed for the unconsciousness they had brought him.

He became aware of the calm that had settled in the car. He no longer had to fight against the incessant, brutal swaying of the train or block the unremitting clack of the wheels from his ears. Best of all, though, was the air. The putrid, stifling atmosphere that had added so much to his miseries in the past few days had been driven out by an abundance of cold, fresh air that streamed through the bullet holes in the roof. He sucked it in as hungrily as he would have eaten food. It tasted indescribably clean and good. He looked at the holes in the roof. Perhaps they have saved my life, he thought, recalling how it had seemed to him before the attack that it would be impossible to breathe the foul air of the car much longer. It struck him as odd that bullets had saved his life.

He braced himself for the effort of sitting up. Rolling onto his left side, he brought his hands together on the floor and pushed. At the first go he succeeded in propping himself into a half-sitting, half-lying position against the wall. The maneuver had cost him less effort than he had expected. Nevertheless, it was several minutes before he recovered his breath and the pounding in his chest slowed down.

He looked around, his eyes well attuned to the dark. They settled first at the far end of the car where a pile of human bodies about four feet high stretched across the entire width of the carriage—a wall built up of the grotesque contortions of death.

Only the strongest and healthiest prisoners had been selected for this train. Yet the first had died even before it pulled out of Buchenwald. Over two hundred men were crammed into each car. The one in which Yaakov sat was among the first to be loaded and sealed, and in the hour or two that they waited on the siding for the other cars to be filled they were without even the small amount of fresh air that would reach them through the skylight once the train got under way. They were so tightly packed together that at first it was impossible to move the corpses. For the better part of the first day, Yaakov found himself wedged between two corpses, with whom, to make matters less disagreeable, he would from time to time converse.

The hours, then the days, wore on. Sufficient space opened up to enable the survivors to drag the corpses to the rear of the car. The deterioration of the air slowed down somewhat, now that there were fewer men alive. But the death rate continued to accelerate, caused now not so much by suffocation as by starvation and thirst. (Each prisoner was provided with less than one day's supply of food and water, as measured by Buchenwald standards, when they left the camp.) Dragging the corpses to the rear of the car demanded enormous expenditures of energy by the enfeebled men. Yaakov saw one man die as a direct result of this activity, collapsing onto the pile to which he had himself moments before helped carry a corpse. Yet even after many days, those who remained alive continued to separate themselves in this fashion from the dead. They did so not only because it created more space for the living but also because, even at death's doorstep, it was necessary for them to hold on to the distinction between life and death.

But on the eleventh day, when no more than twenty men were still alive, the ritual was abandoned. The survivors' strength had given out completely. Much of the time only their delirious ravings showed that there was life left in their parched and emaciated bodies. Most of the men held out, however; and two days ago, when it began to rain, they managed to remove some clothing from a corpse and, placing it under the skylight, used it as a sponge to catch rainwater. Revived by it, Yaakov and three or four other men had found the strength for a short conversation. In painfully whispered half sentences that were scarcely audible above the noise of the tracks, they talked about their destination. All agreed that they were heading south. Dachau seemed the most likely camp. But why, they wondered, was it taking so long to get there?

If only they could get to Dachau soon!

Remembering that conversation, Yaakov wondered where his companions were now. "Hey, how long we been here?" he called out. No sound came from his mouth. He tried to wet his lips, and his throat. At length, they were sufficiently moist. He repeated the question. The rasping sound of his voice surprised him, but he was gratified by its loudness. It seemed minutes before he finished the question. He sat back, his ears alert for a reply.

None came. The silence was absolute—and painful. He clicked his boots together to break it. Reassured by the sound, he repeated it a few times. He felt his thirst again and determined to try to get to the rags under the skylight to see if there was still moisture in them. He collapsed in his first effort to move forward onto his hands and knees and lay huddled in a little fetuslike heap, recovering his breath. His thirst, as if excited by the prospect of the damp rags, suddenly became unbearable. He moaned—a thin, desperate, croaking sound that syncopated with his panting breath. Three times more he collapsed before finally getting onto his hands and knees. The rags were no more than two yards away. Even in his condition it did not take very long to crawl to them.

They were drenched with rainwater. Falling to the floor, he buried his face in them, chewing and lapping at them as though he were a dog.

His thirst was far from quenched, but he forced himself to stop. It was not good to drink too much. Besides, some of the other men might also be needing water. He took it for granted that they were still alive. Or at least most of them. But where were they? Why had no one answered him?

He looked around. About four or five feet away, a group of men were lying next to one another, side by side, in what was virtually a straight line. "Hey! Any of you awake?" he called out. In the dark it was impossible for him to see if any of them were breathing. "Answer me, will you?"

But there was no answer. Gripping one of the rags in his left hand, he crawled toward the bodies. Despite the water, his strength was giving out fast. Twice he stopped, the second time almost falling off into unconsciousness again. He forced himself to stay awake. He had to reach the others, find out how they were and what he could do for them. At last he reached the body nearest him. He shook one of its feet, softly at first, and then with increased vigor, his bony hands clamped tightly over the naked foot. There was no response. Driven now by a surge of fear-inspired energy, he crawled up the length of the body until he was staring his old friend Victor Bezymensky in the face.

Bezymensky's eyes, open but unseeing, confirmed what Yaakov already knew. A little mournful wail escaped from his lips. Desperate now, he climbed over the body next to Bezymensky, and then over the ones next to it. Not one was alive. A sticky substance in his right hand told him what had happened to the last of his companions. The bullets that only a short while earlier he had blessed for saving his life had put an end to theirs.

More than ever before in his life, Yaakov felt entirely alone. If there was no God left in the universe, there had at least been men— friends. And now they too were gone. Lying on his side diagonally across the pile of bodies, his knees drawn up, and with his head on the chest of a Polish rabbi whose name he had never learned, Yaakov Kovner shed a few silent tears. Thin and bony as it was, his mattress of corpses was more comfortable than the wooden floor of the car. He fell asleep.

He woke up not long after. Opening his eyes, he found them directed at the gaunt and emptied face of Chaim Strizower, a fellow Latvian Jew whom he had known slightly before the war as the husband of the sister of his butcher in Riga. He had seen him again, but only from a distance, at Auschwitz. Both men had been sent from there to Buchenwald, where a strong if cantankerous friendship had developed between them.

Half delirious, Yaakov imagined that they were still in Buchenwald, and in his mind he took up again the old and interminable debate with his friend. "Don't you see, wherever you look, that God is no longer with us?"

Without a trace of self-pity—indeed, in an altogether matter-of-fact fashion, as though he were selecting merely one of innumerable possible illustrations of the point he wished to make—Yaakov repeated the details of his family's destruction. How his wife had been raped and then shot (first in the vagina, then in the head) by a Latvian militiaman. How his children, having been forced to watch this spectacle, had then been stomped to death by other Latvians. How, as their most imaginative act of sadism, they had decided to spare Yaakov—"for a while"—so that he would have to live with these scenes forever engraved in his mind. And how, in one sense worst of all, the world had continued blithely on its way while these abominations were being carried out. Lovely clouds were floating overhead, he told Strizower, while his children were being stomped to death in the streets of Riga.

As always, Yaakov's voice grew quieter as he proceeded with his narrative, and his speech slower—almost as if he were bored with the retelling of a rather ordinary set of facts. It was only when he came to the part about the clouds that he became agitated. "How can you still believe that God is any longer with us, Strizower? He has left us. He has left us. . . ." As he spoke, his voice would trail away, sometimes with the calculated effect of a born storyteller, sometimes with the thinness that marks genuine grief.

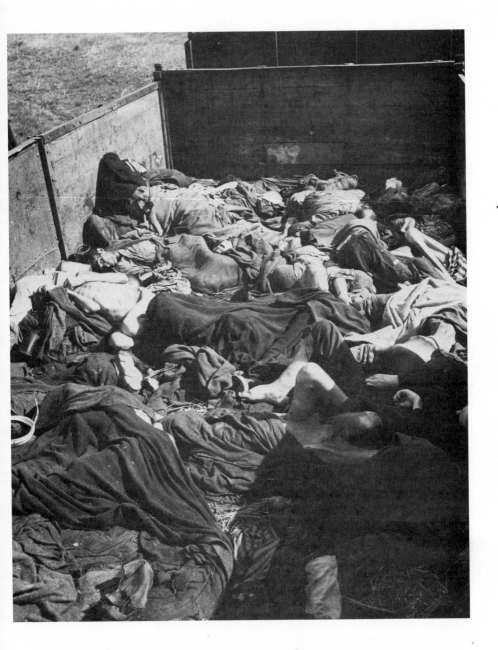

A cattle car loaded with the bodies of prisoners who died while being transported to Dachau from another concentration camp.

"For the sins that we have sinned, you say?" he now asked Strizower, anticipating his every response. "What are our sins, my friend? How do they compare with the Nazis'? And tell me, what were my children's sins?" He paused. "And you, Strizower. What about *your* children? How did *they* sin?"

Strizower was forced into conventional pieties.

"Our lives are *not* in God's hands," Yaakov rebuked him. "Our lives are only in the hands of the Nazis. If they want to kill us, we are dead. If they don't want to kill us, we remain alive a little longer. Come on, now, you know that's a fact. So how can you say that our lives are in God's hands? I'm telling you, Strizower, God has gone. He no longer wants our lives or anything else connected with this world in His hands.

"Don't ask me why, Strizower. If God is not here, how's He going to tell us? And if He told us why, would you really accept that *any* explanation could be good enough for us, after all we've been through?

"Don't look at me so wise and patient," Yaakov continued. "If you had something to say, you would say it, wouldn't you? I tell you, our lives are not in God's hands but in the Nazis', and the only thing left to us is that we, only we, can decide if we *wish* to die. You can't live if they want you to die. But you can want to die. Or want not to die. That much we still have left. Even if they are killing us, we can still make *that* decision!

"So what, you say?" Yaakov persisted. "So everything. Everything, my friend, because that's all we have! And I tell you something." He leaned forward and grabbed his friend's ragged shirt. "I will be willing to die only at God's hand. Then I will die contented, revenged. Because if I am to die at God's hand, He must first return to the universe.

"*Oy,* Strizower, my friend, my poor friend." Yaakov's voice was suddenly clearer, firmer. "Why am I talking to you like an idiot? You are dead, believing it was God's will, and I am alive, knowing that it was a stupid accident that not even the Germans willed. Goodbye, my friend.

"I'll tell you a secret," he added as a hasty afterthought, but with his voice quivering again on the edge of delirium. "Shall I tell

you how I really know about God? You are dead now, so perhaps
you won't be too shocked. Let me tell you. For nearly four years
now, yes, four whole years, not a day has gone by when I have not
cursed God and mocked Him! Look, I'll show you. I even learned
how to do the sign of the cross! Me, Yaakov Kovner, doing the sign
of the cross! Would you believe it, I've told God to drop dead? I've
said things that would have made *you* drop dead, just hearing them.
Every night I've said them before going to sleep. I hoped that God
would be so angry with me that He would come back to the world
just for the moment it would take Him to strike me dead. And perhaps, while He was at it, He would take care of some of those Nazi
swine, too.'' Yaakov paused now, his voice almost pleading. "And
you do agree, don't you, that He would do that? I mean, you can't
imagine that God would come back without punishing them, too? He
wouldn't just punish a little Jew from Riga and leave all those Nazis
roaming around, would He?

"So that's how I figured things out," he explained. "Here,
look." With a practiced hand, Yaakov made the sign of the cross. He
waited a few moments and then pointed out, ironically and triumphantly, "You see? Nothing happens! I go on living. God doesn't return. *'Curse God and die,'* it says in the Bible. Perhaps then, when
God was around, but not now. You understand? Your death doesn't
mean a thing. It doesn't tell of God's glory. Only of His absence.
You died from a stupid accident, my friend, don't you see that?
Nothing can bring Him back. . . .''

Yaakov's body convulsed with sobs, each of which felt like the
sledgehammering of a heart attack. A trickle of thin tears coursed
down his cheeks. Presently they subsided. Still making the sign of
the cross, he muttered, *"Eli, Eli, lama sabachthani,"* before falling
again into unconsciousness.

3. Niederdorf

Niederdorf. A picture-postcard village in the Dolomites. Little more than a cluster of pretty Alpine chalets huddled around a larger one, an inn, to which tourists come in the winter to enjoy the ski slopes nearby. The sun had not yet risen over the vast mountain crags, but darkness had already yielded to the first glimmerings of dawn.

In the inn, a Wehrmacht captain climbed to the second floor and turned down the corridor. A thick carpet muffled the sound of his boots as he made his way hesitantly along the unfamiliar passage. At the far end, outside what he reckoned was a choice corner room, a thin beam of light shone through a keyhole. He found the handle at the first try and opened the door, slowly, in order to accustom his eyes to the bright light.

The opened door at first obscured the far corner of the room. Stepping around it, he saw a small washstand in that corner. At it, a man stood shaving. His brawny body, hairless but powerful, was naked from the waist up. He wore the black trousers and boots of an SS officer.

He did not look around as the door opened. "Put the coffee down somewhere," he said. "And see if you can get me a couple of eggs. Soft-boiled. I'm hungry. This mountain air, I guess."

"Good morning, *Obersturmführer* Stiller." The voice was hard, its politeness unmistakably peppered with sarcasm.

"What the devil!" Stiller said. He turned suddenly, the razor still on his cheek, but managed to avoid gashing himself. "Oh, you're—eh—the fellow from yesterday, no? I'm bad at names." He smiled genially, as he recognized the Wehrmacht captain who had passed through Niederdorf in the afternoon, and returned to his shaving. Concentrating on the mirror, he asked, "What can I do for you? It's a bit early in the morning, isn't it?"

"My name is von Alvensleben," the captain replied. "I am here under the orders of General Röttiger, deputy commander of Wehrmacht forces in this zone. He requires that you turn over to me the prisoners you brought here from Dachau. Then you may return to Munich or wherever it is that you come from."

Stiller did not reply. He continued shaving. Alvensleben could not help noticing that his actions were more deliberate; in fact, almost comically so. At last, to the captain's gratification, he nicked himself. A thin trickle of blood coursed down into a patch of lather on Stiller's jaw. "Damn it!" he muttered angrily. He threw the razor into the washbasin and reached for a towel. Pressing it into the wound, he glared at Alvensleben and growled, "And you can go to hell. I don't take my orders from you or from any Wehrmacht general."

He sat down at the foot of the bed, the feathery quilt billowing up around him.

"I've got to hand it to you," he said with a grin that implied at least a measure of genuine admiration. "You had me fooled yesterday. Really did believe you were just passing through. How did you get to hear about us? The partisans, I suppose, eh?"

"Let me remind you, Stiller, that we are on the same side. The Wehrmacht fights partisans. I assume the SS does also. When it is not involved in *other* matters, that is." More than mere interservice rivalry seemed implied in his contempt. "And let me remind you also, Stiller, that although we are in different organizations, I am superior to you in rank. You will call me *Hauptmann.*"

In measured tones, Stiller responded, "You can shit on your rank and on your Wehrmacht. I have my orders from the *Reichsführer*-SS himself. My mission will be completed when the prisoners are executed. My trucks will be repaired today, and then we take those traitors and Jews for a nice ride into the hills. And then for a little swim, if you know what I mean. And now get out of here. I find you—disagreeable."

Alvensleben did not move. "In that case, your mission has

become meaningless," he said. "You are my prisoner. This village is now occupied by my men. We have set up roadblocks, and the telephone exchange is in our hands. My men outnumber you by, I would say, six to one. Think it over, my friend." He got up. "My command post is at the telephone exchange. Come and see me there when you have decided. And I give you my word, we will not disarm you and your men if you decide to go back peacefully. I've no interest in seeing you become target practice for the partisans." He left the room, making sure that Stiller could catch a glimpse of the self-satisfied smile on his face as he passed through the doorway.

Outside the inn, he was met by a sergeant. The two men marched briskly down the cobbled street to the house in which the telephone operator lived, with his switchboard. While they walked, the sergeant gave his report. The billets of the SS detachment had been ascertained by the sentries. Wehrmacht men had been sent to them and would remain on duty outside. A list had been obtained of the prisoners. About half of them were in the inn. The rest had been billeted in houses throughout the village and were watched over by SS men. There were not enough Wehrmacht soldiers to assign for guard duty at each of these houses.

They reached the telephone exchange. The operator sat at his switchboard. He was wearing a dressing gown and looked disheveled and grumpy. Alvensleben asked if there was a private telephone available. The man said there was not, his voice implying that that was the end of the matter. Alvensleben, however, demanded that one be installed in an adjoining room. Much muttering came from the switchboard, but eventually the operator got to his feet. He shuffled about for ten minutes or so, and then reported in a surly tone that the phone was now ready. Alvensleben thanked the rustic profusely, for he found him amusing, and ordered him to place a call to General Röttiger's headquarters. He wished to speak directly to the general.

It took another ten minutes for the call to go through. The general, evidently, had to be roused from his sleep. He was, Alvensleben could tell, in a foul mood.

"Have you gone completely insane?" he shouted when the captain finished his report. "My instructions were for you to investigate the situation. That was yesterday afternoon. Why did you not report to me at once?"

"There were communications difficulties," Alvensleben replied, rather lamely. "The telephone exchange here was in the control of the SS."

"And you couldn't have sent a messenger, I suppose? Before undertaking this insane action? Do you realize what it means to wage war against the SS? Even in *these* times? You're going to get yourself shot, my friend. And me too!"

"But General, if I may explain. The prisoners here are a fantastic crowd—VIPs, almost every one of them. Kurt von Schuschnigg, the former chancellor of Austria. Léon Blum, the French prime minister. Von Kallay, the prime minister of Hungary. There's a nephew of Winston Churchill, and one of Molotov, too. The prince of Hessen, whose wife is the daughter of the Italian king. Hjalmar Schacht. Pastor Martin Niemöller. General von Halder. General von Falkenhausen—he's still wearing his *Pour le Mérite*. I could go on. A hundred and thirty-seven men of this class, or their wives and relatives. And one small child—Schuschnigg's daughter. She's four."

There was a long pause at the other end. "Christ Almighty," the general said at last. "I thought half of those people had been killed years ago."

"No, sir. It seems that they've been at Dachau all this time, though some were brought there recently from other concentration camps that were too close to the Allied advance. There was a sort of VIP section at Dachau, as I understand it."

"And now, I suppose, Dachau itself has become too near the Allied lines? Where do they propose taking them, to hell?"

"In fact, sir, yes. This is supposed to be the last move. The SS *Obersturmführer* in charge of the party told me that he plans to execute them tomorrow. Says he got his orders directly from Himmler himself. He would have shot them today if two of his trucks hadn't broken down. They commandeered postal trucks in Munich. But they're being fixed, and he's ready to do the job tomorrow. I correct myself, sir, I mean today, Sunday. He's going to take them up into the mountains and dump their bodies in one of the lakes."

"And you want to come in like Don Quixote, Alvensleben, and rescue them?"

"It can be done, sir. They have about sixty men. I have two hundred. But they think I have more."

"Well, you listen to me, Captain," the voice at the other end snapped hurriedly. "I'm having none of this romantic tomfoolery. You get out of there, do you understand? And take every one of your men with you. Immediately, is that clear? My business is not to save men from the SS. Not even women and children. Nor is yours. That's a direct order." The line clicked dead at the other end.

"Of course, sir," Alvensleben said into the dead phone. "Of course." Still holding the receiver to his ear, he hunched forward in his chair, lost in thought. He was still in this position some fifteen minutes later when a corporal entered the room with a steaming cup of coffee.

4. The *Revier*

"Pierre, Pierre! Wake up! I've got something great to tell you!
C'mon, wake up!"

The hand nudging his shoulder sent shock waves, like an earth-
quake, through Pierre Martin's fever-wracked body as he lay on a
cot in the *Revier,* the hospital barrack. "OK," he said weakly. "Stop
pushing me like that." Slowly and reluctantly, his eyelids obeyed the
command to open. In the dim light of dawn he saw Igor leaning over
him. His bony head was traversed by an enormous smile.

"What is it?" Pierre asked the nine-year-old. "Why don't you
let me sleep? I'm feeling so sick still. *Merde!*" he muttered, lapsing
from German, the lingua franca of the prisoners, as the pain in his leg
intensified—mercifully, this time, only for a few seconds. "And
what are you doing here anyway?" he added. "You know children
aren't allowed in the *Revier*. Do you want to get shot?"

"I know, I know," the boy replied, not a trace of repentance in
his voice. "But it's a silly rule. We're allowed everywhere else,
aren't we? What's so special about the hospital?"

Pierre did not reply. He remembered the first time he had seen
Igor. It must have been several months ago, right before one of the
SS Dobermans tore a chunk of meat out of his right leg. Igor had
been playing tag with two other children, both about the same age,
as far as one could tell, and both Russians. Oblivious to anything
else, they were chasing each other around the *Moorexpress,* the horse
cart still loaded with corpses, outside the crematorium. For the first
time in ages, Pierre came close to tears. It was three years since

he had seen his children. These Russian boys, he reckoned, were about the age of his own little son, Claude. For a few minutes he stood there, watching sadly but enraptured by the sight of children at play, and as unmindful as they of the bony limbs sticking out of the cart into which they would from time to time bump.

A shout from one of the guards—"Get back here, you shit, or I'll give myself the pleasure of throwing you into one of the ovens"—had brought Pierre back to the present. He knew that under Article 12 of the Dachau code a prisoner could be executed on the spot, virtually at the whim of a guard. He had seen that happen often enough not to take the guard's threat lightly. He ran back to work stacking bodies in front of the ovens.

But a few minutes later the guard went out to relieve himself. Pierre knew from experience roughly how long it would take the guard to walk over to the execution pit, his favorite watering spot, and return. He rushed out and brusquely told the children to go away and find somewhere else to play. They ignored him. Pierre, knowing he did not have time to stand there and argue with them, smacked the boy nearest him across the bottom. Not very hard, but hard enough to make his point. Then he ran back to the crematorium.

Looking out a short while later, he saw that the children had left. That evening, lying on his bunk, Pierre felt a soft nudge. Turning around, he found himself looking into the doleful faces of the three children. He never discovered how they had managed to find him.

In the next days it became apparent to Pierre that the boys had decided to adopt him. Incredibly, they would from time to time slip him bits of food. And when he was sent to the *Revier* they took up a sort of guard over him. Although they were forever being chased from the hospital barrack, they remained undeterred. At first, Pierre told himself they were as faithful as puppy dogs. Gradually it occurred to him that he was *their* puppy!

"For God's sake, Igor, let me sleep. What do you want?"

"I've got some great news for you, Pierre," the boy said excitedly. "Do you want me to tell it to you?" He paused. "Or shall I go away?"

"OK, OK," Pierre replied wearily. The throb in his leg was getting worse again, and he was feeling desperately tired. "But tell me

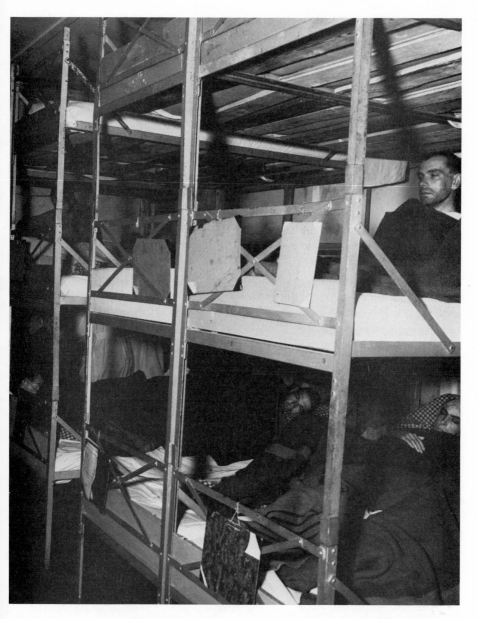

The hospital barracks were so overcrowded with sick inmates that pairs of beds were jammed together in three tiers and each pair had to be shared by three men.

quickly. I must go to sleep again. And don't talk so loudly,'' he
added. "You'll wake everyone up.''

"Well, it's like this. Gregory was sitting outside the window.
The one that's broken in the room where the doctors' office is. And
he heard what the doctors were talking about. You know what they
said? They said that you and the two Poles from the *Plantage* will be
dead by this afternoon! Many others, too, of course, but they mentioned you and the two Poles by name!'' A generous, indeed a bea-
tific, smile spread across the boy's face—a benefactor's smile. "Are
you happy?'' he asked, as though he had brought his friend a
cherished gift. There was no reply.

"Did you hear what I said, Pierre?'' the boy persisted. "The
doctors said that you are going to die today!''

"Yes, Igor, I heard you,'' Pierre said softly. He reached for the
boy's hand and received a reassuring squeeze. "I heard you the first
time. It's awfully nice of you to come and tell me that. Thank you.
But you know, Igor, perhaps the two Poles would not like it as much
as I do. So I think it's wiser that you do not tell them also that they
are going to die. Do you understand?''

"Oh, sure,'' Igor replied lightly. "I wasn't going to tell them,
anyway. You know you're our special friend. That's why we decided
that I had to come and tell you. We'll all come and see you later.''

With that, the boy vanished. Pierre shut his eyes. "I will not
die. I will not die,'' he told himself with absolute determination. As
so often in moments of desperation, he repeated the names of his
wife and sons. "Marie . . . Claude . . . Jean.'' He could not leave
them alone in this world. He had to see them again. With these
thoughts, he fell asleep.

In another room of the same hospital *Block,* chosen as their
meeting place because it was the one group of buildings to which the
SS would never go for fear of contagion, sixteen men sat on benches
around a crude wooden table. In the center of the table, as if reluctant
to illuminate more amply the dreary and colorless world of things and
men on which they shone, two candles gave off a limp light. The
men looked as spent and plastic as the congealed trickles of wax
around the base of the candles, but they were the International Com-

Doberman pinschers housed in these kennels were used by the SS guards to patrol the camp.

mittee of Dachau Prisoners, the *de facto* government of the prison compound. Each of them knew that on their cunning, stamina, and resourcefulness depended the lives of tens of thousands of their fellows.

For days now, perhaps weeks—who could keep track any longer?—the Committee had shouldered a dual burden. The SS, beset with their own cares as the Allied advance came ever nearer, and handicapped by growing numbers of desertions from their ranks, had increasingly relinquished the administration of the prison compound. Someone had to look after the prisoners, thirty thousand famished, frightened inmates, large numbers of whom were desperately sick. That "someone" was the International Committee, which, to the extent possible, had to see to it that the sick were tended, that food was distributed equitably, that the prisoners' morale did not sink too low. And all this had to be done discreetly, for the Committee members knew that the SS would regard the existence of their group as an insufferable act of insubordination.

Looking after the prisoners was one of the Committee's tasks: the easy one. Far more difficult, and desperate, was its responsibility for protecting the inmates from the Nazi Götterdämmerung. It had happened elsewhere that, rather than let a camp be liberated, the SS had slaughtered its entire prison population. The men of the International Committee knew this, and there was plenty of reason for them to believe that it might happen in Dachau, too, at any time—even just hours before the Americans arrived. The Committee's supreme task was to prevent this from happening—to stay the murderer's hand. Was this possible? Could the Committee defend the prisoners against so much as a single Nazi machine gun? Now *that* was a question.

Tonight, though, there was an even more pressing concern to torment the Committee. A couple of days before, they had learned that Weiter, the camp commandant, and Ruppert, the *Lagerführer,* or officer in charge of the prison compound, had disappeared, like so many of their subordinates, presumably to escape the punishment they knew awaited them at the hands of the Americans. The prisoners had breathed a sigh of relief. With Weiter and Ruppert gone, the chance of averting the slaughter of the inmates seemed perceptibly greater.

But then, late the previous evening, had come word that Ruppert was back and wished to speak at once with two prisoners named Hopman and Weinsma. Both these men were members of the Committee.

Surely this could only portend something ominous. Why had Ruppert returned to the camp when common sense dictated that he try to vanish into thin air? And did his demand to speak to the two men mean that the secret of the International Committee's existence had been uncovered?

Hopman and Weinsma had conferred hurriedly with their fellows and then set out for the *Jourhaus* where they were to meet with the *Lagerführer*. The Committee had been waiting for them to return for hours now, but still the two had not come back. The night wore on. The men around the table only rarely expressed the thoughts that raced through their minds. Had Weinsma and Hopman been shot? Then this would be the beginning of it all. . . . Did Ruppert's summons mean that the existence of the Committee had been discovered? Then at the least they would be shot for insubordination, or subversion, or whatever reason. Most bitter of all was the suspicion that Weinsma and Hopman might have betrayed the Committee, and all the prisoners, to save their own skins.

Ali Kuci, the Albanian, walked over to one end of the room, where several field-gray blankets hung over a single window. He peered cautiously behind the flap of one of the blankets.

"We can blow out the candles now," he said in a voice heavy with fatigue. No one stirred. Kuci tugged sharply at a blanket, and then at the others. They fell away, stirring up a cloud of dust as they settled on the floor. The dismal light of dawn filled the room. Picking up one of the blankets, he wrapped it around his shoulders and returned to his seat at the table. Before sitting down, he leaned over to blow out the candles. With the fourth puff, he succeeded in doing so.

"It can't be long now," he said to no one in particular. "One way or another."

On their way back to the *Revier,* Joop Weinsma and Paul Hopman walked along the edge of the *Appellplatz* and then turned left down the *Lagerstrasse* between the seemingly endless rows of barracks. Although Weinsma was desperately thin—down, in fact, to less than half his normal weight—his tall, big-boned body still conveyed an impression of power. Even after three years his military bearing was evident. It was a matter of pride with him that he not conceal it, as many other officers did who adopted the anonymous shuffle of the concentration camp prisoner.

His companion, Hopman, was small and emaciated, with a face that seemed permanently set in a mask of passivity and depression. Although Weinsma was by no means immune from the traditional Dutch contempt for their southern neighbors, he regarded the Belgian Hopman with deep respect. Behind his mask, Weinsma knew, there was a brilliantly resourceful mind.

"I was just thinking that this is the damnedest war anyone in my family has ever fought in," Weinsma said with amusement. "We've been officers for three centuries. More generals than anything else, if you want to know the truth. But this—this is ridiculous. Have I ever told you that during the whole time the Germans were invading Holland I was on my back, sick as a dog? Pneumonia! What is it Clausewitz says? About war as an extension of diplomacy by other means? You know, I've never fired a shot at the Germans! My battles with them have been verbal. I think I'll write a book arguing that diplomacy is an extension of war by other means. I can't believe that that bastard Ruppert came back. Just for a little visit!"

As he talked, his voice became higher, his speech punctuated with increasing frequency by inappropriate chuckling. Almost imperceptibly, he crossed the threshold of laughter. Nervous laughter. He felt a hand close in a viselike grip on his arm.

"For God's sake, man," Hopman snapped. "Get hold of yourself. This is no time to crack."

Waves of uncontrollable heaving seemed to be dragged up by the laughter. Forced to choose between them and the hand tightening on his arm, Weinsma surrendered to the latter. He paused, profoundly ashamed, but grateful, too, for Hopman's presence. He took a deep breath, then another. His body relaxed. "Thanks," he said. "I'll be OK now."

Hopman said nothing, but removed his hand. The two men resumed their march down the *Lagerstrasse* back to the hospital *Block* to report the results of their mission.

So, Weinsma thought to himself, another day has begun: April 29. He was startled to realize that in two days it would be the third anniversary of his arrest. It had hardly seemed possible then that he would survive for a week. How often he had prepared himself to die in these past three years! Most recently, he had done so last night. He wondered whether he would have to do so again—soon.

The recollection of last night's summons triggered off another memory—one that, oddly enough, had lain dormant for a long time now. . . .

He was in the Orange Hotel, as men in the underground called the SD prison in Scheveningen, about three weeks after his arrest. It was early morning, and he was lying in his cell steeling himself for another day of interrogation. The door opened; the guard entered. Weinsma was astonished to notice that he was in civilian clothes. Was he, perhaps, Gestapo? Behind him were two more men, similarly clad.

Wordlessly, they put handcuffs on Weinsma's wrists and led him off. The route was unfamiliar. They came to an office, and there, waiting for him, was—a barber!

Still no explanation. He obeyed a silent command to sit in a chair. The barber placed a towel around his shoulders, trimmed and brushed his hair, and gave him a shave, the first Weinsma had had since being arrested. Surely, he thought to himself, they don't shave a man and cut his hair before shooting him?

He was taken out into a courtyard and pushed into a car. A short ride brought them to a large house. Inside the house he was met by an SS *Sturmbannführer* with a large dueling scar on his cheek. The handcuffs were removed. The officer beckoned him to follow. Still not a word had been spoken, and Weinsma did not even try to figure out what was going on. He wondered if an opportunity to escape might present itself.

They went through the house to the garden at the back. As they stepped outside, the SS officer nodded his head in the direction of a group of men some distance away. Reverently, he said, "You are here to be questioned by *Reichsführer* Himmler himself. Nothing to do with your case, but he wants to gain an impression of the state of affairs in the Netherlands. You will address him as '*Reichsführer*.' "

The *Sturmbannführer* left Weinsma to proceed alone. The group, Himmler at its center, watched him approach. As he came closer, he recognized some of the other faces, including the *Reichs-*

kommissar for Holland and his chief aides. The *Reichskommissar* seemed lame in one leg. Facing the party, Weinsma lost all fear for a brief moment and, recklessly disregarding the convention of reporting himself as "Prisoner Number . . . ," he stood smartly at attention and announced, "Captain of the Royal Netherlands Artillery Weinsma!"

Thickset, but with his high-peaked cap giving him a top-heavy look that verged on the absurd, Himmler seemed startlingly unimpressive to Weinsma. For all that his chest was emblazoned with decorations and badges, he looked more like a clerk than a soldier. But the cunning intelligence of his tight-set mouth—and, no less so, of his porcine eyes, hidden though they were in part by the gleam of his pince-nez—conveyed an impression of sinisterness that belied the otherwise ordinary qualities of his appearance. Weinsma tried to persuade himself that the little man opposite him looked sinister because he knew he was Himmler. But he failed in this attempt. Yet Weinsma felt strangely impersonal in this encounter. He was not in the presence of a human being, it seemed to him, so much as of a phenomenon, one that actually did not seem very *alive*. Himmler's black uniform matched a kind of inner deadness that was readily apparent. It struck Weinsma as surprising, in that moment, that wickedness should seem so lifeless. He had not noticed this quality before in the Nazis with whom he had had dealings up to now. Had he missed it? Or was this something distinctive to Himmler's personality?

These thoughts and observations entered Weinsma's consciousness through a thick filter of astonishment at the morning's events. He no longer felt afraid. Fear was for the unknown or for the all too palpably known: the death sentence, or the SD man swinging a club at him as he sat strapped in a chair: Himmler right now seemed too far removed from such things to appear plausible as their origin. The deference his cronies showed him, *their* fear of him, was as distant to Weinsma as the awe a headwaiter inspires in a busboy is to a customer in a restaurant.

"You are of German blood. Why do you fight us?" Himmler broke the silence. His voice was not unpleasant, but its high pitch startled Weinsma, as did his rather grating Bavarian accent.

"The words 'German blood' do not mean anything to us,"

Weinsma replied bluntly. He felt that he was a spokesman for his nation, and this made him feel proud and responsible. Above all, he determined, he would do nothing that would give these Nazis the impression that the people of Holland would ever accept the German occupation. "Nothing at all," he repeated. "We are Netherlands subjects first and foremost. After all, the English are of German blood, too."

"Yes, they are," Himmler responded, as if he had won his point. "That is why the Führer did not want to wage war against the English."

"Besides that," Weinsma continued, "we love our freedom and are a stubborn people."

"But these are typical German qualities!" Himmler said. "And your national anthem has the line 'Wilhelmus of Nassau, I am of German blood.' "

"It says also, 'I shall be true to the Fatherland even unto death.' "

"You want to be illegal." Himmler's voice had grown raucous and angry. "You don't know even how to begin! We have been illegal since 1923. We know the job, and we know how to deal with people like you."

Himmler paused, as if remembering that he had not come here to get into a stupid political argument with a mere captain in the Dutch Army. In the ensuing silence, Weinsma became aware of a group of photographers clicking their Leicas in his direction. A squad of SS guards marched by. As they approached the group, they changed into a goose step.

"How do you expect to win this war, eh?" Himmler suddenly asked mockingly.

"I'm not very well informed at the present," Weinsma replied, a touch of sarcasm in his voice. "We are not allowed to receive any news. But perhaps the Americans will sooner or later enter—"

Himmler quickly changed the subject. "Our prisoners are well cared for, aren't they?" he asked.

"You shoot them."

"We have to. After all, we cannot allow partisans in our rear. But you—are you treated well?"

Weinsma sidestepped the question. What good would it do for
him to complain? "I've heard that the situation in the prison at Leus-
den is particularly bad," he said.

Himmler shrugged his shoulders. "Have you read *Mein
Kampf?*" he asked.

"I once glanced through it."

"*Glanced* through it?" Himmler asked angrily. "*Glanced
through* it?" His face tightened in anger. He stared unseeingly at
Weinsma for a brief moment and then launched into a violent rhap-
sody about the Führer, whose genius these stupid Dutchmen seemed
unable to appreciate. After the first few sentences he was shrieking
and gesticulating as though he were addressing a huge throng of the
Party faithful in the *Sportpalast* in Berlin. Weinsma was mesmerized
by the performance—but not to the point of wondering why the second most powerful man in Nazi Germany should deem it necessary to
harangue a single insignificant prisoner. Later it would occur to him
that perhaps this was part of Himmler's technique for controlling his
subordinates. And for inspiring desperate fear in them.

The diatribe ended as abruptly as it had begun. With a peremp-
tory flick of the hand, Himmler dismissed Weinsma. He was led
away. Another prisoner stepped forward.

"So," his guard said as he brought him back to the car. "What
do you think of the Bloodhound, eh? He means well by you Dutchmen."

Evidently Himmler had indeed meant well—by Weinsma, in
particular. The next evening an SS *Obersturmbannführer* whom he
had never seen before came to his cell. "The *Reichsführer* was very
impressed by your bearing," he told Weinsma. "And he has ordered
me to tell you that he will allow you to join the SS to fight in Russia.
You will have the equivalent rank that you had in the Dutch Army:
Hauptsturmführer. That means, of course, that your death sentence
has been revoked. My congratulations!"

He reached forward with a smile to shake Weinsma's hand.
Weinsma did not extend his. "I am an officer in the Royal Netherlands Army," he told the man coldly. "I live as one. And if necessary I will die as one."

As it happened, Weinsma's sentence *was* commuted. In Poland's Katyn forest, the Germans stumbled across the graves of some twelve thousand Polish officers who had been murdered in cold blood by the Soviet Union. Eager to make propaganda out of this discovery, Berlin halted all executions of political prisoners in the Western countries. Those slated to die during that month were shipped off to concentration camps instead.

A door of the room in the *Revier* where the Committee sat waiting creaked on its rusty hinges. Kuci, the man with a blanket wrapped around his shoulders, was the first to rise to his feet. One by one, the others did the same. The hollow thump of wooden clogs came toward them—two pairs of clogs. The door opened.

Hopman stood before them, and Weinsma. The others rushed forward to greet them. Only one man remained at the table. "Let's get the meeting together, please," he commanded in a voice that was cool and authoritative. "Joop. Paul. We're glad to see you back," he added, as the men returned to their seats. "Frankly, I had almost given you up."

"You think only you have the luck of the Irish, Connally?" Hopman answered, his face creasing into a little smile that seemed quite out of character.

Jim Connally ignored the remark. "Now, tell us what happened. First, do they know about the Committee?"

"Not so far as I could tell," Weinsma replied. "I think it was just a coincidence that Ruppert sent for both Hopman and me. It wasn't at all what we thought."

"Then why were you gone so long? It must have been at least seven hours." The way the others looked at Weinsma and Hopman made it apparent that many of them, at least, shared the suspicion, implicit both in the question and in the tone of Connally's voice when he asked it, that some double-dealing might be afoot. At Dachau you survived by trusting your comrades—and by not trusting them more than was realistic. But what *was* realistic in the world of Dachau? The extraordinary selflessness and heroism that were daily occurrences? Or the treachery that led someone to steal the scraps of food and clothing on which another prisoner's life depended? No one could answer these questions with any degree of confidence. No one

who was not guilty of treachery would feel offended if others—even
close friends—questioned their motives. You were entitled to your
suspicions. And they were to theirs.

In particular now, Weinsma recalled the deep anxiety that they
had all felt when a prisoner had arrived in the *Revier* with word that
Ruppert wished to see him and Hopman at the *Jourhaus* immediately.

Two weeks earlier, a Greek prisoner whose fluent command of
German had won him a coveted job in the camp's administrative of-
fices, had managed to read a top-secret directive, signed by Himmler's deputy, Ernst Kaltenbrunner himself, which had just arrived
from Berlin. The directive ordered Dachau's commandant, *Sturmbannführer* Weiter, to evacuate the entire population of the camp
before they could be liberated by the advancing American armies.
The VIP prisoners held at Dachau were to be sent to the Dolomites,
where "special arrangements," as they were called, would be made.
The Aryan prisoners from Western countries were to be sent to Switzerland. Both of these groups were to go by truck. The rest of the
prisoners were to be marched on foot into the Tyrolean mountains
with the intention of eliminating them all en route.

The SS would see to it that their opponents would not survive
the destruction of the Third Reich.

Only the first stage of Kaltenbrunner's order was carried out,
with the evacuation, on April 25, of the 137 VIP prisoners and their
dependents. The group destined for Switzerland was never assembled, evidently because Weiter was unable to round up sufficient
numbers of vehicles for this purpose. Weiter then decided—on his
own initiative, it would seem—to send the entire camp population of
some thirty thousand people on a death march into the Tyrol.

This plan was also thwarted. On the twenty-sixth, the prisoners
were ordered to ready themselves for evacuation immediately after
Appell. They were told to assemble in national groups on the *Appellplatz,* where, after receiving rations, they would be moved out of
the camp. "For your own safety," as Ruppert, the SS officer in command of the prison compound, told them.

The International Committee, however, recognized this order as
a revised version of the directive from Kaltenbrunner. At an
emergency meeting, a plan for dealing with this situation was hastily

drawn up. The essence of the plan was to stall, to delay, to play for time, not to cooperate with the Germans in any way.

It worked like a miracle. The distribution of rations, which normally would have taken about an hour, was stretched out endlessly. Placards identifying assembly points on the *Appellplatz* were moved around, and some simply disappeared. The SS did not dare intervene. To do so would have meant mingling with the prisoners, thus exposing themselves to the typhus that had reached epidemic proportions in the prison compound. Moreover, the SS staff was already seriously demoralized, and its numbers had been decimated over the past week by the desertion of officers and enlisted men alike.

Only at ten o'clock that night—fully twelve hours after the assembly had begun—were the first groups ready for departure; 1,759 Jews were put on a train for which a locomotive engineer and coal had been found at the very last moment, and 6,887 additional prisoners, of whom about half were Jews and half Russians, were sent on foot toward the Tyrol. By then, the SS had had enough, and the rest of the prisoners were sent back to their barracks for the night. The next day, in accordance with instructions from the International Committee circulated through the camp, the prisoners stayed away from the roll call. Only about 200 turned up, and they were marched out of the camp and never heard from again.

That same day—April 27—the Greek reported to the International Committee that Weiter, Ruppert, and most of the senior SS officers had fled. A large number of enlisted men had also taken to their heels. It seemed that fewer than 250 SS were left to guard the camp. That was the good news.

The bad news was that a new directive, signed by Himmler personally, had been received that morning from Berlin. Noting the failure of plans to evacuate the camp, the *Reichsführer* ordered the immediate execution of the entire prison population in an operation code-named *Wolkenbrand*, "Firecloud." "Not one prisoner must be allowed to be liberated by the Americans," Himmler commanded. The Greek did not discover how *Wolkenbrand* was to be carried out. He had managed to read a sentence ordering that the *Nacht und Nebel* prisoners (political prisoners who had been arrested and brought to the camp without notification to their next of kin) were to be killed first, and that they were to be shot. But details about the liquidation of the rest of the prisoners were on a page that he didn't have a chance to read before the *Oberscharführer* in whose office he was working returned to his desk.

It was against this backdrop that Ruppert's reappearance and his summons to Hopman and Weinsma on the night of the twenty-eighth seemed so ominous. For both men were *Nacht und Nebel* prisoners. Their execution would herald the implementation of *Wolkenbrand*.

Now they had returned—to report what had happened and to explain themselves. It was Hopman who answered Connally's question of why they had been gone so long. He spoke in his usual terse fashion. "We stayed because Ruppert told us to stay. In the *Jourhaus*. There are new men in the guard towers. He has no authority over them and said they would probably fire at us if they saw us moving in the dark. I don't know where they got their reinforcements from or how many there are, but evidently there are fresh SS men here. Though for all we know, most of the old hands who were here yesterday morning have followed their buddies out since then. Anyway, it was Ruppert who told us to stay until it was light."

"But what was Ruppert doing back at the camp after disappearing the day before yesterday? Can you explain that?"

"I think we can," Weinsma said. "You see, when we got to the *Jourhaus* we saw, on the road leading up to it from the other side, a convoy of Red Cross trucks. Perhaps twenty of them. They're from Switzerland, filled with food. For us."

The eager expressions on his companions' faces urged him to continue. "What Hopman and I reckoned is that Ruppert saw them coming here—on the road; he was probably going in the opposite direction—and decided to come back with them. I got the definite impression that he did not want the new SS units to know he was here."

"What do you mean?" someone asked.

"Well, he said he had no authority over the men in the towers. My guess is that the new units are so undermanned and unfamiliar with the camp that it was possible for him to sneak in with the convoy right under their noses. He is, after all, an *Obersturmführer*, and I doubt whether the reinforcements are commanded by anyone of higher rank. So with his rank and his familiarity with the camp he was able to get in without any of the new people knowing about it. He had three SS privates with him, but they are people who've been here for a while. Their faces were familiar, though I don't know their names. And Ruppert seemed anxious. As if he was afraid that someone would stumble on us at any moment.''

"Are you asking us to believe that Ruppert, out of the goodness of his heart, risked his hide to sneak back here and bring us food? Come on. That simply doesn't make sense'' Oskar Müller, the camp's Senior Prisoner, whom the SS had appointed as their liaison with the other prisoners, was speaking. "You know as well as we do that he's one of the biggest bastards that's ever been in this place.''

"Of course he is," Hopman snapped. "But what Joop is saying is that we think that Ruppert's trying to save his own hide. Make a good impression, if you know what I mean, with the Red Cross. He stayed until we left. But I had the feeling that he could hardly wait for it to get light enough so that he could get out of here as well."

"And what about the Red Cross?" Connally asked.

"The trucks were being unloaded. A number of them left before we did. But the Red Cross official stayed on. He's probably left now. He said he was returning to Switzerland."

"Was he Swiss?"

"Yes. The bastard sat on a table smoking cigarette after cigarette and never thought of offering us any. But I managed to tell him at one point that the situation here is desperate, medically and politically, and that we have to have help immediately. I doubt if anything will come of it, though. He said there wasn't anything he could do, but he would report to his boss. I asked if he had a radio with him, and he said no."

"But did you tell him *how* urgent it is?"

"I said things are desperate," Weinsma replied. "But I had only a few seconds while Hopman was talking to Ruppert."

"And what did you say to Ruppert?" Müller asked Hopman.

"I warned him that he and his friends would be held responsible by the Americans if they tried to liquidate the prisoners. I said that we had information about Himmler's orders. He didn't deny that's what they're planning to do. He said only that orders were orders, that things weren't up to him, anyway, and that he had shown his goodwill by escorting the Red Cross in. Then he shrugged his shoulders.''

There was a long silence. Instinctively acknowledging him as their leader, the men turned to Connally and waited for him to speak.

''I think Joop and Paul are right,'' he said at length. He stared in deep concentration at the candles on the table, and spoke in low, measured tones. ''And that is what worries me a great deal. Ruppert is a savage, one of the worst we've ever had here—which is saying a lot. But don't underestimate him. He's no fool. On the contrary, although he's a fanatic Nazi, he's also a very shrewd man. Devilish. And now he's here trying to win good marks for himself.'' He

The Jourhaus, *entrance to the Dachau concentration camp.*

paused, slowly looking at each face in the room. "Why? *That,* my friends, is the question. Is it because he thinks that will make up for all the things *we've* seen him do in the past years? Certainly not. As I've said, the man's no fool. And so I'm led to the conclusion that he's trying to protect himself from what he believes is *going* to happen. Not from what has already happened. And that, my friends, is why I'm worried. Very worried. Ruppert knows, or believes, that *Wolkenbrand* is going to be carried out. It's not *us* he's trying to impress, because he doesn't think we'll be around. He wants to show the Americans—courtesy of the Red Cross—that he's a good guy. Dead men don't tell tales. But he thinks the Red Cross will."

5. The Athlete

Ernst Kroll stepped out of *Block* 8 and was careful to shut the door quietly behind him. He had slept badly last night, what with one thing and another, and now every muscle and joint in his body felt stiff. For some minutes he flexed his arms and legs. His movements were awkward and inelegant, as he himself ruefully recognized. But he reminded himself that there were probably not a hundred men in the camp whose muscle tone was any longer as good as his. Spurred on by this thought, he forced himself to do some knee bends. He collapsed at the very first one and with a good-natured smile picked himself off the ground. No point in overdoing things, he told himself. It's been a long time since you were swimming champion of Munich. He rubbed the mud from his hands onto his striped uniform.

Exhausted, he walked to a small pile of rubble a couple of feet away and sat down. He took a deep breath to control his panting, and then several more because the air felt so fresh and good after the stagnant atmosphere in the *Block*. Puddles on the ground showed that it had been raining last night, but now the sky was clear and aglow with the rising sun. He felt good. On an impulse, he pulled his feet out of the wooden clogs he wore and dipped them in a puddle, rubbing them against each other to remove at least some of their accumulation of grime.

Kroll was by nature a gregarious and tolerant man, and three years in the solitary confinement bunker at Dachau had taught him to be particularly appreciative of human company. Nevertheless, he relished the solitude of this moment. Indeed, there had been times in the

72

past few days, and especially yesterday evening, when he had felt that he would almost have preferred being back in solitary. He did not believe the rumors, and he detested the excitability that accompanied them. "We are going to be poisoned." "We are going to be transported to Austria." "They're going to shoot us here like a pack of wild dogs." "They've decided to burn us all with flame-throwers."

And each report, of course, was from an unimpeachable source. Or at least from someone who had heard it from someone who had gotten it from an unimpeachable source. Kroll had noticed that some of the prisoners were creating a new kind of status system in the camp. You lost standing if you could not top the latest rumor with an even more ghastly one. And at times it seemed to him that there was almost relish in the way in which they anticipated the end. Yesterday evening, especially, people had been so worked up by the situation that it had been impossible to get to sleep until midnight.

Kroll resented this because he had to get up earlier than the others to work at the crematorium, where double shifts were now the order of the day. Even more to the point, though, he thought that all this talk was senseless. As far as he was concerned, the camp was too real, too substantial, to disappear in a puff of smoke. Things just did not happen in that way, not even when the Nazis were in charge of them.

Kroll had spent almost his entire adult life in Dachau. He was now thirty years old and had been sent to the camp a few months after it opened in March 1933. It did not seem miraculous to him that he had survived here for twelve years. In some strange way, the brutality of this place, the evil that was its *raison d'être,* seemed to him so normal a part of life itself that, even though he had seen literally thousands of people die here, the continued existence of the camp was something he took for granted. And if the camp continued to exist, then with a bit of luck people like him could also continue to exist in it. It did not occur to him to believe that his luck might now be running out, or that Dachau itself would disappear with the system that had created it.

As for his luck running out, there had been only one time when he believed that was happening. For two months after his arrest he had been kept in the Gestapo headquarters in Munich. He knew the Nazis were desperate to discover the names of other members of his cell. He knew that some of them had been arrested along with him. And he stubbornly clung to his story that he did not know them or any of the other people whose names were mentioned to him during the interrogations. He belonged to no organization. He was not a Communist. There was nothing he could tell the Gestapo, much as he would like to. Felix Schmidt? No, most certainly he had never heard of anyone called Felix Schmidt.

Schmidt, who was the chairman of Kroll's Munich Communist Party cell, was brought into the interrogation room. "Do you know this man?" the Gestapo officer asked him, pointing at Kroll. Schmidt stared at his old friend for a couple of minutes. "Yes or no?" the Gestapo man roared. "Do you know him?"

"Yes!" Schmidt at last replied, the word barely audible as it came through his bruised and swollen lips. "Yes, I do."

In that moment, Kroll knew he was lost. Schmidt, his old comrade-in-arms, the man who had fought alongside Rosa Luxemburg herself: Schmidt had given in. They must have done terrible things to him, Kroll assured himself, even as his panic grew. But how could Schmidt betray him like this?

The Gestapo officer beamed triumphantly. "We have you now, you swine!" he said gloatingly to Kroll.

The thin, broken voice spoke again. "His name is Kroll. Ernst Kroll. Everyone knows him. He's the swimming champion of Munich. My factory team competed against him every year!"

The Gestapo officer blanched. "Get that bastard out of here!" he roared.

Schmidt was led away, and Kroll's belief that he was under the protection of a lucky star was born. It never left him during his twelve years in Dachau. "If you believe in destiny," he once said to a friend, "then you have to believe that our destiny is to suffer. In order to suffer, you have to be alive. Therefore, we have to live."

He pulled his feet out of the puddle and leaned over to dry them on his trouser bottoms before putting them into the clogs again. As he had so often before, he now thought of how good it would be to be able to swim again. To feel the shock of the cold water as you dive

in. The pressure of the water on your face as you climb to the surface. The sudden clarity as the water slips away from your eyes.
And, above all, the surge of your body as it propels itself along.
These sensations, although last experienced so long ago, remained as
vivid as ever. He had clung to them during the long brutal hours of
interrogation and in the desperate isolation of the solitary confinement bunker. They not only refreshed his soul, they acted as an infusion of vigor and endurance into his body.

He glanced at the watch he had been given when he was assigned to the early morning shift. The *Kommando* assembled at the
Jourhaus gate at six forty-five. It was time to go.

He got up and walked between the *Blöcke* to the *Lagerstrasse*.
Many years ago, he had helped build the *Blöcke,* along with the SS
barracks and the workshops outside the prison compound. That had
been a terrible time. The SS set impossible schedules for the construction work and then imposed punishments on the prisoners for not
completing each phase ahead of the scheduled time. Everyone knew
that the SS men did not care about the schedules and that they used
them as a new way of venting their sadism. One day the *Kommando*
in which Kroll was working was warned that two of their number
would be shot if the wall of a workshop they were constructing was
not completed by noon. The men set to work as though their lives
depended on it, which indeed they did. At eleven thirty the SS
overseer diverted a load of bricks from Kroll's *Kommando* to another
one. Kroll and his men did not have enough bricks to finish the wall.
At twelve noon precisely, two men in his *Kommando* were shot.
"Malingerers!" the SS man said. "That'll set an example for the rest
of you!"

All the same, Kroll was a worker in every sense of the word. He
believed in work, which he would always insist was the very essence
of life. "Work *does* make you free," he would sometimes urge his
comrades, quoting the odious inscription on the camp gates. "I can't
explain that exactly, but when you work you are doing something for
yourself. Even if someone else is telling you what to do. These buildings," he would add, pointing all around him, "we made them.
They're our prison, but *we* made them. And we can be proud of
that!" The others seldom saw his point. But Kroll meant what he

said, and while he recognized that the buildings weren't exactly beautiful (except for some of the SS officers' quarters, but he hadn't worked on them), he was proud of the fact that he had helped construct these sturdy structures under such difficult conditions.

In the past few months, however, the camp had deteriorated terribly. The Spartan appearance it had formerly possessed had appealed to Kroll as neat and efficient-looking. Not, to be sure, that he regarded these as architectural ideals. His tastes were for the ornate. But certainly the camp had not looked a mess; and once you got used to its appearance it was—well, *reassuring*.

He felt terrible for the thousands of people who had been shipped to the camp in the past few months. Their condition was so bad, for the most part, that the old-timers here in Dachau regarded themselves as positively healthy in comparison. Like many of them, Kroll did what little he could to help the newcomers. Occasionally there would be a scrap of food he could spare. The crematorium was a good place for picking up extra clothing, and many of the newcomers were in desperate need of that. Often Kroll exposed himself to considerable risk to smuggle clothing out of the crematorium enclosure and back into the prison compound. There were other things he also did for the newcomers. Often their biggest need—their only need—was to have someone to whom they could talk in the few moments before they died. A painfully whispered last message for wives, or parents, or children. Some only wanted their names known before they died. Others seemed to need no more than to have their hand held in that last moment. Whether Communist or priest, Jew or Gentile, they were all comrades in the great struggle, so far as Kroll was concerned. His feelings of class solidarity extended to all of them.

But his compassion, which was genuine, did not stand in the way of his irritation and disappointment at the disorderly and messy appearance of the camp. He *did* blame the newcomers for that, but he also held the SS and his fellow veteran prisoners responsible. They should have taken more care of the place. Flimsy lean-tos had been added to the walls of the barracks, most of them consisting of no more than four thin posts and a couple of blankets draped over them. Pieces of clothing and bedding and debris of all sorts littered the ground around these ramshackle structures. The road between each *Block* was about thirty feet wide, yet the disorder was so great that you could hardly walk five paces without having to step over something. The scene reminded Kroll of photographs of Calcutta that had been shown at a lecture on British imperialism in India that he had attended many years before in Munich. They had made a deep impression on him then. And now the camp that he had helped build with his own hands was beginning to look like Calcutta!

He reached the end of the *Block* and turned right, up the *Lagerstrasse,* the wide, straight road that cut through the prison compound. Here, at least, a sense of order still prevailed. Gaunt, tall poplars lined the road, and if one looked straight ahead to the *Appellplatz,*

A pile of clothes stripped from cremated prisoners.

toward which he was now heading, it was still possible to recapture a view of how the camp had been in earlier days. Provided, that is, you didn't look to either side at the messy alleys between the *Block* rows. The huge open space of the *Appellplatz* was a welcome contrast to the overcrowding everywhere else in the camp. Its graveled surface, which Kroll would always remember helping to lay—what agony it had been!—had absorbed the rainfall and was not littered with muddy puddles.

Reaching the end of the *Lagerstrasse,* Kroll paused for a moment to glance appreciatively at the *Wirtschaftsgebäude* on the other side of the *Appellplatz*. The huge building (it was about two hundred yards long) housed the prisoners' kitchens and showers, depositories for their possessions (the ones that the SS didn't steal, that is), and a number of workshops. It, too, was still in excellent condition. And despite the colossal size of the building, its high-pitched roof lent it an appearance that was almost snug and homey. Kroll had a special affection for that roof. He had helped build it.

Kroll now felt fine. His irritation at the disorderly mess that had greeted him when he stepped out of the *Block* was gone. Things were as they should be. He turned onto the *Appellplatz* and headed for the *Jourhaus,* the big guardhouse that enclosed the main gateway into the prison compound. In front of the gate he could see a number of men, prisoners, waiting for the arrival of the SS guards. He hurried to join them, for latecomers were severely punished. As he approached, he was struck by the strange observation that the men of the bakery *Kommando* were, for the most part, standing, while those in the crematorium *Kommando* were sitting or lying on the ground. The lucky devils in the bakery *Kommando,* he thought, I'm sure *they* get enough to eat.

He joined the men and made a point of standing on his feet. He glanced at his watch. It was now six forty-seven. Damn, he thought, this watch is fast. But at least that's better than being slow.

In fact, his watch was not fast. The SS supervisors were late today and did not arrive until nearly five to seven. There were four this morning; which was odd, and only one of them, a *Scharführer,* came up to the gate. The other three entered a side door and disappeared into the *Jourhaus*. Kroll noticed that one of them was carrying a white bundle. Idly, he wondered what it was and why, for the first time in his memory, the SS men had arrived late.

The *Scharführer* watched his companions go into the *Jourhaus* and then addressed the prisoners on the other side of the gate. His voice was strained into a high pitch, and he seemed agitated. "You prisoners," he called out, "all of you. You return to your quarters. Stay there. No work for you today. Go!"

Kroll wasn't one to argue with such an order, and he quickly turned back toward the *Lagerstrasse*. I knew it was going to be a good day! he thought to himself. It never occurred to him to wonder why the work details had been canceled.

He was halfway across the *Appellplatz* when low but excited

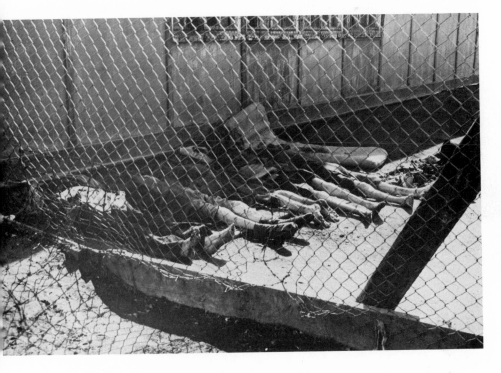

Bodies of prisoners who had died during the night lie behind each barrack, waiting for the Moorexpress *to pick them up and take them to the crematorium.*

sounds from the group of prisoners behind him made him stop and turn around. The men were all staring up at the *Jourhaus*. "What the hell?" Kroll said aloud as, astonished, he saw a white sheet flying from the flagpole on the roof.

6. White Flag

His eyes open, Piet Maas saw the stooped form of Herman Plaga, the Czech journalist, coming toward him. A vigorous curse in Polish broke the quiet of the room as Plaga's foot accidentally grazed the chest of one of the men sleeping on the floor. Plaga ignored it and bent over to whisper in Maas's ear.

"You won't believe it, Piet, but there's a white flag waving from the top of the *Jourhaus.*"

"What did you say?" Maas shouted, raising himself on one elbow.

"Shh!" Plaga replied. "Be quiet. You'll start a stampede in the room. I wanted you to be the first to know. Come. I'll help you to the window."

With great dexterity, Maas pushed himself upright and swung the stumps of his legs over the edge of the bunk. The two men with whom he shared the bed didn't even stir and continued their snoring without interruption.

Plaga had already taken Maas's crutches and was holding them out to his friend. Maas looked at them and at the carpet of men sleeping on the floor and raised his eyes questioningly to Plaga. "How the hell am I going to get to the window without waking everyone up?" he asked.

"So wake them up. The lazy bastards are oversleeping, anyway," Plaga answered with a grin.

In fact, the crutches found a way between the bodies without waking up a single man. It was Plaga, rather, whose feet created a trail of shouts and curses as the two men wound their way to the window.

"You see?" he said triumphantly, pointing through the grimy window with one hand and steadying his friend with the other. "Do you see, Piet?"

"Holy Jesus!" Maas muttered, staring as if hypnotized at the roof of the *Jourhaus*. For a couple of minutes the two men said nothing more. Their eyes seemed riveted to the white flag.

"I knew it all along," Plaga finally said, his voice quivering on the brink of sobs. "I knew I would live to see the end of the war! And here it is. I can't believe it, Piet. I just can't believe it." Maas saw the tears running down his hollow cheeks. Freeing his left hand for one precarious moment, he gently patted his friend's back. "Plaga, old fellow," he said gently. "Don't go too fast. We don't know what it means. Let's continue to be scared, and cautious, until we see the Americans step through the gates."

Just then a commotion erupted in the room next door. A moment later the door into their room burst open and a man stepped in, shouting at the top of his voice. "They're surrendering! A white flag! On the *Jourhaus* roof! They're surrendering!" In an instant, pandemonium broke loose. Men jumped to their feet, shouting wildly at each other in almost every language spoken in Europe and rushing wildly for the door. Maas watched them run out. In less than a couple of minutes the room was empty, except for him and Plaga and eight or nine bodies of men who had not made it through the night. "Fools!" Maas shouted angrily after them. He turned his head slowly toward Plaga. "Haven't you noticed that the guard towers are still manned?"

"You're a skeptic," Plaga replied jocularly. "Come, let's go outside too."

"Not me," Maas said firmly. "There's a crazy crowd outside, and there are the same Nazi swine on those towers who have always been there. I don't know what's going on, but I sure as hell am going to play it carefully." He could tell that Plaga was unimpressed by his reasoning.

"I'm going out. I'll come back and tell you if I find out anything," Plaga said as he headed for the door.

Before he reached it, Maas called out, "Hey, there's a chair underneath that bunk to your left. Do me a favor, will you, and bring it to me?''

"Sure,'' Plaga replied, hurriedly pulling out the chair and placing it by the window. He helped Maas sit down on it.

"Thanks,'' Maas said as his friend left the room. "Be careful, will you?''

Leaning his crutches carefully up against the windowsill, Maas reached into his tunic pocket and pulled out a tattered notebook and a pencil. He turned to a fresh page and, in bigger letters than usual, wrote the date at the top. Then he began writing the first entry for the day:

> *0700. Plaga comes in. A white flag is flying*
> *on top of the command tower.*

He finished writing and looked down at the entry. Tears welled up in his eyes, and from nowhere, seemingly, a sob rose up within him. He smiled limply. "I'm as excited as Plaga after all,'' he said to himself. He looked slowly around the room, shaking his head sadly as his eyes rested on the corpses who were now its only other occupants. His gaze returned to the diary on his lap. He added two more lines to the same entry:

> *Am looking at white flag on main entrance tower.*
> *Cannot say anything else about it. A white flag!*

Maas had believed in his luck for a long time. There was no other explanation for the fact that he was still alive. He needed to hold on to that belief now—and to his luck itself. He allowed his mind to recall times when it had pulled him through in the past. . . .

There was the day he attacked a target drone that was being towed by another plane over the sea near Den Helder. The burst of bullets from his twin machine guns lacerated the drone, but they also cut through the wire cable—no more than three millimeters thick—by which it was being towed. This was not an unusual occurrence, and the crew of the tow plane had with them a spare drone for just such contingencies. As they tried to let it out, however, it slipped from their grasp and fell into the sea. There was now nothing to do but cancel the target practice and return to the base. Maas landed and taxied over to the apron. The ground crew put blocks on the wheels and then stared in astonishment at the propeller. Apparently, the synchronizing mechanism that enabled the machine guns to fire through the propeller had malfunctioned, and the guns had blasted away a portion of the blade. Later, Maas would try to calculate the odds against his survival on this day. They seemed like one in a million that he should have shot the cable *and* that the second drone should have been lost before he could dive down to attack it. The odds against his having survived that dive would have been even longer. The stress of the dive would have torn off the damaged propeller, the engine would have exploded, and he would have been hurtled helplessly into the sea.

But he did survive this fantastically long shot. Just a few weeks later—it was April 19, 1936—his engagement to Elisabeth was announced. That day, he was on a training mission with his squadron. They were flying in close formation, and the plane behind him collided with his tail, shearing off a portion of it. It took him several of the worst moments in his life thus far to regain control of the craft, but the damage was so extensive that he knew he could not bring it down safely. He would have to bail out. For the present, however, he was flying over Utrecht, and he had to keep the plane aloft until he was clear of the built-up zone. Somehow he managed to do this. Then, cutting off the motor, he pulled open the cockpit and jumped. The plane crashed harmlessly into a field. Maas's parachute opened and carried him gently down to the ground. He thereby became the first Dutch Air Force pilot to save himself by parachute.

And then there was that time in the prison at Amersfoort when he was lined up with ten other men who were to be shipped off to the concentration camp at Natzweiler. Two of the men in the group were twin brothers. An SS officer came into the room to inspect the group. His name, Maas learned later, was Cottelle. Without a word, he walked along the line, merely glancing at each man's face. Then he walked back again and turned to inspect the men once more. He was halfway down the line when suddenly, without warning or reason, he kicked one of the twin brothers with the full force of his heavy boot in the groin. The man fell to the ground screaming in agony. Word-

Two pages of the diary in which Piet Maas recorded his experiences at Dachau, showing his entries for April 29, 1945.

lessly, Cottelle began kicking him in the kidneys, in the stomach, and then in the face. After the first few kicks, the screams ceased. Presently the writhing of the body ceased too. The man was dead. Without a further glance, Cottelle left the room. In the surge of terrible emotions that overwhelmed him at this spectacle, Maas did not fail to notice that once again his luck had held out. Cottelle had chosen his victim entirely at random. It had been a matter of luck that he had not picked on Maas.

Or again, when Natzweiler had been evacuated in face of the American advance and he had been put on that terrible train to Dachau. The cattle car in which he was traveling quickly became a rolling morgue. Four days later, when they reached Dachau, Maas was on the verge of death. Unconscious, he was lifted out of the train along with the mass of corpses it contained and carried on a cart to the *Appellplatz*. The bodies, after all, had to be checked by the SS before cremation. Night fell before this could be done. Maas regained consciousness on the *Appellplatz,* lying in a row of corpses. He knew where he was, and in the brief moments that he could open his eyes, he stared up at the stars that shone so brightly in the dark sky. He was desperately cold—it was November—and he was wearing only the thin striped uniform that was standard issue in Natzweiler. He was too weak to move, let alone to crawl away to safety. He hoped that he would die before he was thrown into the ovens, but he accepted the possibility that he might not.

All of a sudden he heard a shuffling sound a short distance away, and then a hand gently shook his shoulder. A voice called his name. With all the strength he had left, he uttered a small groan so that the man might know he was alive.

"Piet," he now heard the voice say, "this is Felix Schwartz, from Natzweiler. I recognized you when they brought your transport in. I just knew you were alive. I've come to get you. No, don't move." Recognizing that Maas was freezing, Schwartz took off his own coat and put it around his friend. "You are married, and so it's much more important that you return home one day than I. Take it." And then he grabbed Maas's shoulders and, on all fours, crawled away, dragging the half-dead Dutchman along with him to the safety of the nearest *Block*. Two months later, Schwartz was dead from

typhus. By that time, Maas had recovered to an amazing degree. He
had held Schwartz's hand while he died. . . .

He looked down at the diary on his lap. Without knowing it, he
had turned to the back of the little book. Here, on page after page,
were the names of men he had known in both Natzweiler and Dachau. Their names. Their home addresses. And the dates of their
death. He sighed. Could it really be that the list was now complete?
That there would not be more names to add today? And tomorrow?
And in the weeks and months and years that stretched ahead? He
doubted it.

But certainly, he, Maas, had been fantastically lucky so far. He
looked out the window again. Yes, the white flag was still flying over
the *Jourhaus*. Men were milling around the *Appellplatz* in small,
fluid groups that reformed into new clusters with each moment.
Again that fatally enticing thought occurred to him. How he would
love to be able to move through the elements, speeding forward,
soaring and diving, as he once had done! He could almost feel the
joystick in his hand again, and the manly challenge of overcoming
the confusion in his stomach and head as he put the craft through its
paces. He looked down at the floor. There was no point in allowing
himself to get carried away by these thoughts. Without legs he would
never fly again.

He reminded himself also that Lady Luck had not always smiled
graciously on him. After all, how lucky could any prisoner in a concentration camp consider himself to be? His mind went back to the
night of September 1, 1941. . . .

For fourteen months he had been active in the Dutch underground, his missions connected primarily with intelligence-gather-
ing. A set of drawings of German defense installations under construction along the coastline fell into his group's hands. They were of
great importance. Maas and two companions were ordered to take
them to England. A route was planned along the canals to the open
sea. A small fishing boat was obtained. For three nights the German
guard posts along the route were checked. Maas was heartened to discover how lax the guards were. At one key point, where they would

have to pass under a canal bridge, the sentries marched by only every twelve minutes.

They set out. All went well. They were near the sea, with only one more bridge to pass under, when the deep rumble of an approaching flight of bombers reached their ears. A moment later, the night sky was pierced by a score of searchlights, and all around, antiaircraft guns opened fire. The three men gazed up in fascination as one plane was caught by a searchlight. It weaved its way to one side and the other in a desperate attempt to shake off the fatal light. But to no avail. A shell exploded in its tail, and the big plane plummeted to the ground. Only two parachutes opened.

In the noise of the raid, Maas had felt free to open up full the engine throttle, confident that the gunfire all around would muffle its loud chugging. Now that the British bomber had been shot down, however, the German sentries would be on the alert for the fallen bomber's crew. The bridge loomed directly ahead, and it was too late to ease up on the throttle. Maas made an instant decision: Full speed ahead, and perhaps we'll catch the sentries by surprise.

The boat passed safely under the bridge, and they were already some yards from it, preparing to celebrate their luck, when a burst of machine-gun fire opened up from the sentry box. One of the men was killed instantly. Maas took three of the bullets in his legs, and at once passed out from the pain. The third man was unhit. He seized the tiller and steered the boat in a zigzag course away from the gunfire. A bank of fog sheltered them from view, and another burst of gunfire splattered harmlessly into the canal only five feet away from the boat. A few minutes later, they were out of the canal and on the sea. Maas recovered consciousness only to discover that they were drifting helplessly on the high waves. A round of bullets, he learned, had torn through their fuel tank, emptying its gasoline into the water. A short while later, they were picked up by a German patrol boat.

Had it not been for the air raid, they would probably have been able to cross to England without incident. It was one of those things you couldn't allow for: bad luck.

Bad luck. There had been other times, too, and none that Maas remembered more vividly than that time six months earlier. Then, too, the Americans had been close—to Natzweiler. Then, too, their planes had flown overhead and the sound of artillery could be heard clearly in the distance. And then, too, the prisoners had been certain that their liberation was imminent. Just a matter of days. Just a matter of hours. Every sign pointed to it. The worried looks on the SS men's faces. The burning of the camp's records. And hour by hour the gunfire came closer.

But there was no liberation for the men of Natzweiler. At a time when the German artillery was coming from *behind* the camp, thousands of men had been assembled on the *Appellplatz* and had been mowed down by machine guns from the guard towers. The rest, among them Maas, had been hurriedly packed into a freight train and shipped off to Dachau. The Americans, it was said, were no more than one hour away. One single hour! That is all that had stood between Maas and liberation six months before.

He reminded himself that he was lucky not to have been murdered by the machine guns. Particularly lucky because the Germans could not have expected much by way of useful labor from a man without legs. Yes, he was lucky to have gotten to Dachau. But that wasn't a very consoling thought. He would have been far luckier if the Americans had arrived at Natzweiler just one single hour earlier.

And now there were all the same signs. He had seen them for days. The anxiety of the guards. The restlessness of the prisoners. The rumors—infinite in their variety, absolute in their authenticity—that swept through the camp by the minute. The Americans were coming. The Third Reich was *kaput*. Soon we will be liberated.

There were other rumors as well, which had particular credibility for men like Maas who had hurriedly been shipped from other concentration camps, in the path of advancing Allied forces, to Dachau. These men knew that the Germans would not quietly hand over the keys of a concentration camp to the enemy. They knew that elsewhere the Germans had tried to hide the evidence of their crimes. Burning or shooting the inmates. Burying them. Or shipping them off to Dachau. Now, with the Americans advancing on Dachau, there was nowhere else to send the few still healthy enough to be of use to the Third Reich. And because there was nowhere else, it was logical to suppose that this time *all* the survivors would be liquidated. Per-

haps, at the very end, Dachau would remain true to the prisoners'
saying—their response to the SS's *Arbeit Macht Frei*—that the only
way out of Dachau was through the crematorium chimney.

Maas checked himself. A few moments ago he had been congratulating himself on his good luck, and yet now he was as depressed and fearful as it was possible for him to be. He forced himself to look up again, through the window, at the white flag on the
Jourhaus.

There it was, fluttering in the breeze.

7. Natalie

Only a few feet away from where the International Committee was meeting, Natalie Walter's disease-wracked body was heaving in the throes of a dream. She was running frantically across an open field, light brown in color, trying to escape from the SS. She could not see them, but she knew that her life depended on her getting away. The field stretched to the horizon on every side. There was nowhere for her to hide. The stubble of the harvested crop pierced her bare feet painfully as she ran. A cave opened out from the side of a little hill. She ran there to hide, but when she got close, she saw that the mouth of the cave was sealed off by steel bars. Behind them, naked men and women crowded, their faces distorted by insanity. She ran up to warn them of the SS, but they responded only with lunatic screams and gesticulations. "You must escape," she cried. "You must escape!" They ignored her.

Despite the nightmare, Natalie knew the moment she woke up that her fever had broken. She smiled softly. Her limbs still ached terribly, and her thirst was so great that it seemed to her as though an ocean full of sweet, fresh water would not slake it. But her mind was clear again, and the nightmarish, semiconscious delirium of the past few days—she had no idea how many days it had been—was already beginning to feel like a distant memory. She felt a profound sense of gratitude. She still did not know whether she would live, whether the fever would return, whether some other terrible doom awaited her. But for the immediate moment these anxieties, although present, were distant. They, too, attested to her recovered consciousness. All of a sudden, she felt a yearning to see cornflowers growing in a field, to pluck a bunch of them and rub the jagged edges of their petals against the tip of her nose as she had done long, long ago when she was a little girl in Austria. That yearning, too, resolved itself into gratitude at the memory of her childhood. Gratitude. She was not sure to whom she owed it, yet words dimly remembered from the past stirred within her. *Shehechiyonu.* She paused, uncertain. Yes, here they were. She whispered the ancient invocation, loudly enough to be audible to herself. *Boruch ato adonai elohaynu melech ho'olom shehechiyonu vekimonu vehigiyonu lazmon hozeh.* "Blessed art thou, O Lord our God, King of the Universe, who gave us life and established us and brought us to this time." Again she smiled, almost shyly. Fancy my saying a prayer! she thought. And still that feeling of gratitude lingered—and with it, a sense of something unremembered, a pleasant something, which also was contributing to that feeling of gratitude. She couldn't find it.

There was something else she had to find. This it took her only a moment to remember. She reached under the blanket into the pocket of her dress. Her grip tightened on a neatly folded piece of cloth—a handkerchief. She pulled it out, unfolded it, and held it up in front of her. The bright designs on the white cloth were vivacious, cheerful. When she squinted her eyes, the colors resolved themselves into names. Hildegard. Wassily. Hans. Wladimir. Lisabeth. Puck. And many others. For now, the people whose names these were remained indistinct. Their faces, their nationalities, the concentration camps at which she had known them, the conversations she'd had with them, the things they had done for her and she for them—none of these was invoked by their gaily embroidered signatures on the handkerchief. Rather, the sight of those names aroused in her, in their mass, that infinitely pleasing sensation of closeness to friends whose loyalty, concern, and devotion are beyond doubt. The kind of feeling you can almost snuggle up to, to which also is added a conscious appreciation of your own value as a person.

This was a feeling that Natalie had had only in a most tenuous and intermittent way before her arrest. It had been difficult to acquire it as the only Jewish girl in her class in Vienna, when the viciousness of children was joined with, and encouraged by, the viciousness of

Natalie Walter's handkerchief, embroidered with the signatures of the camp inmates who had become her friends.

their parents' racial fanaticism. It had been difficult to acquire it in
Paris, when the miseries of being a defenseless Jewish girl were
joined by those of being a refugee, of being a German (as her school-
mates insisted she was), and of being consumed by fear for her missing father. And when word came that he had been killed by the Nazis
in a camp outside Munich, she had felt, for many days, that the
world was such a vile place that she did not wish to be happy in it, to
be liked by other people, or to care for them. Then one day her
mother announced that they were going to move to Amsterdam, in
Holland.

There, everyone was kinder. She felt herself surrounded by decent and honest people. She was grateful to them, and in large part it
was her gratitude that prompted her to enter nurse's training. In some
measure, she would repay the Dutch people for their kindness, which
slowly came to seem to her not only a kindness to her personally but
a testimony to the sort of world for which she yearned, but which so
little in her experience up to now seemed to make plausible. For the
first time now, as a nurse, people looked to her for help and comfort;
and they responded, not to her racial origin or her political beliefs or
her nationality, but to the abundance of compassion and skill that she
was so happy to lavish on them and that made her, no less than
them, feel human.

All the same, her work in the hospital left many needs unsatis-
fied. Patients were not friends. They responded to what you did for
them, not to what you were. They got better, or they got worse and
died, or they were moved to another ward; and one way or another
they were soon out of your life. What Natalie still yearned for were
real friends. She had never had one.

The desperate needs of war led her to extreme acts of self-
sacrifice, of giving to others. In the hospital in Amsterdam, the Germans, learning of her exceptional skill, asked that she be transferred
to the ward where German soldiers and political prisoners were being
cared for. Natalie resisted the transfer for fear that her Austrian background and Jewish religion would be discovered. She refused to
agree—until the hospital director himself came to her and told her
that he had been threatened by the Germans and must move her to
their ward. Natalie gave in, with deep misgivings. One day the hospi-

tal director came to see her again. The Dutch underground had attacked a German convoy, and one of their men had been captured. It was imperative to know whether he was in the ward where political prisoners were being treated. Would Natalie make inquiries? And if she did discover that he was in that ward, would she pass on to him details of the cover story on which the other underground men, now being interrogated on suspicion that they had participated in the raid, had agreed? Natalie found the man—he had been badly wounded—but unfortunately he was unconscious. She asked the duty nurse to give the cover story to him the moment he regained consciousness. The woman refused to do so. She was married. She had children. She couldn't risk everything for a stranger. She was sorry, but no. Let Natalie find someone else.

There was no one else to be trusted. In desperation, knowing that the man would be executed if his cover story were broken, she wrote down the message she had to give him on a scrap of paper and placed it in his pajama pocket. Hoping that he would read it before the Germans came to him again. Hoping that he would regain consciousness before the Germans discovered the note. But her luck ran out. A German doctor, examining the unconscious man, found the note. He read it and called the Gestapo.

Even now, Natalie had a chance to escape, for word reached her almost immediately of what had happened. But she knew that the Germans took hostages, and she feared that they would come after her stepfather if they could not get hold of her. So she decided to allow herself to be captured in order to spare her stepfather.

To be able to give—that was a balm for her wounded soul, and it was a disposition she brought with her to the camps. Five months after her arrest, during which she was shunted from one prison in Holland to another, she was sent to Ravensbrück. No sooner had she stepped into the camp than she again found ways of helping others. Marched from the train along a sinister black path made from crushed cinders, she passed a group of prisoners who had evidently been at Ravensbrück for a long time. Never had she seen anyone look quite as ghoulish as these women. Not in the Dutch prisons. Not even in the cancer wards. They were like thin wisps of people—bones, really—with a little bit of fleshless skin clinging to them. They shuffled rather than walked; and their heads seemed to career recklessly on their necks as they did so. Huge eyes bulged ominously from faces that otherwise were drawn and entirely expressionless. Natalie did not believe it was possible for human beings to be reduced to such a condition. A vast surge of horrified pity overtook her. She reached for the three dried slices of bread that she had hidden in a pocket, broke each into four pieces, and distributed each to a prisoner. As she handed out the last piece, a guard saw her. He sneered contemptuously. "Generous, huh?" he asked. "How long do you think it will be before you look like them?"

It was on that first march into Ravensbrück that she passed a cage, with bars on it as though in a zoo, filled with naked, horrendously emaciated women, each contorted in postures and grimaces of insanity. The Dantesque vision became the source of a nightmare that would haunt her almost every night thereafter.

But it was at Ravensbrück, too, that Natalie found her first friends; and while this experience did not wipe out the terrible realities of that place—the ceaseless hunger and anxiety, the abominable filth, the frequent bouts of despair whenever she thought about the future—it was nevertheless exhilarating. Friendship, she discovered, somewhat to her surprise and relief, did not mean intimacy here. To share of yourself with others required in the first place that you delve into yourself, and into your past. Faced with the incessant struggle for physical and emotional survival, this was a luxury that one could afford only rarely and briefly. Too rarely, in fact, for it to be the basis on which friendship could be built.

Rather, friendship here meant sharing. Food, when it could be spared; and clothing. It meant looking after one another: protecting each other, to the extent possible, from the omnipresent hardships, and consoling each other when that protection failed. And above all, at least for Natalie, it meant sharing childish delights. To inscribe your name on another person's handkerchief or to have her inscribe hers on yours was like becoming a blood relative. To find a piece of brightly colored cloth and to pull out some of its threads with which to embroider these signatures—and perhaps to barter some of your threads for someone else's—was like exchanging licks from ice-cream cones. And then there were the recipes—even entire menus—

that Natalie and her friends would exchange as they huddled close together for warmth on the narrow bunks. Dishes and meals that were dreamed of only by Parisian chefs at the height of their careers. Or, just as often, food that was so commonplace in ordinary life that it would seem necessary to bring a newspaper to the table while one ate. Friendship, Natalie learned, really meant above all having a good time doing things you liked with people you liked—and who liked you. It was no more complicated than that; and yet that was something she had never experienced before. For that experience, without doubt the most beautiful in her life, she had to thank Ravensbrück and Dachau. It did not strike her as bizarre that it was in these places that she learned what friendship was all about, and tasted of it.

The happiest moment in her life, she thought, had been last Christmas, when she was in a work camp at Munich. Conditions there were in almost every respect as bad as in Ravensbrück. True, it was possible to "organize" extra bits of food, and even coal for the little stove in the barrack, to a degree that was unheard of in Ravensbrück. But offsetting that advantage was the desperately dangerous and hard work to which Natalie and the other women had been assigned: clearing away rubble after Allied air attacks. Once, a wall had collapsed and buried three of the women. The SS had not even allowed the other prisoners to try to rescue them. And there was always the fear of unexploded bombs.

This was her first Christmas as a prisoner. When she was a child in Vienna, her family had always celebrated Christmas, even though it was a Christian festival. In Paris she and her mother had not had the heart to do so, but once they moved to Amsterdam they began celebrating it again. Partly for her stepfather, who was a Gentile, but also because she always felt that Christmas was one of the loveliest days, and she saw no reason why a Jewish girl should not share in its delight.

In Munich, Natalie lived in a cellar, with about forty other women, in what had once been a school. For many days she and the others had hoarded small pieces of bread, saved from their meager daily allowance. These were kept in a common box, and despite the terrible hunger that wracked their stomachs incessantly, the women had enough faith in each other to know that no one would steal from

that box. Margarine was also deposited there, and—most marvel-
ously—a small amount of artificial strawberry jam. On Christmas
Eve the bread was broken into small squares—perhaps an inch and a
half long—and each of these was smeared with a bit of margarine and
an even skimpier bit of jam. There was enough to give each woman
three of these little delicacies. They ate them slowly, but gleefully
and with excitement. Thus sated, they formed a circle in the dimly lit
room and sang carols. Some of the songs were familiar to almost all
the women. Then three women sang a song from their native Poland,
and were followed by Slovak women singing one of theirs. Everyone
was happy. No one talked about previous Christmases, at home with
their families, or wondered where they would be spending next
Christmas. For Natalie the joy of sharing these moments with the
other women, feeling so completely accepted by them in their celebration, feeling so close to them, was a happiness she had often
dreamed of but never expected to find in her own life.

After several carols had been sung, one of the women, an exqui-
sitely lithe little Dutch girl named Marie, got to her feet. Malnutrition
and hardship had not flattened her finely sculpted face or dimmed the
deep softness of her blue eyes. She possessed, Natalie thought, an in-
extinguishable beauty, which the ugliness of their surroundings
served only to heighten. Wordlessly, she raised her hand, ran it
through the short blond stubble on her head, and then, transforming
the movement into one of tender self-love, caressed the rim of her ear
and the length of her cheek with her fingertips.

"A dance from Bali," she said softly in Dutch. And for the next
five minutes she moved her limbs with the soft, delicate beauty of
drops of dew sliding down a rose petal in the early morning stillness.
Her arms glided like a snake; her neck swayed like a young palm tree
in the tropical breeze. It was pure magic. Natalie felt herself absorbed
into the movements. She floated along with Marie's undulations. It
was the serenest moment of her life.

And when it was over, Marie returned to her place in the circle.
No one spoke or applauded. Only a few muffled sobs broke the
silence in the room. Natalie got to her feet and walked over to where
Marie sat. She knelt down in front of her and embraced her. She
kissed her cheeks, and her tears mingled with those of the other

woman. Natalie had never before known such happiness, such close-ness.

Lying in bed now, Natalie remembered that night. She crumpled the handkerchief hurriedly and returned it to her pocket. Marie's name was not on it. On Christmas Day she had been killed by a guard. He had tried to rape her. She had resisted, and he, in his fury, had broken her neck with one blow of his hand. The brute, his lust undiminished, had penetrated Marie's lifeless body and, when he had finished, had walked out of the room with as much concern as if he had just blown out a match. Natalie had watched the whole episode. So had most of the other women from the previous night. There was nothing they could do to save their friend.

Remembering Marie, Natalie cried. She ran her hand over her head and along her face as she recalled Marie doing. The gesture was soothing, and she repeated it several times. How good to have friends, she told herself. Even if one has to mourn their deaths.

This comforting thought brought back all of a sudden the one that she had not been able to seize hold of earlier. It was her fever! A limp smile crossed her face. Typhus with fever, she remembered, could be contracted from drinking polluted water, and not necessarily from body lice.

Lice! She remembered her first horrified discovery of them on her body many months ago at Ravensbrück. She had felt so violated then, as if her body had been taken over by those vile little beasts. Panic had seized her; she had wanted to run away, leaving her in-fested body behind for the lice to crawl over. And when that panic died down, there came instead a profound sense of shame. She was polluted, filthy, unclean, just as they always said Jews were—and she was a carrier of infestation. How could she ever return to her spot-lessly clean home, where even the doorstep was scrubbed? How could she ever hug her parents or move among civilized, decent people—she who was now a lice-infested pariah?

That the other women in the camp were also covered with lice was no consolation to Natalie. It did not diminish the shame she felt, which was excruciatingly her own.

Would people back home know that lice were widespread in the camps? Would they think that she had them? What would they think of her if they knew? These questions worried her incessantly. Perhaps it would be possible to lie about it, she thought, and to minimize the extent to which lice were found in the camps. But when typhus broke out and reached epidemic proportions she knew that this would be impossible. What if she too got typhus? That the disease might prove fatal to her, as it had for so many thousands of prisoners, sometimes worried her less than the proof it would constitute that she too had been infected by the lice. And then how would she ever be able to look decent people—*clean* people—in the face again? You couldn't deny that you'd had typhus, and they would know. . . .

Now at last she knew what she had been feeling so grateful for. It was not she who had been polluted, but the water! Didn't the fever prove that?

8. The International Committee

"You're absolutely wrong, General," Connally said in a voice that was none the less confident for being quiet. "Absolutely and *dangerously* wrong," he added.

The Russian was affronted. He was not used to having his judgment questioned, at least not on this side of the Oder. Like Connally, he had a natural air of authority that even the SS acknowledged—not just in the exuberant way in which they mistreated him, but in the slightly tentative manner in which they did so, rather like schoolboys who know that they can get away with twitting their teacher but nevertheless are surprised that they can.

Connally was aware of the general's formidable personality. He respected his courage, his dignity, and the leadership he exercised over the Russian community in the camp. But he did not trust him. The Russian was, it seemed to Connally, congenitally addicted to playing games of one sort or another. There was always something behind any statement he made or action he took. And what that something was was invariably a source of bafflement to Connally—and all too suggestive of deviousness. Not that there was anything wrong with being devious, in Connally's view. He was, after all, one of the most successful spies of the war, and you don't become that without having a lot of tricks up your sleeve. But all too often the general's behavior was cunning when it did not have to be, when there was nothing to be gained by it, and when it served only to breed mistrust and undermine effective action. Connally had never had dealings with Russians before, but it was not difficult to sense in the

101

general's manner the fear, uncertainty, and instability that character-
ized Stalin's world.

He was not going to let the general rock the boat now. Not now,
of all times. There was a personal grudge at stake. Connally had been
one of three men to suggest that a camp-wide committee, representing the major national groups of prisoners, be formed to represent the
prisoners' interests as best they could and to deal with the stresses—
no one at first had anticipated the present crisis—that would inevitably accompany the closing days of the war. Hopman had been one of
the other two men, and the Pole Natlewski was the third. The national groups, often housed in the same barracks, had developed their
own leadership in a natural way; their leaders were well known as
such in the camp and probably to the SS, too. To bring them all
together in one organization was, as Connally and his two colleagues
knew full well, a risky undertaking. If word of a committee—or of
attempts to form it—reached the ears of the SS, the three men's lives
would be worth even less than they had been before. Yet it seemed to
all three that it was a risk worth taking, indeed that they were obliged
to take, for the common good. And it had been in that spirit that the
representatives of the other nations had agreed to participate in the
Committee.

The first meeting could have given any observer a clear understanding of why the League of Nations had been such an ignominious
failure. Common good or no, the Russians claimed the right to the
Committee's presidency by virtue of their large proportion of the
camp population. On the same grounds the Poles made the same
claim—the Poles, half if not more of whose number was made up of
Jews whom the Poles viewed with little less contempt than the SS
themselves did. The French, for their part, were not only unwilling to
see the presidency of the Committee go to one of the eastern nations,
but magisterially insisted on some unspecified *droit* that entitled them
to this post. In the end, Connally, the British representative, was
elected. Not because of grand speeches that he made—for he made
none. And not because of any back-room lobbying—for he did not
engage in it. But because he was manifestly the best choice. He was
patient, willing to listen to others, and yet able to make cool and rational decisions that others readily accepted. And more than most

men in Dachau or anywhere else, he had experience in dealing effectively with the SS and Gestapo in ways that were particularly well suited to the present need.

So Connally became the chairman of the International Committee, and the Russians boycotted it. For Connally this was a personal affront. Hence his grudge against the Russian general. But it was not only that. Connally knew perfectly well that with a third of the camp population unrepresented in the Committee, decisions that it made would be even more ineffective than they might otherwise be. How powerful could the Committee be at the best of times, representing and coordinating some thirty thousand diseased, famished, and powerless prisoners against the deadly machinations of the SS? Not very effective, to be sure. But with the Russian boycott, even that minimal effectiveness was likely to be undermined.

Nevertheless, the Committee carried on as best it could. The camp was bursting with rumors, many of them entirely false and most of them capable of triggering actions by the prisoners that would inevitably be self-defeating, either because they were too optimistic or because they were too pessimistic. A principal task of the Committee, therefore, was to gather and centralize accurate information about the course of the war, about the morale of the SS, and above all, of course, about the SS's intentions toward the prisoners. The daily influx of hundreds and often thousands of prisoners during the past four months, while creating calamitous conditions in every other respect, had at least this beneficial effect, that it enabled the Committee to obtain a measure of information from the outside world. Reports from men sent to work in *Kommandos* outside the camp were likewise sifted. And it was from a trusty who worked in the camp secretariat, a Greek who spoke fluent German, that the Committee had learned of the orders from Berlin to liquidate the entire population of prisoners before the Americans arrived at Dachau.

Accurate information would not save the prisoners, but there was no hope of preventing a final holocaust unless the Committee kept itself informed as best it could. With the information it had acquired, it had been successful on several occasions during the past few days in frustrating the SS plans to evacuate large columns of prisoners who were to be led off to their doom in the mountains to the south. Connally and his partners knew little if anything about an extraordinary man several thousands of miles away who had developed techniques of noncooperation with an overwhelmingly powerful opponent that would lead, two years hence, to the fall of the British Empire. Yet the tactics employed under the Committee's direction when the orders had come to prepare for evacuation a few days before were those of the Mahatma. You can't march off columns of men unless the men fall into those columns. And by creating confusion, interminable delays, ignoring orders while seeming not to, and simply not turning up when and where they were expected to, the prisoners had in good measure foiled the plans for the camp's evacuation. The organization of this disorder was the work of the Committee.

But such tactics could only postpone a showdown. They could not prevent it from taking place, and they could not ensure the prisoners' success when it occurred. In fact, they offered hardly the slightest chance that the prisoners would be able to emerge successfully—that is to say, alive—from that showdown. And so the Committee, with an audacity that was the hallmark of its chairman, set out to acquire an arsenal. If the SS moved to exterminate the prisoners, the prisoners would at least have a chance to fight back.

The objective was truly heroic, outrageously unrealistic, and doomed to failure from the outset. And yet the Committee had no alternative but to try. Not because anyone seriously expected success from these efforts but because failure to undertake them would have been to acquiesce in one's own destruction. The people of the Warsaw ghetto had known this. And so did the people of Dachau. To fight back even when there was no chance of winning, even of surviving, was to hold on to one's dignity, to assert one's human stubbornness and hence one's humanity when there was nothing else to be gained by doing so. And there could be no illusions on this score. The arsenal assembled by the International Committee presently comprised two revolvers, with twenty-five rounds of ammunition. And a few knives.

Perhaps all this was at odds with the pacifist strategy adopted by the Committee against the order to form columns for deportation a few days before. But no one gave thought to questions of ideological consistency under these circumstances. What mattered was to survive. Or to die with dignity.

And the Committee had made other efforts to bolster morale. It tried to obtain extra food supplies—and sometimes succeeded. It organized a rudimentary school for the Russian and Polish children who, appallingly enough, were incarcerated in the camp in the same conditions as the adults. It made efforts to mitigate the desperate plight of the sick.

None of this could have been done by one man. In fact, it depended on the remarkable solidarity between prisoners of different nationalities, religions, and political convictions that was such a striking feature of the camp's life—except when it broke down. Connally was not the Committee, therefore, and the Committee's achievements were not his own. But more than any other man in Dachau he was the guiding spirit of organized resistance to the SS. It was his farsightedness and persistence that had brought the Committee into being and made possible its functioning.

Laboring under fantastic odds, which were compounded by the results of prolonged torture and malnutrition, Connally did not have much patience for the Russians' behavior. In the past, their obstructionism had been frustrating but only potentially calamitous. Now, however, the chips were down. The Americans were close at hand. And so was *Wolkenbrand,* the cold-blooded liquidation of the entire prison population. This was no time for political games—or, for that matter, for humoring the Russians as Connally had occasionally forced himself to do. The final crisis had arrived. If the Committee was to do anything to save the prisoners' lives, it would have to do it *now*. And with everyone, including the Russians, acting in unison.

The general, however, was being insistent. "There is no evidence for what you say, comrade," he replied. "What we have are rumors, hearsay, gossip. Old wives' tales. We have no evidence that the Germans are planning a thing. Not one shred of evidence. All you can point to—the only fact—is that they sent back the work *Kommandos* today and hung some sheets from their flagpoles. What does that mean? My opinion is that it means they are clever and know the game is up. Soon the Americans will be here, and the SS want to surrender and go home. That makes sense, no? Isn't that what you would do? So why do we listen to the provocateurs among us, whose advice will only incite the SS to something catastrophic against the entire camp? I say, let's leave things as they are and wait quietly and peacefully for the Americans to come.''

"Since you've been absent from our meetings in the past few months, you aren't familiar with all the facts at our disposal,'' Connally was about to tell the general. He checked himself. Better to let some of the others take on the Russian first, before settling him once and for all. Besides, the fact that he had bothered to attend this meeting showed that he, too, recognized that serious new developments were taking place. If he really did not believe that the SS posed a threat to the prisoners, then at least he must acknowledge that the prisoners themselves might do something (as the Russians saw it) to bring all hell down on their heads unless they were restrained from doing so. Either way, the general evidently recognized that he needed to cooperate with the Committee. To participate in plans against the SS or to persuade the Committee not to provoke the SS needlessly. He could not stand aloof any longer. That was why he was here now. His hand had been forced.

While the others talked, Connally thought back to the times when he too had brushed aside or minimized the dangers that confronted him. What a terrible price he had paid for that. And how much more terrible was the price others had paid for his mistakes. Men who had trusted his leadership. Fine, brave men whom the Gestapo had tortured to death.

Above all, there was the matter of Paul Cole. His treachery had been unmasked not long after Connally managed to establish the Organization as a going concern for rescuing Allied airmen and smuggling them back to England. Cole had pleaded for his life. The others had argued with Connally that the evidence against him was circumstantial and inconclusive. That to execute him now would leave each member of the Organization with a heightened feeling of danger—not only from the Germans but from their own fellows. If Cole could be executed on mere suspicion, then any one of them might find himself in the same position in a few days' time, or in a few weeks.

Connally *knew* he should shoot Cole. The evidence of his treachery was not conclusive, true, but it was very strong. And the danger of *not* killing him if he had indeed become a Gestapo turncoat was far greater than the danger of being guilty of a terrible and irremediable injustice. Moral philosophers might argue the point, of course, in their seminar rooms. But the streets of Marseilles were not a seminar room, and here you stood to lose not face but your life.

The question became moot. While they wavered and argued, Cole made good his escape from the bathroom in which they had locked him. Connally sometimes wondered whether they had locked him there in the hope that he would escape and thus spare them the decision they knew they would otherwise have to make. After all, every man in the room knew that the bathroom had a window that opened up onto a ledge wide enough for a drunken sailor to take a stroll. . . .

Had he been soft, he wondered? Was that the reason he had not done what his intuition and training alike had told him must be done? Sure, that had been part of it. That and the fact that he was a doctor. His business was saving lives, not putting an end to them.

But that was a fatuous argument. Cole's treachery cost many more lives than one, lives that were vastly more noble and precious than his. Why, in the crunch, had Connally protected that one despicable life and thereby helped throw away those of his brothers-in-arms?

The answer, it seemed to him, had more to do with the unreality of the life he was leading, of the decisions he had to make, and of the world in which he lived than with anything else. No matter how much he *knew* the facts, it still seemed impossible to believe and feel in one's guts that anything and everything that was real and solid and living at one moment could be extinguished in the next. That it was all so fragile and vulnerable. The unreality of war is all the greater for those who fight not in uniforms on the battlefield but as members of the underground. They appear to be just ordinary citizens going about their ordinary lives. They *must* give this appearance, and one of the things that enable them to do so is that in some measure they come to believe it themselves. Layer upon layer of deception and invention envelop the individual. But the fact is that while he must believe some of it in order to be convincing in his disguise, he must disbelieve it, too, not only in order to hold on to his sense of self but to function effectively as what he appears not to be, but is: a spy. That, Connally decided, was the gist of the problem. Becoming unreal, you lose sight of what *is*. Not completely, of course, but in part. Or else, which comes to the same thing, you *fear* that you are doing so, that you are inventing phony realities or blinding yourself to the obvious. You overreact, or else you don't react at all. Or perhaps you catch hold of what is undisputably real and are so grateful for its concreteness that you hold on to it long after it has crumbled to dust.

Cole, it seemed to Connally, despite the evidence, was what he appeared to be: a comrade. It was too bizarre to imagine this person with the familiar face and voice and bearing for what he really was: a traitor. He wasn't a person you shot in the head with a revolver.

But whom *did* you shoot in the head with a revolver? What realities *did* you alter so utterly? He remembered Hopper, the cowboy of the outfit, who shot with revolvers in both hands as they did in the movies—and with a deadly accuracy that you thought existed only in the movies. On more than one occasion, Gestapo men had been seen running away from a shoot-out with him. And with good reason, for he had killed more of their number, probably, than any other Resistance operative in France. And this Hopper, cornered in a Parisian café with his wife, a French girl, had been captured. The last shot he fired was into his wife's head, to prevent her from being taken by the Nazis and tortured to death. Is that the kind of thing you do to the person you love? To your wife? It seemed impossible to accept as real a situation that made such an act the deepest expression of your love. Can reality be so altered that that is what you must do? And is reality so trivial that, having done that, the person you love is no longer in existence? Hopper did not know. He was, poor fellow, an engineer-turned-spy. The training he had received in the Imperial College of Technology had not equipped him to answer such questions. He was haunted by uncertainty, despite the terrible tortures of the Gestapo and the desperate suffering in Dachau. "Did I do the right thing?" he asked Connally, not once but dozens of times. "Of course, old chap," Connally would reply. "Of course you did."

It was so much easier to avoid decisions. Easier, not so much because the consequences of those decisions might be fearsome or because the actions they called for were difficult, but because of the threat to present reality that was implicit in them. That reality to which perhaps you have at least become accustomed. On which you have finally managed to grasp hold. That must now be changed, and a decision to do so becomes necessary. And then the whole process of adjusting to the new reality begins again.

There were times when such considerations—this mood—tied Connally's hands, diverting his emotional and intellectual energy into minimizing dangers and justifying inaction. Such had been the case with Cole. There had been other times when, by the same token, they had led him to take appalling risks that any sensible person would have avoided. Like the time in the camp at Saarbrücken, to which he had been sent after Fresnes. There was an RAF raid one night. The bombs did not discriminate between military and civilian targets, between soldiers and defenseless women and children. The toll had been heavy.

The next morning, an SS officer came storming into the camp and ordered the British prisoners to line up. His name—Connally would never forget it—was Heinrich Hornetz. His face quaking and red with anger, he demanded of the British prisoners an explanation for the RAF raid. "What do you call that?" he spat into each man's face. "What do you call that?" The men did not answer. Until, that is, Hornetz had gone halfway down the line and was staring into Connally's face. The stocky, dark-skinned man, almost Gallic in appearance, did not turn away his eyes timidly—or prudently—as the others had done, but calmly replied to the question "What do you call that?": "I call that Coventry."

The reply came in a most matter-of-fact way. And, after all, wasn't Connally justified in giving it? Certainly he was. But the beating he received from Hornetz almost killed him and rather forcibly impressed a different reality on Connally's mind when he regained consciousness a few days later. Some of the men admired Connally's bravery. Others were appalled by his foolhardiness. Perhaps both were right. But to Connally's way of thinking, what prompted his remark was more a need to hold on to commonsensical reality than anything else. The RAF raids *were* a response to the murderous attacks by the Luftwaffe on civilian targets in England. And in the moment of his confrontation with Hornetz he could not blind himself to that reality, or do anything less than assert it unequivocally, without risking the loss of his sanity.

These considerations did not make Connally a philosopher or even an introvert. He was, in fact, a man of action, brave and effective in fighting the enemy. And for him, at least, an important reason that he was effective—and indeed an element of his bravery—was his recognition of these considerations. They helped him scrutinize his own decisions before he made them final—and to recognize the impulse to avoid making a decision. And when he did act, he understood more clearly than is often the case the fact that he *was* acting and the momentous, possibly fatal, consequences of doing so. His bravery was not reckless or foolhardy but a conscious confrontation with torture and death.

But one thing that Connally had long since learned was that no degree of circumspection, no amount of training and planning, could guarantee the successful outcome of a venture. A dozen times he and his men had rehearsed their landing in France. But how could they have anticipated the customs cutter that came into the bay at just the wrong moment? And what could they have done about it even if they had anticipated it? Or again—Roger. A member of the Organization, a courier who had asked for a meeting with him in a routine enough way. Not all the precautions in the book could have prepared him for the fact that Roger had become a traitor, and that every man in the café was a Gestapo agent. Above all, though, Connally remembered Jean. He did not know his last name; he never saw his face. Jean occupied the cell next to his at Fresnes and, through the ventilation shaft they shared, told Connally his story. He was an eighteen-year-old boy working as a grocer's assistant. His life was ordinary and uneventful. And yet one day someone—he did not know who—reported to the Gestapo that he was a member of a Communist cell that had recently been rounded up by the Nazis. Jean was arrested, placed on trial, found guilty of subversive activities, and sentenced to death. Three days after being brought to Fresnes, he was taken out and hanged. An innocent boy who knew so little about life—killed with a horribly cruel lack of reason or purpose. Against the randomness of fate, even the best-laid plans could prove pathetic in their impotence.

That randomness, however, could sometimes prove a boon. Connally recalled an incident about a year and a half before when he personally had escorted two British airmen through Occupied France down to Marseilles. It was a terribly hot day, and the train from Lille to Paris was crowded. Connally decided that what he and his two wards needed was a beer. After much jostling and pushing, the three men reached the dining car only to discover that the only three empty seats available were at a table at which two German officers were already sitting. Since the airmen spoke no French it would be dangerous to sit down at that table. But a waiter was beckoning them to it, and it would be equally dangerous to refuse to sit with the Germans and to wait for another table. Connally quietly ordered the two airmen to leave all the talking to him. They sat down, and the waiter brought three tall glasses of ice-cold beer. One of the airmen was particularly nervous, and when the train lurched slightly, he spilled his beer—right on the pants of the German officer who sat next to him. An outraged howl pierced the air. The waiter rushed up with a cloth. Connally expressed his deepest apologies to the Germans, who, it transpired, spoke no French. The Germans decided to be gracious about the accident, and a few moments later had calmed down. A tense silence ensued, the Germans thinking whatever they were thinking, Connally and his companions realizing that the incident could cost them their lives. The airman was sweating with anxiety. Suddenly a stifled rumble came from one of the Germans. It quickly became less stifled and more loud. The Kraut in the wet pants was laughing! Connally, realizing this, broke into laughter too. Helpless, hysterical laughter. In a few seconds all five men were shaking out of control with mirth. And the Germans, to show that they were good guys, despite what one might think, insisted on standing the three men another round of beer. It would have been impolite to refuse. . . .

You could never tell what might happen next, Connally reminded himself, but you had to act and think as though you could. George Pallavicini, the dreamer, was speaking passionately, poetically. Painting in gory detail the fate that awaited the prisoners. As if he were enjoying the drama of the spectacle he envisaged.

"There's no point in continuing this," Connally interrupted impatiently. "None of us knows what the white flags mean. But what we do know is that the SS has orders from Berlin to liquidate us. We have seen the first stage of these orders implemented when the VIPs were transported and the first large columns taken away. We know the Americans are very close at hand. That's what we know for facts. And another fact is that the cooking *Kommando* was sent back to their barracks. That means no food today—think of all those Red Cross supplies we can't get our hands on!—and no food today means an impossible situation in the camp. I don't think we can maintain order here if the food is withheld. And my guess is that that is what the SS wants. I think they may try something against us whether or not we riot. But if we do riot, they will use that as an excuse. And I believe at this stage they would feel happier operating with an excuse than without. These are my views as to what the facts are and what they probably mean. The white flags do not mean that we are going to have a calm and pleasant day today—April twenty-ninth, or whatever it is. I think they're a trick. And the final crisis is here, my friends, do not doubt that for a moment. Anyone who tries to persuade us not to act will lead us into a position of criminal irresponsibility that could cost the lives of tens of thousands of men. I for one will not tolerate that.''

He looked pointedly at the general. The brusque tone of Connally's voice, and the vehemence of his remarks, revealed a side of him that the other members of the Committee had never seen before. The Connally they had known was patient, tolerant, willing to let a consensus emerge—though it usually seemed to reflect the position he had hinted at at the beginning of a discussion. This newly disclosed side of him had a tonic effect. Even Pallavicini seemed sobered.

"I know we are taking a risk, General," Connally said to the Russian in a more conciliatory tone. "There *is* a chance that we are misjudging the situation. But I think that's a chance we must take.''

The Russian was quiet for a moment. He shifted uncomfortably in his seat, his eyes cast down at the table. Presently, he swelled his chest and, drawing himself erect, announced in a solemn and formal tone, "As the Soviet representative, I announce my concurrence with your analysis.''

Connally suddenly felt enormously tired and weak. He hadn't

eaten more than half a slice of bread since yesterday morning. The wound in his thigh, a memento of his encounter with Hornetz, was throbbing painfully. No one spoke. They all seemed to be waiting for Connally to do so—to outline a plan that would brilliantly extricate everyone from the terrible danger just ahead.

But the stupid confrontation with the Russian had cost Connally more energy than he would have thought possible. He wanted to sleep, to run away, to curl up and hide. He felt he just didn't have the strength to continue.

"So what are we going to do?" It was Jokarinis, the Greek representative, who broke the silence. The clear, forthright question purged the atmosphere in the room, among other things dispelling Connally's cloud of self-pity. For a moment he experienced the shame of it. Certainly this was not the time to be weak or to feel sorry for oneself.

But what *was* the answer to Jokarinis's question? Was there indeed something the prisoners could do? Connally's faith that there is a solution to every problem was shaken momentarily as he recalled more keenly than ever before the fate of seven men for whom no such faith was possible.

It had happened at Mauthausen, the notorious concentration camp in Austria to which he was sent after Saarbrücken. The guards there regarded him as something of a VIP because one day an officer had come from Berlin for the sole purpose of recruiting Connally into the SS. He told him of Cole. Of the fine villa outside Berlin in which he was living. Of the generous salary he was being paid merely for advising the SS on certain matters from time to time. Connally, who knew so much more than Cole, would be regarded as an even more valuable friend if only he would agree to act as a consultant to the officials at headquarters from time to time. Connally declined the honor, but the fact that it had been offered became generally known and led the guards to become almost deferential toward him. For all any of them knew, Connally might one day accept the honor of working in Berlin. And then he would be in a position to revenge himself on any mere concentration camp guard who had treated him badly in Mauthausen.

He was assigned one of the easiest jobs in the camp—a comfortable, low-key job as lackey to the *Kapo* in charge of *Block* 5. This *Kapo* was a German, Schmidt by name, serving out a sentence for murder.

One morning early in December, Schmidt announced to the men in his *Block* that it was soon going to be Christmas and that he had already decided what he wanted as a Christmas gift this year. There were seven Jews in the *Block,* he pointed out, two of whom were a father and his eighteen-year-old son.

All the Jews, Schmidt said, were to be dead by Christmas. *That* was going to be his Christmas gift.

As a concession, in keeping with the festive season, he was not going to say how the Jews should kill themselves, who should go first, or anything like that. He would leave the details up to them. Though he would be glad to help out if necessary. But he did want them all dead by Christmas, one way or another. His oxlike frame shook with merriment.

Now *there* was a problem, Connally reminded himself with a humorless smile. Did it have a solution? To hide in another *Block* was impossible. To kill the brute was feasible, despite his size, but that would bring down the vengeance of the SS, not only on the seven Jews but on countless others, too. Really, there was no solution to that problem. One by one, during the next three weeks, the Jews had killed themselves. *Kapo* Schmidt got the last installment of his gift on the night of December twenty-third, when the father and his young son ran into the camp's electrified fence.

But right now Connally did not want to remember the details. Jokarinis had asked a question, and what mattered now was finding the right answer to it. If there was a right answer.

Connally's instinct at once prompted him to think of a strategy of subterfuge. If ever there was a moment for playing the grand bluff, this was it. But looking at the faces of the men around the table, he decided against even trying to come up with such a scheme. Not only because he would have a hard time persuading the Committee of anything that was really audacious, but also because audacity required minds that were alert and quick, and the tired, dispirited faces he saw around him, as well as his own physical and mental exertion, indicated that neither he nor anyone else was capable at this time of devising and implementing a piece of effective trickery.

"I think our plan—whatever it is—should be simple and realistic in terms of our resources and of the SS mentality," he said aloud. It was hardly a brilliant beginning, but perhaps it might trigger off some suggestions and, no less important, abort at the outset fanciful suggestions from Pallavicini and some of the others.

"I would not be able to disagree with that," the Russian general replied, nodding his head as he gave the sarcastic tone in his voice free rein. "Yes, we should be realistic."

And, in fact, Connally's banal remarks *did* seem to revitalize the meeting. "Our immediate objective should be to get the food," someone said. "That at least will keep the camp relatively quiet, white flags or no."

Presently, a plan of action emerged. A delegation would present itself to the SS commander to demand the midday meal. It would also sound out the officer and, if appropriate, warn him that he would be held responsible for any drastic action against the prisoners. Discreetly, he was to be reminded of the imminent arrival of American forces. The International Committee, whose existence was now to be disclosed to the SS in order to impress them with the extent to which the prisoners were capable of coordinated action, would guarantee the maintenance of order within the camp.

It did not amount to much, this plan. The threat it posed to the SS was about as grave as a platoon of peashooters would be to a herd of stampeding bull elephants. But the hope was that it would show the SS that the prisoners were not entirely passive and, indeed, were capable of their own initiatives. That the initiatives were not exactly potent ones *might* matter less than the fact that they were taken. They *might* give the SS pause to reconsider whatever fiendish moves they were intending.

That, at least, was the hope.

It was quickly agreed that the delegation would be made up of two men: Hopman, the little Belgian, and Müller, the German who was the Senior Prisoner. The Committee drew up orders requiring all prisoners to remain inside their barracks. The meeting was temporarily adjourned.

9. At the *Jourhaus*

The jostling, pushing, excited crowds on the *Lagerstrasse* were too much for Piet Maas. Twice he had nearly been pushed over. Not that falling down was a disaster, of course, but this was one day that he wasn't going to be taking any chances. Particularly because he didn't trust the mood of the crowd. They were like children, blind to anything but the most obvious facts, in which they invested all their enthusiasm—in this case, the white flags that hung from the *Jourhaus* flagpole and from the guard towers. Maas still felt uneasy about them. He did not yet know what they meant and was not prepared to take them at face value. The thought suddenly struck him that if the SS were surrendering the camp, it would make sense for them to have white flags at its main entrance, which he had never seen but knew to be more than a mile away from the *Jourhaus*. Perhaps there *were* flags there. But the thought nagged at him. If addressed to the Americans, the flags were unnecessary. In that case, they might be intended for the prisoners. But why would the SS want to tell the prisoners they were surrendering? To lull them? And to lull them for what purpose?

He sensed danger. From the flags, from the Nazis, but most immediately, now, from the excitable mob of prisoners. He decided that he would continue to respect his inner warning signals. It was safer and more comfortable to be back in the *Block* with the corpses. He sat down on the chair by the window that he had occupied earlier and pulled out his diary. He made a fresh notation:

0800. Lagerstrasse looks like a Byenkorf [“beehive”: the name of a chain of Dutch department stores]. Everyone looks surprised, unbelieving, in wonder, dismayed . . .

116

He stopped. *Dismayed?* Where had that word come from? he wondered. He shrugged his shoulders and continued to write:

> . . . *laughing, cursing, quietly raging. All at the white flags.*
> *Strong wind. 4/10 cumulus between 600/1,000 meters. Clear*
> *blue sky. Much fighter activity. North of us an artillery spotter*
> *plane flies slowly back and forth.*

He enjoyed putting down that bit of meteorological information. The feeling it gave him was—he shuddered—a bit like stretching one's legs after a long period of inactivity. Would he ever put that expertise to use again? Other than for diary writing, that is? For the first time in years the sense of freedom and excitement of flight—not of mastery but of complete cooperation with the elements—returned to tempt him. He felt an overwhelming yearning to take a plane up into the sky again.

He snapped the diary shut. If there was one thing he could not allow himself to do, now perhaps more than ever, it was to dream about what he could never have again in his life. Legs. And the ability to fly.

Piet Maas struggled with the desire to believe—and to dream. But it was from his pilot's memory that he found the strength to do so. He remembered how careful he had always been, even on short flights, to enter his destination and arrival time in his logbook only after he had landed. One step at a time, and don't tempt fate. That had been his motto. He told himself he would do well to hold on to it now.

Had he really written *dismayed?* Yes he had! But why? Surely a very odd word, wasn't it, in this context? But it had come spontaneously, and he had noticed it only after he finished writing it down.

The more he pondered the matter, the more firmly did he recognize that there *was* a mood of dismay on the *Lagerstrasse*. Half dazed, perhaps half crazed, the men seemed to be cursing *at* the white flags no less than at the Nazis who had put them there. They weren't expressing rational opinions, of course, but unconscious anger and, yes, dismay. Maas was sure that if he had stopped any man in the crowd and asked him to describe his feelings he would have said, "The Nazis are surrendering, and I'm delighted." And certainly that would have been true. People were delighted, and they had every reason to be. But behind, beneath those feelings there were different ones.

What were they? Maas shuddered again. Dismay meant that you didn't want something to happen. The something in this case could only be the arrival of the Americans and the liberation of the camp. Could it really be that at a certain level they didn't want to be set free from the ghastly torment of Dachau? And why was that? Was there something in the camp that the men didn't want to lose? Or something out there, in the world where life was lived, that they were afraid of?

And even as he thought about these questions, another one rose to trouble him: Who were *they?* Only that frenzied horde of gaunt, diseased, famished, desperately abused, and frightened men in striped uniforms out there on the *Lagerstrasse?* Only them? Or was he, Piet, one of them? Did he detect their dismay because—he shared it?

He wiped beads of nervous sweat from his forehead. As he did so, he saw two men striding purposefully across the *Appellplatz* toward the *Jourhaus.* He recognized them at once as Hopman and Müller, the Senior Prisoner. The thoughts of a moment ago were at once dispelled by new questions: What were these two men doing? What was the International Committee planning? What was going on?

Paul Hopman ran his eye over the geometric patterns of the iron grillwork on the gate. Never having worked on an outside *Kommando,* he had passed through that gate only once: the night he first entered Dachau fourteen months before. But then it had been too dark to make out the details; and he did, after all, have other things on his mind. The gate held a special fascination for him; there was something magical about it. And because it was on the perimeter of the prison compound, he, like other prisoners, was careful not to approach too close to it for fear of being shot by one of the guards.

So this was the first time that he had had a chance to inspect it from close up. It struck him that the gate really did mark the boundary between freedom and slavery. In other words, it really was a gate, functioning (as so few gates any longer do) as the metaphor it had become. He wondered who had made it. A prisoner, surely, but who? He took it for granted that the man had known he was making this particular gate—presumably he was a prisoner at Dachau. How had he felt about constructing the gate that locked him into hell? And about the inscription in the center of the gate: *Arbeit Macht Frei*. "Work Makes You Free." Had he enjoyed this joke, which mocked him so viciously? Possibly, Hopman thought, though without recrimination, the man had enjoyed his task, this unexpected chance to work at his old trade. Who knows but that during this *Arbeit* he did not indeed feel *Frei?*

He and Müller were not speaking to one another now. Tacitly, each recognized that it would be inappropriate for them, as mere prisoners, to chat with each other while awaiting the arrival of the SS officer. Hopman's instinct, in fact, was to stand apart from Müller lest their solidarity be interpreted by the guards as insubordination. But he checked that instinct. After all, they were here to demonstrate the prisoners' solidarity. They were doing the right thing, he decided. To talk with each other would be going too far. To stand apart from one another, not far enough. Although a lawyer by training, Hopman had never before felt so acutely the need to ensure that every nuance of every word or gesture was the correct one. He felt oddly elated by this. It was a familiar enough situation to be in, in one sense, representing the interests of his clients against a hostile adversary. And if he overlooked for the moment, as he was able to, that his adversary was judge and executioner as well; that the interest of his clients was nothing less than their lives; that his clients numbered over thirty thousand souls, including himself—if he overlooked all these considerations, then it was easy enough to feel familiar in the role he was now playing, and to enjoy flexing his old, unused legal muscles. Though I've never done it on such an empty stomach before, he thought to himself with a cynical smile. And these clothes would definitely not be acceptable in the Palais de Justice in Brussels!

These thoughts made him conscious of his affinity with the unknown man who had wrought the iron gates in front of which he was now standing. He was glad that he had not felt bitter about him.

He felt less affinity for Müller. He looked at his companion. Even now he was a handsome man; imposing, in fact. Hopman knew almost nothing about him beyond the fact that he was a German, a political prisoner, and obviously well educated. Most German politicals in the camp were Communists, but from the tenor of Müller's comments at the Committee meetings, Hopman had guessed that he was probably a Social Democrat. Also that he was a university professor. But there was no way of knowing that for a fact, or indeed almost anything else about him. Like Hopman, Müller was naturally taciturn. His rank and responsibilities, for all that they were imposed on him by the Nazis, set him apart from the other prisoners to the point where many treated him with deference and others thought of him as aloof.

Looking at Müller's drawn, dignified face, Hopman felt a sudden surge of compassion for him; in a sense, despite himself. Although the prisoners were joined together by real feelings of solidarity, national as well as political differences quite often came between them. Even the Dutch and the Belgians were sometimes at each others' throats. But these were, for the most part, somewhat petty and familiar animosities, and no one made too much of them. A special set of feelings, however, was almost universal in the prison compound when it came to the Germans. Despite the recognition that they shared the same plight as the others, the Germans were viewed with hostility and mistrust. Of course, almost everyone knew that not all Germans were Nazis (or even sympathizers), just as they also knew that not all Nazis were Germans. That, indeed, they often knew from the most bitter personal experiences with collaborators in their native countries. Poles and Czechs, Frenchmen and Danes were to be found in the ranks of the most vicious Nazis.

Yet despite this recognition, the feeling was widespread that there was something all too German about Nazism—and Nazi about the Germans. And even if one made the effort to think through that feeling to the mere prejudice that underlay it—and Hopman did that from time to time, possibly more out of a conviction that prejudice crippled one's judgment than that it was wrong—there was still a feeling that the Germans were all responsible for the whole barbaric, tragic mess the world was in. Sure, the German prisoners, or at least the politicals among them, had been opposed to Hitler. (You couldn't always be sure of this, of course, since it was so easy to be denounced as an enemy of the state in Nazi Germany; and, in fact, more than a few of the German politicals were about as non-Nazi as Hermann Göring, who, as it happens, was sentenced to death by

Hitler.) And sure, it was unjust to blame them for not having been more effective in their opposition to the Nazis. But the question remained: Why *hadn't* they been more effective? Why hadn't they been more extreme in their attempts to wipe out Nazism before it became a serious threat to humanity? Why hadn't they assassinated the Nazi leaders? There were still now—in 1945, after all the world had gone through—Communists here in the camp who repeated the argument of the early thirties that Hitler's rise to power was welcome because it marked the last stage of capitalism.

These were questions to argue about rather than to answer, perhaps; but they reflected a widespread feeling in the camp that all Germans, including the ones here, were somehow responsible for Hitler. And there were other factors that shaped the prisoners' attitudes toward their German fellows. Whenever news trickled into the camp of a German defeat, the prisoners rejoiced; a German victory plunged them into gloom. The German prisoners shared these feelings—up to a point. For although *they* were in the camp, almost all of them had friends and relatives who were fighting in Germany's armed forces, and whom they wished well even while they recognized that their welfare could only prolong the sufferings of the men in the camp. Or again, nothing cheered the prisoners so much as the sight of British and American bombers and fighters winging their way to or from German targets. This was a common sight these days, and recently even the sound of bombs exploding could often be heard quite clearly. The prisoners rejoiced, the Germans among them. But for the others there was always the suspicion that the Germans' pleasure was less than total. That they were not entirely thrilled at the thought of bombs shattering the houses in which their families lived, the streets along which they had once walked, the places where they had studied or worked or played.

It must be difficult to be a German here, Hopman thought, and for Müller those difficulties were surely compounded by the isolation and anxieties of his position as Senior Prisoner. But genuine as his sympathy was for the German—and perhaps despite himself—Hopman could not entirely suppress his fear and contempt for the Germans and for everything German.

Nor was he convinced that Müller was an appropriate choice for the present mission. Hopman was sure that he would remain cool and steadfast. But was it a good idea to have a German along to represent the prisoners? He was afraid the SS officer might seize on Müller's nationality to rail against his disloyalty to the Fatherland, etc., etc., and after an impassioned speech send the two of them back into the prison compound.

Yes, indeed; it would probably not take much to rouse the SS man's fury. On the other hand, the fact that Müller was Senior Prisoner might possibly make a good impression on the Nazi. It would show that he was dealing with equals, in a sense: one authority with another. Perhaps this was something to be emphasized—discreetly.

Hopman's thoughts were cut short as he saw an SS officer, accompanied by a sergeant, walking casually down the road that led up to the gate. Hopman cursed his self-indulgence. At a time when he should have been formulating phrases and deciding on just the right approach to the Nazi officer he was, instead, letting his mind wander freely around these other topics. That was no way to play at being a lawyer, he told himself hurriedly; cut it out. But he could not shake off an eerie feeling at the prospect of a meeting in which he would be surrounded by Germans on every side. He half expected that they would, as Germans, all gang up against him—Müller along with the SS.

In fact, the meeting went off smoothly and in a low key. Despite his appearance as what Hopman enthusiastically joined Goebbels in calling the Aryan beast, the SS officer seemed relaxed and almost cordial toward the two prisoners. He sauntered casually up to the gate and, separated by it from the two delegates, introduced himself as *Obersturmführer* Skodzensky. He was, he explained, almost as if apologizing for his rank, only the acting commandant of the camp. What could he do for the two gentlemen?

Müller introduced himself as the Senior Prisoner and gave Hopman's name and nationality. "We are here as representatives of the International Prisoners' Committee of Dachau Concentration Camp," Hopman declared, pausing to see whether his disclosure of the existence of the organization would have any effect on Skodzensky. But no expression crossed the SS officer's face, which was frozen in the slightest suggestion of a polite smile. Hopman continued, "It has been brought to our attention that the work *Kommandos* were ordered back to the barracks this morning."

"You're not complaining of that, eh?" Skodzensky chuckled. "Today's Sunday, you know. A day of rest." He turned toward his sergeant, whose face was already registering appreciation of the officer's sense of humor.

"We are not complaining about anything," Hopman said in a level tone. "But one of the *Kommandos* that was sent back prepares the food for the prisoners. If they are not allowed to work today, the men will go without food. It is our view that an extremely serious situation will develop if that happens. The prisoners will probably riot. It will be impossible to control them." He paused, and then added significantly, "The International Committee will be unable to maintain discipline in the prison compound if the prisoners do not receive their food today."

The suggestion of a smile did not leave Skodzensky's face as he listened attentively to the Belgian. He turned slowly toward Müller and asked quietly, "And what, Herr Senior Prisoner, makes your Committee believe that it is responsible for discipline in the camp, or that the authorities here are unable to maintain order among the prisoners?"

Müller rose to the challenge splendidly. In a patient tone, but without a trace of condescension—as though he were giving a lecture on a complex subject—he replied, "It is apparent that the Americans are very close at hand. Possibly they will arrive here today, or tomorrow at the latest. That is apparent to every man on either side of this gate. In view of this, special circumstances have arisen in the camp, among which is the withdrawal of the regular units commanding the camp and their replacement by a far smaller unit—your own. These circumstances are well known to us, *Herr Obersturmführer*. Because of the excitement and tension they have caused, we are concerned about the men's behavior if they are not given their food. We are, as you may know, not very well fed here. We are as interested in seeing to it that order and security are preserved in the prison compound as you must be. Therefore, we have a shared interest. It is necessary that the men be fed. That is up to you. For our part, the International Committee will guarantee order and security in the prison compound until the Americans arrive."

He spoke without hesitation, and Hopman listened admiringly. One pause to find the right word or phrase, one expression of uncertainty over whether or not it was advisable to speak as forthrightly as he had done, and Müller's speech would have been a fiasco. As it was, he spoke with complete conviction, and his tone did nothing to disturb the veneer of propriety that had graced the meeting up to this point.

"Your Committee will maintain order and security, you say, eh?" Skodzensky asked, his voice almost imperceptibly more severe and menacing now. "Well, tell me one thing, Herr Senior Prisoner. How many heavy machine guns does your Committee possess? Are they located on towers overlooking the prison compound? And how many men armed with rifles, bayonets, and machine pistols do you have at your disposal? Tell me that, and then we can discuss how you will cooperate with us!"

Müller remained unperturbed. "The prisoners do not possess any weapons," he said in a matter-of-fact tone.

"And you will maintain order and discipline—security, you said, no?—without machine guns. That is not how we do things in the Third Reich. And *we* have machine guns." He smiled, a twinkle in his eye, at Hopman.

"You also have white flags flying from the top of this building and from the guard towers," Hopman answered laconically.

"Ah, so you noticed my little flags, did you? They're silk, you know—real silk. From the officers' quarters here. Did you know that they slept on silk sheets? That's not what you sleep on, I bet. Nor we—" He checked himself.

Next, the man will be telling us that we are brothers because none of us sleeps on silk sheets, Hopman thought incredulously. But what he said, in the same direct tone in which Müller had spoken, was, "We assume that the flags are addressed to the Americans. I must repeat what Herr Müller here has said. If the food is not provided, there will be serious disorders in the camp. I must warn you that in that event you personally will be held responsible for the consequences." Hopman looked the SS officer straight in the eye. Skodzensky's lids screwed up in anger, but he could not return Hopman's glare and he turned his head awkwardly away.

"Well, we mustn't stand here arguing, must we?" Skodzensky answered. "You probably think that I am some kind of terrible man-eating beast, but of course I'm nothing of the kind. My predecessors were in a hurry to leave, and I'm trying to get everything in order before the Americans arrive. Food supplies here are nonexistent. We've checked that this morning. I have telephoned Munich, and a convoy of special food—good, wholesome food—is on its way. But I think it will not come before about two o'clock. At that time I'll have one of your *Kommandos* help prepare it for distribution.''

He paused, his face entirely impassive now. ''And the Committee, I understand, will join in the effort to maintain order among the prisoners, yes? It would be such a shame if any of you got hurt just before the Americans came here to set you free.''

Without another word he turned and walked away. His brightly polished belt and boots glistened in the sun. Hopman and Müller stood silently and watched the two figures retreat. Then they walked back to the *Appellplatz* and down the *Lagerstrasse,* conscious of the thousands of eyes that by now were directed at them.

''What do you think?'' Müller asked Hopman.

''We were right,'' the Belgian replied.

''About what?''

''About *Wolkenbrand*. He said there was no food in the camp, that 'special' food was being sent from Munich. He doesn't know we know that the Red Cross convoy brought food for us last night.''

''There's no way that someone could have stolen all the Red Cross food this morning, is there?'' Müller asked. But it wasn't really a question.

''No. No way at all.''

They walked on. ''Those dirty, filthy bastards,'' Hopman muttered, almost to himself.

10. The Man with Half a Face

For Joachim Berenson, jostled and jostling on the crowded *Lagerstrasse,* the extremes of gaiety and anxiety between which he had been oscillating were almost more than he could bear. Soon these feelings were engulfed by alarm, which alone possessed the strength to subdue them. The wild humming that never left some place hidden deep inside his head and threatened to dislodge his mind . . . sights that at one moment pulsated with life and vigor and in the next seemed to be stretched out by some unknown force and to become distended and motionless—mimicries of themselves almost ghoulish in their menace and unreality . . . the sounds of the crowd around him suddenly slowing down, dissolving almost into their separate vibrations playing lazily and senselessly on his eardrums . . . the danger was becoming extreme.

His body had been bruised and violated to a spectacular degree in the past two years. Yet he still carried the expectations that his six-foot frame and the burly construction worker's muscles he once possessed entitled him to. He tried to push his way out of the crowd. He might as well have been a swimmer trying to free himself from a powerful undertow. Fragile and almost as translucent as a drop of water though each man in the crowd was, when combined as now with thousands of others like him, and animated by a frenzied enthusiasm, he became part of an irresistible stream. Against it, Berenson was helpless; he could only allow himself to be swept along.

In the moment when disbelief at his helplessness was about to give way entirely to desperation, Berenson suddenly found himself free and alone—nakedly and fearsomely alone. He turned and gazed in astonishment as wave after wave of men came swirling to the end of the *Lagerstrasse*. Here, no longer hidden from the guards in their towers by the rows of barracks, they exposed themselves momentarily in the vast open space of the *Appellplatz* before wheeling back into the security of the *Lagerstrasse*. A second ago, Berenson had wanted only to be free from the crowd. No less urgently, he now wanted to escape from the menacing isolation and exposure of the *Appellplatz*. He squeezed himself against the end of the nearest *Block,* facing the coming tide, hoping somehow to slip past it into the security of the next side street. He failed and was swept out again onto the *Appellplatz*. A second time he tried, and again he was pushed out, this time so forcefully that he fell backward onto the ground. A cold sweat broke out onto his forehead as he got to his feet and once more pushed his way back into the crowd. The hard surface of the building pressed painfully into his back. His ribs were no less painfully compressed and bruised by the elbows of men rushing past him. But this time he made it to the end of the building and turned into the side street. He collapsed on the muddy ground between two lean-tos that jutted out from the wall.

Lying on his side, he gasped for breath but succeeded only in lapsing into another of those excruciating coughing spells that had been tormenting him for the past few weeks. His chest seemed to tear itself apart with each cough, while the blood squeezing out of his lungs into his mouth and then trickling down his cheek did not lubricate those coughs but felt, rather, weird and poisonous—like something brewed in a witches' caldron. And in the background, breaking through in the pauses between his convulsions, the banshee howling of the mob on the *Lagerstrasse* offered an appropriately ominous counterpoint to the rasping of his breath. He fainted.

When he came to, he found that he was feeling better, physically and mentally. Even the humming inside his head, though still audible, had died down considerably. He yearned for the familiarity, the security, of his own bed in the *Block,* which, at least for now, was his home. He got up without a great deal of difficulty and thought about how he might best return to his *Block*. He needn't have worried. The crowd on the *Lagerstrasse* was much thinner than before, and the frightening frenzy that had gripped it seemed to have dissipated.

The sudden change spelled danger to Berenson. He looked around for a familiar face, but there were only Poles and Russians in sight and he did not have the energy to engage one of them in the belabored pidgin-German conversation that would be required before he could learn what was going on. He headed for home.

"What's been happening?" he asked a fellow Frenchman as he crossed the *Lagerstrasse*.

"You haven't heard?" the man replied.

"I wouldn't have asked you, would I?" Berenson snapped. "So tell me."

"The Committee has announced it's taking over the prison compound at ten o'clock. That's a couple of minutes from now," he added, looking at the watch he wore, with some pride, on his wrist. "They've ordered everyone to stay inside his own *Block* until the Americans get here."

"They ordered that a couple of hours ago. And no one listened to them then. What's changed?"

"Don't ask me. Perhaps the fact that they are taking over the compound."

"And what about the food?" Berenson asked. "Have you heard anything about that?"

"Yes," his companion replied. "The Committee also announced that the Boches are going to be distributing it sometime in the early afternoon."

"Thanks," Berenson said as he turned away to his own *Block*. "And good luck to you, my friend," he called after the man. As he walked to the entrance of the building, he was careful to avoid catching sight of his own reflection in the windows.

The *Block* was curiously quiet, though not at all calm. Men sat around in little groups whispering excitedly to one another. Some glanced at Berenson as he entered, but since he ignored them they did not call out to him. He walked over to his bunk and climbed to the top bed, which in all these months he had managed to keep exclusively for himself. It was one of the choicest pieces of real estate around, for a large skylight opened just above it and provided a view of the perimeter of the prison compound in every direction.

Lying on his bed he noticed, for the first time, the almost incessant sound of artillery fire and heavy machine guns. He was not a military man and could not judge how far away they were, but he was certain that he had never before in his life heard the sounds of war so close at hand. And almost every few minutes the pane of glass above him would shiver from the powerful throb of flights of fighter planes overhead.

The overall effect of this noise was to create a sound that was at once primitive and strong and—tranquilizing. They were not startling, shocking noises but rather sounds whose deep resonances acted to massage and reassure him as their vibrations passed through his body. Soothing him thus, they allowed him for the first time that day to confront squarely the terrible anxieties that had been besetting him since he woke up.

Waking up was the worst time of the day for him. Not that he slept tranquilly. Hardly a night went by when he did not dream about his capture, just eighteen meters from the Swiss frontier. The dream was almost factual in its recapitulation of the event: the one middle-aged, ineffective-looking SD man with his Luger—yes, just one man had caught up with him—and a whole squad of well-armed Swiss frontier guards standing passively on the other side of the wire, watching. Just watching. Knowing that a terrible fate awaited him. Knowing full well that they could have rescued him by just a discreet little violation of their precious neutrality. But refusing to help. Berenson had been too proud—stupidly, perhaps, but who knows?—to entreat them. But he had looked at them, hoping that by some magic he could burn scars of shame into their faces. But even when the SD man made him lie down—facing Switzerland—so that he could handcuff him and then, as much to taunt the Swiss as for any other reason, kicked Berenson in the ribs—the third kick fracturing one of them—even then the Swiss did not move. Not one man had so much as clicked off the safety catch on his rifle.

That was one dream that returned almost nightly to haunt him. How he hated the Swiss! Possibly as much as he hated the Germans themselves. And then there was that other dream. The one in which he was strapped into that wooden armchair. A rather nicely made oak armchair, in fact, though from the outset there had been something terribly sinister about the black-webbing straps that hung so casually from one arm. Those straps that had tied him to hell. . . .

No, he did not sleep tranquilly. But to wake up, for him, was to enter the real nightmare of his life. He would never have imagined that it would be possible to go on living with such incessant pain. Or, even more incredibly, that it would be possible for pain to be so incessantly acute. He often thought of Job these days, and found it almost amusing to think that Job's tragedies were trivial in comparison to his own. To weigh less than half one's normal weight. That was bad enough, for starters. To have TB, that was also bad. To have a bomb fragment removed from the right eye by a devoted but unskilled surgeon in the concentration camp, whose equipment would be considered unfit for a slaughterhouse, and to lose most of the sight of that eye, that also was pretty bad. Wasn't all this more than one man should have to endure in his life without . . . ?

Even now, more than a year later, he could hardly bring himself to think about the other thing. Even so, he found it fantastic that he was able to live with the pain and—still more fantastic—that he was able to live with the knowledge that this had been done to him. That was, if anything, the worst thing of all. That they had done such a thing to him.

Insofar as *thinking,* or even just being conscious of, these matters was concerned, it was easier for him to be aware of the others there. Of the men who were put into high-altitude pressure chambers without protective gear—ostensibly to see whether they could be revived. Of the men who were exposed to prolonged immersion in tanks of supercooled water—ostensibly to see what the effects of freezing were. Of the man who was placed naked on a stretcher, covered only by a sheet, and then taken out into the freezing winter night to be sluiced down with a bucket of cold water each hour until he died shortly before dawn. Of the men who were shot "for experimental purposes," for instance in the spleen, to test the effectiveness of coagulants.

These were the ones he knew of, either because he had seen them happening or because he had been told of them. Nothing he had seen before in Dachau had prepared him for these things. Not the elaborate, inventive tortures at the *Bock* (stocks) and *Pfahl* (stake), not the animal brutality of a guard on the rampage or the calculating sadism of the SS in their quieter moments.

But he could never have believed that doctors could do such things. Even German doctors. One might expect lower standards from them, perhaps, but not that they should use human beings with as little fellow feeling as one might have for a guinea pig or a rabbit. And how they held on to their medical disguise! White coats and stethoscopes; clipboards on which to record the reactions of their "patients," as they called them. *Herr Doktor,* they called each other, except for the elderly one, whom they respectfully spoke of as *Herr Professor.* He was the one who looked for a cure for malaria by infecting men with it and then watching them die—very scientific in his observations of their agony.

How could doctors do such things? Berenson would have had less difficulty with the notion of regular SS men doing them. There was nothing that you wouldn't expect from an SS beast. But men who apparently cared enough about suffering to want to become doctors, to heal the sick and wounded—how could they make people sick, how could they deliberately wound people, destroying rather than saving them? And what about the elaborate medical rigmaroles that they played? Did they really need those, the white coats and all, to persuade themselves that they were doing this for the sake of medicine, science, and humanity? Or were they, in fact, so oblivious to the enormity of their deeds that they did not see any discrepancy between who they were supposed to be and what they were actually doing? In general, Berenson did not trouble himself about people's motives. His hands were full enough dealing with the consequences of their motives—with their deeds. But these physicians, so-called, they were something else. A genuine curiosity moved him, quite often, to try to understand them, to get a sense of what it was that made them tick. He did not get far in his speculations, though.

And today, certainly, there were other things on his mind. To the horror of waking up this morning—the normal, everyday horror a man might have who has had half of his face cut away in the name of science—to that horror was added a desperate anxiety.

As soon as he had awakened this morning, he had realized that he had overslept, the first time he had ever done so in his years at Dachau. Yesterday, the prisoners had boycotted *Appell,* except for a couple of hundred who had shown up despite the Committee's orders. But those orders had come in only at the last moment, when the men were already awake and ready to step out for *Appell*. But today—today there was no *Appell*.

The assembly of the entire prison population twice a day on the *Appellplatz* was the most regular, the most predictable ordeal that the men faced. Nominally, the exercise was intended to ensure that no prisoner had escaped, that the deaths of the men who had not made it through the past hours were registered. That was the nominal purpose. But the actual purpose was purely sadistic. The prisoners had to stand at attention through the whole *Appell*, which seldom lasted less than forty-five minutes. A prisoner whose posture was less than perfect would be beaten to correct it. Or else beaten to the point where there was nothing left to correct and he presented nothing but a certain disposal problem at the crematorium. Especially when dysentery was rampaging through the camp, a prisoner would be forced to relieve himself standing in his place—at attention. This the guards always thought very amusing. And if a prisoner was missing, which rarely happened, or was unaccounted for, which happened quite often, if only because the guards deliberately miscounted, the *Appell* might last for hours. Last winter there had been an *Appell* that began at seven in the evening and continued until four in the morning. In a driving sleet storm, the men had had to stand rigidly at attention for nine hours. At least twenty-seven had died that night.

So *Appell* wasn't one of those routines whose absence you miss. And in one sense, of course, Berenson was grateful that today, at least, he would be spared the ordeal. But in another sense, the disruption of the camp's routine was a source of alarm to him. It was a portent, certainly, and, in the nature of things at Dachau, almost certainly an ominous portent. Change was change for the worse, and that in itself was reason for anxiety. But added to that concern was the deeper dread that a failure in the basic routine of camp life aroused in Berenson.

He knew of the rumors that had been agitating the camp for the past few days, of course: "The Americans are coming, and soon we will be free." "The Americans are coming, and the SS are going to liquidate us before they get here." It did not take him long, on waking, to connect those rumors to the fact that there was no *Appell* this morning. Then news of the white flag on the *Jourhaus*—later on the guard towers—seemed to confirm that connection.

But these were two very different sets of rumors, and the former—soon we will be free—was one to which Berenson could scarcely relate. It wasn't necessarily a question of disbelieving it, though he had a hardened skepticism insofar as good news was concerned. Rather, it was that freedom now seemed to mean nothing to him because it was so totally, ludicrously, removed from his experience.

The other version of the rumor—the SS are going to liquidate us before the Americans get here—was one that he could very much more easily credit. *Very* much more easily. Killing was so much more appropriate to the reality of Dachau, after all—indeed, it was its inherent reality—than liberation. In one sense, in fact, the latter rumor, by harmonizing with reality, was less disturbing than the other, which was so completely at odds with it.

Death was a commonplace to Berenson, more so than to most other men in Dachau. In ways that few others could imagine, he knew how little separated life from death. Inject a few malarial germs. Lower the body temperature by not all that many degrees. It didn't take much to cross the threshold, just as it didn't seem to take very much, here at Dachau, to push others across it. And Berenson had been close to death so often that it was scarcely fearful to him any longer.

But today he feared it more than he had for months. It still did not seem to him that he particularly wanted to go on living, but it seemed imperative to him that the camp not be liquidated by the SS. It wasn't at all a question of self-sacrifice for him. Even if the occasion should arise, he was not sure whether he would do anything at the risk of his own life to save the others, to prevent the final destruction. Nor was he driven by feelings of love or concern for the other men here. It was more a question of not letting the SS get away with their last act. And of having men alive who could testify to the world about the horrors that had taken place here.

Berenson's anxiety about the rumor of the camp's liquidation was in these senses an impersonal one. It was rooted in hatred and bitterness, but was none the less strong for that. And insofar as he had a desire to remain alive himself, it was for only one purpose: revenge.

Revenge? For all that he had suffered? It wasn't a question of getting them to atone. It wasn't a question of repairing wrongs. It was a question of hatred—a burning desire, perhaps the only desire left in him that was truly personal, to inflict some suffering on them. With his own hands. Slowly and crudely. He never supposed that it would undo anything that he had suffered. But that did not make him want it any the less.

On the *Lagerstrasse* this morning he had been caught up in the excitement, the anticipation of joyful liberation. He had been caught up in the fear of having it plucked away from his grasp at the very last moment. The joy and fear, swinging wildly into one another, was something he had picked up from the crowd. It had intoxicated him, had threatened to unhinge him. But they weren't really *his* feelings. Lying on his bunk now, he still did not believe that they were going to be liberated—let alone today. *Today!* The thought was too bizarrely unreal. And—he tentatively asked himself this now, explicitly—would he really welcome it if, against all probability, it turned out to be true? Did he want to start life again? *Could* he? It seemed too much to ask of himself.

"Hey, Joachim!" someone called out from below. "Look out and see if anything's going on, will you?" It was a fellow Frenchman, Beauvoir. His voice sounded happy and excited, a "When?" rather than an "If" tone to it.

Raising himself slightly, Berenson could see over the expanse of sloping roofs to the perimeter of the prison compound. The *Appellplatz* seemed completely deserted, as was the little stretch of the *Lagerstrasse* that he could see. The white flags were still on the *Jourhaus* and the guard towers. In some of the latter, he could dimly see the forms of men standing behind their machine guns. He reported this to Beauvoir and then lay back again. He did not feel particularly interested in what was going on. All he wanted was to be left alone with his thoughts. Or whatever else it was that was churning his mind.

A moment later, he felt a tug on his elbow. Looking down, he saw Beauvoir again, conspiratorially putting a finger to his lips.

"Don't say anything, Joachim, but I've got a bit of black bean soup that I made this morning while everyone was running around outside. It's good. Here's a bowl of it for you." He passed it up to Berenson and then vanished.

The slop that passed for food in the camp—a so-called soup made of potato peels and bits of turnip, and one or two slices of stale and often moldy bread—would have seemed heaven-sent to Berenson at this moment. But black bean soup! Now that *was* unbelievable. He checked the impulse to wolf it down and forced himself, instead, to drink it in small sips, crunching each bean lovingly against his gums. How on earth had Beauvoir managed to "organize" this? And hardly less miraculous, where had he gotten the extra bowl from? Bowls were almost as precious a commodity nowadays as the food that from time to time was put in them. And Beauvoir hadn't even asked for it back! "Organizing" was a fine art in the camp, and there were certain individuals who were well known as masters of it. But Berenson knew that Beauvoir was not one of these. So where *had* he gotten this from? Had he been saving it for the day of liberation?

And then the thought hit him, a shock like none other that morning, that Beauvoir had given *him* the food! Berenson was a loner by nature, but the other prisoners also kept him at a distance. That they didn't like to look at him he could well understand. He was at least as anxious to avoid a glimpse of his own face reflected in the barrack windows. He was not offended by this; in fact, he enjoyed at least one consequence of it, which was that in the crowded *Block* he alone was able to have a bunk all to himself. Anyone would prefer sleeping on the floor, or even crammed into one bunk with two other men, to waking up in the morning staring at Berenson's half-cut-away face. Only dimly did Berenson also perceive that the other men were not only repelled by him but also in awe of him. Not many men had emerged alive from *Block* 5, nor had many there ever undergone what Berenson had. He had never told anyone this, but word had nevertheless gotten around somehow that when they cut away half of his face—for an experiment whose object no one could really figure out—they had not used anesthetics.

So the men kept aloof from Berenson, repelled by his appearance, frightened that the very misery of his experience might rub off on them, ashamed of their relief that they had been spared his fate, and ashamed, too, of their recognition that no consolation they could offer would be commensurate with the agonies he had endured. He was to them both hero and pariah. His isolation from the other men was by and large welcome to him. It suited his personality, but also seemed consistent with his destiny.

Beauvoir's gift, so out of context with everything familiar, touched him deeply. Perhaps precisely because it was an irrelevant gesture, unrooted in his relationship with Berenson or in Berenson's place in the social life of the *Block,* it seemed to open up, for Berenson, the possibility of a world of spontaneous, caring behavior, of giving and, no less, of taking. And this suddenly made Berenson care passionately for life. He still wanted revenge, but that was no longer his only reason for wanting to live. Life itself became the paramount reason. Again.

And with this awakening of that simple, yet infinite desire, Berenson's anxiety lest he be robbed of life when liberation was so close at hand intensified. And became, for the first time, intensely personal.

11. Noon

Ten miles west of Dachau, Yaakov Kovner stirred in his sleep as he dreamed that the train's motion seemed increasingly uneven. There were angry, deep groans and hurried, chattering rolls. Sometimes the two were interlaced, and sometimes only one or the other could be heard. And every now and then it was quiet, though the silences were only brief lulls. Alarm and curiosity beckoned Yaakov Kovner out of his dream. This was no way for the train to be moving. What was going on?

He soon realized that the sounds were not accompanied by movement. That the train was still stationary. That the noise was coming from some distance off. It took him a few moments to recognize the deep booms of artillery, the staccato rattle of machine-gun fire.

Unpredictable, insistent, the noise demanded that he focus all his attention on it. Not on the terrible weariness and, again, the thirst he was feeling. Not on the mattress of bony bodies on which he was lying. His first guess, he now realized, had been correct. The guns—both machine guns and artillery—were firing on both sides of him, to the left and right. Which side were the Germans on, he wanted to know, and which the Allies? There was no way for him to tell. He didn't even know who the Allies here were. Russians? English? Americans?

He was not excited to hear the sound of Allied guns, the first he had ever heard on the ground. He could not, for one thing, distinguish between their guns and those of the Germans. Nor did he gloat over the fact that *some* of those explosions, at least, were ravaging German bodies with red-hot splinters of steel, killing and wounding them terribly. Had not Allied guns, friendly guns, killed his companions here on the train?

Without knowing why, he assumed that the train was standing on open ground—an exposed target sandwiched between two armies. Oh, my God! he thought to himself. What if a gunner decides to have fun blowing up the train? He persuaded himself that that was unlikely. There were enough other targets around, surely, and much more useful ones. But what if someone misses and hits the train by mistake? Or if one side advances to the train and uses it as a shelter to hide behind? What if . . . ? The anxious questions shot at him like an artillery barrage from which one cannot hide. Except in an exposed train in the middle of a battlefield.

Imperceptibly, these anxieties translated themselves into a recognition that Yaakov, even in his weakened state, found astonishing. He did not want his train to be shelled or raked by machine-gun fire. He was scared that he would be killed. He didn't want that to happen. So very, very desperately, he did not want that to happen. He wanted to—live.

To live. Not in order to taunt God, let alone for the joy of seeing the Nazis defeated or for the unimaginable pleasure of not being hungry and in pain. But to live because—there was no *because* in Yaakov's mind. He merely wanted to remain alive. Caught between two warring armies, half dead himself and sprawled out on a mattress of corpses, Yaakov Kovner no longer needed a reason for wanting to live. His desire to live had returned.

He *recognized* this desire. But before the welter of questions and feelings it was capable of arousing presented itself to him, it suddenly occurred to Yaakov that he had been entirely mistaken all these years. God had not withdrawn from the universe but had, all along, been guiding its destiny. This revelation came in a calm and wholly self-assured way that precluded any possibility of doubt.

The peace this brought him lasted little more than a moment, however. For no sooner had Yaakov recognized that everything that had happened to him had taken place in accordance with God's will than he also remembered that he had never said Kaddish for the dead. For his children, Rochele, Dovid, and little Channah. For his wife,

Shaineh. For his mother and father, Rivkeh and Moishe. They, his beloveds, had all been dead for three years, and he had never said Kaddish for them! The pain, the shame, the guilt that this recognition brought—the overpowering sadness—seemed too much to deal with. He felt he could die of a broken heart (he knew such things happen), and now was no time for him to die, not only because he still had to say Kaddish but also—because he wanted to live.

He would say Kaddish now. For his children, for his wife, for his parents. For Strizower and all the others he had known; for those whose names he remembered and for the ones he had forgotten or never knew. For all the dead. For everyone. A grandiose surge of piety filled him; there was no limit to the blessings he would now invoke on God's newfound goodness, and on the memory of the dead. He would atone for his neglect and defiance of God; he would throw his soul into the task confident that it would emerge cleansed and reinvigorated for the life he hoped was still ahead.

But the fact was that Yaakov could not remember the prayer! Try as he might, it eluded him. He sobbed with shame at his forgetfulness and then at his impiety in hoping that he could, in this one time, erase the burden of his failure to say Kaddish for three years. For a moment he was sidetracked. Might a person say Kaddish without a minyan of ten adult Jewish males? He could not remember the ruling on this. Perhaps he would be forgiven now if he did not say Kaddish. And in the next moment he hoped that his anguish at forgetting the ancient words would in itself be the equivalent of saying them. Or that the more deeply he felt his anguish, the more God would be tempted to implant the words of the prayer in his mouth. He felt himself going insane with the desire to remember, at almost the same time as he felt appalled that he was using himself up in this quest.

And suddenly an indescribable joy seized him as words from long ago came racing through his mind:

> Where were you when I laid the earth's foundation?
> Tell me, if you know and understand.
> Who settled its dimensions? Surely you should know.
> Who stretched his measuring line over it?
> On what do its supporting pillars rest?
> Who set its cornerstone in place,

when the morning stars sang together
and all the sons of God shouted aloud?

But no! This was not Kaddish, it was from— Absurdly, intellectual curiosity awoke for a moment in Yaakov. He frowned as he tried to recall the passage and the words that came immediately after it. But he reminded himself that he was not a little boy being quizzed in the heder about a passage from the Bible. He was a dying man who had never said Kaddish for his family and could not remember the words. With a pitiful groan, Yaakov again lapsed into unconsciousness.

It was midday, and Ernst Kroll was feeling gratified. Proud, in fact. Once again the correctness of the Party line was evident to him; and once again he congratulated himself on his good fortune and good sense in having recognized its superiority so many years ago.

The *Block* was more crowded than he had ever seen it before. Even those who ordinarily lived outside in the lean-tos had come indoors for shelter. In this moment of crisis the thin asbestos walls of the barracks seemed to offer a degree of safety that did not exist outside. Drawn by a herd instinct, the men gathered to find security in the overcrowded rooms. They were excited, still, and tense, milling around in small, fluid groups that constantly reformed themselves and posing, interminably, the same questions and offering the same answers to them: "What's going on?" "Do you think the Americans are going to get here in time?" "What do the white flags mean?" "Are we going to get our meal today?" "Yes." "No." "The Americans will get here." "No, they won't." "The Germans are going to kill us." "No, they're not." "The food is about to come. . . ." It was incredible to Kroll that these men, who looked like living skeletons, still possessed—or had suddenly found—the energy to expend on these matters. Except, that is, for the men who were too weak to do anything but stare blankly into space. And those who were already dead.

Kroll and his comrades, however, were immune from the frenzy of the moment, and they had been all day long. They had stayed aloof from the hysteria on the *Lagerstrasse* earlier in the morning

when, without even receiving word to do so, they had gathered—
each man of his own accord—in this room to hold a cell meeting.
There were eighteen of them left—only five down from their original
number. Quietly and calmly, they appraised the situation and worked
out various strategies for dealing with the new situations that could be
expected to develop. All were agreed that the International Committee could not be trusted. With the exception of the Russian general,
who held aloof from the German Communists, the members of the
Committee were bourgeois, and even now they could be expected to
act in accordance with their class interests. The same held true of the
Senior Prisoner, Müller, who, although a German, was a Social
Democrat. It was resolved that the cell would cooperate with the
Committee insofar as necessary and desirable. But not a single step
further. On this, every man was emphatic. Beyond that point, the cell
would act on its own initiative and continue, as before, to protect its
own members.

There was no agreement yet on what this entailed. But that did
not alarm Kroll or, it would appear, any of the other men. They had
been in such situations before, when it was easier to agree on what
they would *not* do than it was to come up with a concrete plan of action. Sooner or later, Kroll knew, there would be the right suggestion, everyone would recognize it, and then all would be settled.

For now, he had no ideas to offer, though there was a thought
way at the back of his mind that he could not quite grasp. Instead of
trying to get hold of it, he basked in the sense of cool confidence that
he and his friends, the comrades, were displaying in this moment of
crisis, and that set them apart so strikingly from the undisciplined and
fruitless agitation of the other men. And he felt great joy in learning
that his comrades explained the wider situation in terms that resembled his own thinking. All along, he had known that the Fascist
regime and the corrupt monopoly capital that had supported it would
be overthrown. With its downfall, the next stage of the dialectic
would inevitably commence. He personally believed that this would
be the workers' state of which he had always dreamed. Others, however, suggested that there would first be some intermediate stage.
Kroll was not an argumentative type, and he knew what he hoped for
much more clearly than what he believed. So perhaps the workers'

state would not yet be established, but there was no doubt in his mind that now, perhaps within the very next few days, he would witness a great leap forward in the historical development that had led up to it. And that was a prospect that filled him with enormous joy.

And there was another thing, too. Katerina. It was years since he had last heard from her. In that letter she had told him she had bought a wolfhound puppy to keep her company until he was released from the camp. That was in 1935. Ten long years ago. Somehow, he was certain that she still had the dog, and that there was nothing else—no man, that is—to replace him in her affections. Sure, ten years was a long time for any woman to wait. But twelve years was an even longer time for any man to spend in a concentration camp. Katerina knew that. And she was a true Party worker.

". . . food." The word focused his attention back on the cell meeting. Someone was talking about the food situation. It was Krieger, the Frankfurter, a good Party man though a bit too humorless for Kroll's taste. "I don't trust the Fascists," he was saying. "I have this feeling that they're going to try something with the food. Poison. That's what I think they have in mind. Don't ask me why, but I think it's going to be the food. I just have a hunch."

That was the thought that had been at the back of Kroll's mind earlier, the thought he hadn't been able to get at! "I agree," he said hastily. "That's just what I'd been thinking." Quietly, he excused himself the little lie, and continued, "It's only a feeling I have, but I just don't think the Fascists are going to say to the Americans, 'Here is the key to Dachau, come and liberate thirty thousand prisoners.' They *are* going to try something—it's in their nature—and for days we've known that they have plans. And I don't see what else they can do now. They can't bomb us because they don't have the planes anymore. And their regular troops have their hands full with the Americans."

For want of any other plan of action, the men agreed to Krieger's proposal. "We won't eat the food they hand out today. Now's the time to use up our emergency rations. And if the food they give out today turns out to be all right, we can always eat it tomorrow. But I propose the emergency rations for today. This *is* an emergency!"

She was aware of someone sitting beside her on the bed. "Hello, Natalie!" The voice was gentle. "I've brought you some soup. You must try to eat it. It'll give you back your strength."

She opened her eyes and saw the Frenchman looking down at her. A warm smile lit up his face, creasing almost every part of it into thin wrinkles. The wonderful Frenchman! She couldn't remember his name, only that he was the Baron de something or the other and that he had nursed her from the time she had been brought to the *Revier* from Munich. She smiled back at him. "You've been so good to me, Doctor," she said weakly. "Almost every time I opened my eyes, you were here looking after me. Thank you."

"Nonsense," he said gruffly. "We all look alike, anyway, so you don't know if it was me or not. Now stop talking and drink." He held the bowl toward her.

"I *know* it was you," she replied, managing to sit up enough to take a few sips of the soup. It was thick and warm, the best she had had in months. Potato soup. It felt wonderful. "Thank you, Doctor," she added after a few sips. "I don't think I can take any more."

"Stop 'doctoring' me," he said. "I'm about as much a doctor as I'm a monkey. My name is Henri. And you must eat the soup. The whole bowl. So many people have died here in the past two days, we've got more food than we've ever seen before. And if you eat it, all of it, I'll tell you something wonderful!"

She ate the soup. There were real chunks of potato, not just peels, and the liquid was thick enough not to taste like warm, polluted water. She could feel the nourishment course through her body, bringing new life and comfort to her, massaging her insides. The sensations were so encompassing that she could be aware of nothing else. And she forgot about Henri's promise to tell her something wonderful.

"So, do you want to hear the news?" he asked, almost disappointed at her lack of eagerness.

She smiled. "I'd forgotten. The soup is making me feel so good, I'd forgotten what you said. Am I going to get better?" she asked, as if to anticipate the news.

"Of course you are, Natalie. We'll have you up and about in a few days, I promise you!"

A look of alarm swept across her face. Up and about. That

meant—back to Munich, back to work, back to the horrible brutali-
ties from which the hospital and her own illness had temporarily
shielded her.

"But that's not what I was going to tell you. Listen," Henri
said, taking the empty bowl from her hand and gently pushing her
back onto the pillow, which was one of the few "luxuries" allowed
patients in the *Revier*. "Lie down and don't get too excited." He laid
a hand on her wrist and, massaging it softly, said, "Natalie. Wonderful things have been happening in the last few hours. The Germans
are surrendering! They have white flags on the *Jourhaus* roof and on
the guard posts, and soon—today, or at the latest, tomorrow—the
Americans are going to be here to liberate us. I promise you that's
true. It's no dream. Do you hear the shooting outside? That's the
American Army. They're only a few kilometers away, and they're
coming for us. Then we will be free and we can all go home!"

Dimly she could see the Frenchman looking eagerly at her.

"Natalie! Natalie! Did you hear what I said just now? The
Americans are coming! Soon, only a few hours, we're going to be
free!"

She did not respond. The warm, wonderful feeling inside her,
that massaging of her guts and throat, was all she could be aware of
right now. Her eyelids felt very heavy. She wanted to sleep. That
was all she wanted. She closed her eyes and turned her head to one
side.

"Natalie!" the voice insisted. "Hear me. Hear me. By the time
you wake again, I think the Americans are going to be here. You
must hear me before you go back to sleep! We are going to be liberated today!"

Natalie opened her eyes slightly, battling against the urge to
sleep. In a remote sort of way, she understood what Henri was saying. Why is he so happy? she thought to herself. Why is he so happy
to be free?

And before falling asleep again, she muttered, "Doctor, I'm
afraid."

Climbing up the ladder had been the most difficult part of it all.
But with Plaga pushing his butt from below, and with his own relatively powerful biceps to pull with, Maas at last managed to reach the

rim of the roof. From there it was easy enough to crawl up to the peak, something that Plaga, with his gangling legs, found rather more difficult. On the northern pitch of the roof, they were shielded from the men in the guard towers. Maas checked to see that the ladder was still securely in place. He needn't have worried. The pile of corpses into which they had wedged the foot of the ladder hadn't allowed it to move at all.

The roof felt pleasantly warm as he lay sprawled out on his back, against it. Idly he wondered if it had been warmed by the sun or by the ovens underneath, which only yesterday had still been hard at work in a futile attempt to diminish the huge piles of corpses inside and outside the crematorium.

The view was partly blocked to the west by some of the larger workshop buildings. But to the south and east there was an unrestricted view of the Bavarian countryside rolling gently away into the distance. A few farmhouses, one or two small villages, but mainly fields and woods. He was surprised to discover what an attractive country Germany was. "It's funny, Plaga," he said to his comrade. "You know, this is the first time I've seen anything of Germany, except before the war when I could see it in the distance from my plane sometimes—but that was a part that looked just like Holland. Somehow I thought it would be a really ugly place. You know, I think I half expected it would be a desert. But look at it! It's charming, no?"

Plaga didn't answer. A slight smile played on his face as his eyes darted back and forth. "Look at that!" he muttered, almost to himself. "That's Schleissheim getting it over there. Can you believe that? I never thought I would live to see such a thing." His voice trembled as he turned for a moment toward Maas, and tears filled his eyes. "Just *look* at that, Piet!"

Only now did it really sink into Maas that he was looking at a battlefield—not just at a charming rural scene. True, small forests and villages dotted the landscape. But so did brilliant, energetic geysers of smoke and fire that seemingly sprang out of the ground and then disappeared—only to reemerge a few moments later in another spot. At times the whole countryside seemed to be erupting with these explosions. Occasionally Maas fancied that he could see columns of vehicles, but a second glance never confirmed that. These sudden eruptions of fire and smoke were all, really, that he could see of the war that was raging just a few miles away. It did not seem particularly dramatic or lethal, except, perhaps, on the few occasions when a round of artillery shells found a target—a tank, perhaps, or an ammunition dump—which they sent on its way with spectacular dispatch.

Seeing all this go on, oddly enough, made the boom of artillery fire and the rattle of machine guns that had been filling the air all morning seem less rather than more dramatic. The artillery, in particular, which had sounded so foreboding, produced only those bright, ephemeral eruptions, which, when they had passed, seemed to leave everything just as it was. The machine guns appeared to produce even less impressive results. By far the most frightening sound came from the shells that whistled overhead. Only they made it feel as though a war was really going on. Maas had the impression that there were many more shells passing from the American positions to the north than from the German positions that lay behind, to the south, between Dachau and Munich.

Plaga, who had seen service as an infantryman, echoed his thoughts. "Do you notice how many shells are coming from there?" he asked, pointing to the north. "My guess is that the main German positions are now behind us, between here and Munich. And they're probably firing rather blindly at the Americans out there."

"So you think those are mainly German shells we see exploding?" Maas asked, a disappointed tone in his voice.

"Probably not. There're a hell of a lot more explosions than there are shells coming from behind us, as far as I can make out. A lot of what we're seeing is probably American artillery zeroing in on German infantry positions. That's all that's left between the Americans and us. Really! It's just a matter of hours before they'll be here."

Maas didn't reply. They must have been mad to take the risks involved in climbing up here to watch the action. It had been a sudden impulse on his part. As if all the common sense and caution he'd displayed earlier in the morning had been overwhelmed by the desperate hope that rose up in him. Plaga, astonished at the suggestion, had nevertheless agreed at once. And so, despite the curfew, despite their own recognition of how foolhardy it was, they had crept out of the *Block* and somehow managed to get to the crematorium without being seen. Maas now understood why he had wanted to do this. His skepticism was as strong as ever. He did not believe that the camp would be liberated—that the Nazis would just let the Americans march in and hand over thirty thousand living witnesses of the crimes they had carried out over the years. And this is what his feeling had been: If the Nazis are going to wipe us out just before the Americans get here, I want at least to have the satisfaction of *seeing* the American Army fighting the Nazis.

In this respect, their adventure had been not only foolhardy but disappointing. There was so little, in what he was seeing, to suggest the battles that were raging just a few kilometers away. Still, there was nothing to be done about that. If he was going to die, he would at least have had the satisfaction of seeing American artillery shells explode on German targets. If necessary, he would decide for himself which had been the American shells and which the German. But he noticed that he was feeling numb now, more than anything else; not particularly excited or frightened or gratified.

"Well, so that's that. You know, unless my memory is mixing me up, that doesn't seem like very heavy fighting that's going on out there. I bet you the Americans are advancing at one hell of a pace." Plaga smiled. "We'd better be getting back now, Piet. I'll go first and help you down the ladder. I'm not sure how we'll manage that; perhaps you can sit on my shoulders."

"No. Not just yet. I want to do something first." He reached into his pocket and pulled out the notebook and pencil. "Give me a couple of minutes, will you? I want to write this down."

"Our Dachau correspondent! For God's sake, Piet, do that later."

Maas ignored him. He wrote hurriedly:

*1200. Artillery fire has Schleissheim and
some other targets under fire. On roof of
Totenkammer. Saw hits. Shells fly and
whistle over the camp. German machine guns
near Plantage. Heavy fire.*

Not exactly Hemingway, he thought to himself as he read the entry over and put the diary back into his pocket. "OK. Let's go," he said to Plaga.

And they returned to their *Block* without incident.

12. Von Alvensleben

It was a delicate juggling act, and he had no experience in such matters to guide him. He felt out of his depth. Yet Alvensleben was determined to see the thing through. So much was at stake here. The lives of the 137 men and women mattered, among other reasons because they were such important personages. Not letting the SS get away with one more massacre mattered. Redeeming the honor of the Wehrmacht and not hiding behind the immobility and apathy of his superior officers mattered. And so too, God knows, did his own skin. The Allies, he thought, could be expected to wreak a far more fearful revenge on Germany now than they did in 1918. And this time they would have rather more justification for doing so. The thought did not entirely escape him that his role in saving the lives of the distinguished Dachau prisoners would possibly be acknowledged in a positive fashion by the Allies.

Since midmorning, Stiller had been strutting around like a cock, delighted and a little amused to discover that the Wehrmacht captain had only 200 men at his disposal. "You had me fooled there for a moment!" he kept on repeating to Alvensleben. "Not bad at all," he chuckled.

Exasperated, Alvensleben replied, "Except that we also have two armored troop carriers. Not to mention the reinforcements that General Röttiger has sent me. They'll be arriving this afternoon."

"Sure, sure," the SS officer replied. "But where do you think we'll be by the time the Wehrmacht arrives here, my friend? Where do you think we'll be?"

148

"Exactly where we are right now," Alvensleben answered, staring Stiller directly in the eye.

Did the Nazi believe him? Alvensleben hoped rather than thought so. It was a game of bluff. But then, so much in life is, he told himself. For now, at least, the two armored personnel carriers gave him a definite edge. What is more, the British intelligence chief, Sigismund Best, who had been captured so ridiculously by a Gestapo ruse at the beginning of the war, had told him of a conversation he had had earlier in the morning with Stiller.

"Herr Obersturmführer," Best had said, "you told me that your orders were to ensure our safety until you were able to hand us over to our advancing troops. Now we've heard a lot of rumors that seem to indicate that you are either unwilling or unable to carry out this intention and that plans are afoot to liquidate the whole lot of us."

"No, Herr Best, really. I want the best for you—you have nothing to fear from me. Your Colonel Stevens knows me well and can tell you that I have always treated prisoners well. It's all the fault of Bader—he's my commanding officer in Innsbruck. I had a big row with him last night when I told him that I would not allow any of you to be harmed, and he threatened to put a bullet in my head. You can count on me to do anything I can to help, but I can't do anything with Bader."

"Well, you say that you want to help us but that you can't," Best had countered. "But that's not much good to us, and we are most certainly not going to allow you or anyone else to murder us. We have therefore decided that I shall take over command from you until the arrival of our own troops. Do you agree? Can I count on you for your loyal cooperation?"

At this point, Best told Alvensleben, one of his companions, General von Bonin, had stood up at the table at which they were sitting and pointedly allowed Stiller to see that he had a Luger machine pistol tucked into his waistband. Stiller, it seemed, had realized that the men were quite prepared to shoot him on the spot unless he assented to Best's proposal. He had assented.

Alvensleben was not impressed by Best's story. The crude ruse that had enabled the Gestapo to capture Best in Holland was widely known in Germany and hardly inspired great respect for the British spy's judgment and tactical sense.

"And you believed him?" Alvensleben asked Best, trying to hide the incredulous tone in his voice.

"I think so," Best replied. "He knows the war is finished. And he wants to come out looking good."

"Did you ask him to disarm his troops?"

"It *was* something we raised," Best answered. "But Herr Stiller replied that it would be in our interests not to do this since the hills around here are apparently crawling with German deserters who are armed and dangerous."

"I hope they're not more dangerous than the SS."

"Now don't you worry about it," Best responded, adopting a gratingly paternalistic tone of voice. "I'm sure that everything will work out well."

Alvensleben had more useful ways to occupy his time than in discussion with Best. "I hope so," he said, and walked back to his command post at the telephone exchange. Appalled as he was at the Britisher's naïveté—did he think they were playing a game of cricket?—he had to acknowledge that the prisoners were still alive. Something was restraining Stiller. Perhaps only a reluctance to execute the prisoners in Niederdorf, where there would be witnesses. Evidently, then, Stiller did not feel he had a free hand. And while the Wehrmacht presence was not overwhelming, it certainly was not a factor that Stiller could overlook.

But how long could Alvensleben remain in Niederdorf? The general had given him explicit orders—and he had, no less explicitly, gone on to disobey them. If he kept out of touch with the general, he could probably stay on here indefinitely. On the other hand, unless he got in touch with the general, there was no chance of getting the reinforcements that he had boasted to Stiller would shortly be arriving. They had to be sent. Which, in turn, meant that he had to ask for them. Otherwise, Stiller would call his bluff. And while he did not mind the prospect of shooting it out with the SS men (he was, after all, better armed than they), common sense told him that this was something to be avoided if at all possible.

He put in a call to General Röttiger's headquarters. No one

seemed to be able to find him—a call from a mere captain apparently inspired no great sense of urgency at the other end of the line. He extracted a promise from a lieutenant that the general would be notified of his call. He waited.

Presently Stiller turned up at the telephone exchange, accompanied only by an *Unterscharführer*. A playful, sardonic smile, which Alvensleben found infuriating, lit up his face as he stood in the doorway. "The Britisher Best came to me and said that the prisoners want to hold a church service. Today's Sunday, you know. And would that be OK with me? Seems they have two bishops with them. So I said of course, so far as I'm concerned, but that really it was a matter for you to decide." He paused, the smile on his face transforming itself into a sneer. "After all, you're the senior German officer here in Niederdorf."

"It's OK with me," Alvensleben responded, though the thought of all the prisoners being packed into the one church, an easy target for the SS, caused him some alarm. Stiller gave a Heil Hitler salute and left.

"Take one of the personnel carriers," Alvensleben ordered a sergeant, "and eight men, and place it near the entrance to the church. Find the side entrance, if there is one, and put two men there. SS men can enter the church only if they are disarmed. Your job is to make sure nothing happens to the people in the church. Is that understood?"

The phone rang. Hurriedly, Alvensleben picked it up. It was the lieutenant from headquarters. His voice, urgent and tense, alarmed Alvensleben the moment he heard it. "I don't know what's going on in Niederdorf, Captain," he said, "but I thought you should know at once what's just happened here. Orders came through a few minutes ago relieving General Röttiger and General Vietinghoff"—the latter was Röttiger's immediate superior—"and placing General Scholtz in command."

"Scholtz, did you say?" Alvensleben asked. *"The* Scholtz?"

"Yes, Captain. *The* Scholtz. Excuse me," he added hastily. "I cannot talk more now. I will try to keep you informed, if that is at all possible."

Alvensleben did not even have a chance to thank him for the

news. Not that he was thankful for it, for Scholtz was known to every officer in the Army group as a fanatical Nazi. It made no sense to place a man like Scholtz in charge at the very time that the entire German war effort was in its final stage of collapse. Alvensleben was deeply disturbed. He knew that there was no point at all now in appealing for reinforcements. If Scholtz knew what he was up to, he would, at the very least, require him to cooperate with Stiller. In fact, he would more than likely give orders to have him shot for insubordination. At all costs, Stiller must be prevented from finding out about this new development.

For want of anything better to do, he wandered over to the church to check that his orders had been carried out. And indeed they had been. Two sentries with submachine guns stood at the side entrance. The armored personnel carrier, a heavy machine gun mounted at its front, was parked outside the main entrance of the church. Two soldiers manned the machine gun; five others stood guard in a semicircle that arced toward the church door. It struck Alvensleben that they looked just a bit on the provocative side, and he ordered the men into a more informal pose. He asked the sergeant for a report. No incident had occurred, the sergeant reported. About sixty or seventy prisoners were inside the church. Not a single SS man had shown his face.

Indeed, the whole village seemed deserted. The villagers could tell that something was going on—or was about to happen—that threatened the peacefulness of their remote region. During the entire course of the war they had not seen so many soldiers at one time. With rustics' instincts they had responded to the situation by locking themselves in their houses and keeping their shutters drawn. The pretty village, deserted by its inhabitants, seemed like a film set onto which the cast of another movie had mistakenly strayed.

Rounding a corner, three men entered the square in front of the church. All were in civilian clothes—rather ragged ones at that—but two of them carried rifles and had bandoliers slung across their chests. Confidently, they strode toward the personnel carrier. As they came nearer, Alvensleben saw that the man in the middle of the group, a short, stocky little man, had two Lugers tucked into the waistband of his baggy trousers. The German soldiers tensed in anticipation of danger.

"I am looking for Captain von Alvensleben," the stocky man said to the sergeant, who had gone forward to meet him. "I am General Sante Garibaldi. You will tell him that I wish to see him." He spoke fluent German, but with a heavy, almost comical accent. Alvensleben recognized the Italian soldier's name as belonging to one of the distinguished Dachau prisoners. He was astonished, however, that the Italian general—even after having been incarcerated in a concentration camp—should look so, well, *undistinguished*.

He stepped forward and saluted. "I am Captain von Alvensleben, General," he said. "What can I do for you?"

The general did not return the salute. "I have just been speaking to your compatriot Stiller," he said, "and what I have told him I now have to tell you." He looked tired and drawn, but confident nonetheless. Alvensleben was tempted to make a remark dissociating himself from the SS man, but he couldn't think of one that wouldn't sound apologetic. And after all, for better or for worse, Stiller *was* his compatriot. He waited for the general to continue.

"This morning, I made contact with the partisan brigade in the vicinity. As you know, there is a large Italian population here, and, in fact, until your Führer annexed this region, it was a part of Italy. But never mind that—that is something that is going to be settled soon enough, anyway."

Suddenly irritated, Alvensleben said, "Is that what you have come to tell me, General?"

Garibaldi smiled, a friendly smile. "Don't be touchy, Captain," he said. "I know who you are and what you have done for us, and I appreciate it. What I told Stiller is this. My partisan brigade is in the vicinity. It will not be long before it arrives here in force to take command of the village and to liberate us. Stiller has agreed, and I hope you will, too, to place his forces under my command. This will ensure order and the security of the area."

Alvensleben had not lost his sense of humor. "General, an hour ago, Herr Best came to me and told me that *Obersturmführer* Stiller had agreed to place his men under Herr Best's command. Forty-five minutes ago, *Obersturmführer* Stiller came to me and acknowledged that *I* am in command of this area. Now you tell us that he has placed himself under *your* control. Herr Best told me that the American Army will arrive in a few hours. You tell me that soon the partisans will be here. And now I have to tell you that soon I will be receiving reinforcements from my divisional headquarters.''

The general laughed.

"But why do we stand here?'' Alvensleben asked. "Will you join me for coffee in my command post, and we can continue our discussion there?'' Garibaldi readily agreed. With the two partisans as their escort, they returned to the telephone exchange. The corporal on duty reported that all was in order, no incident had occurred. No SS man had been seen since the captain had left. Alvensleben wondered what had become of Stiller and his men.

"Believe me, General, I know the SS mentality better than you do. Do not allow yourself to be tricked by this man, and don't let's make his job any easier for him by squabbling among ourselves over who is in control here. At this moment, I am in command of the village, and my forces are superior to any other. I will carry out my mission as ordered until American troops arrive here. At the same time, I will welcome the cooperation of your partisans. When *they* get here.''

He was about to continue when the corporal entered. Not with the coffee but to say that there was an urgent phone call from headquarters. Alvensleben's heart sank. In trying to persuade Garibaldi of his position, he had almost come to believe it himself. With a sense of foreboding, he walked to a room next door and picked up the phone.

It was the young lieutenant again. "I have a call for you from the general, Captain von Alvensleben,'' he said in a flat, noncommittal voice. "Please hold the line.''

"Alvensleben?'' a gruff voice said at the other end. "What have you been up to since yesterday, eh?''

"General Röttiger, sir?'' Alvensleben stammered.

"Well, who the devil else do you think I could be?''

"I'm sorry, sir,'' Alvensleben replied, still stammering. "But I was told just a short time ago that you'd been replaced by General Scholtz. I'm very glad to hear that is not the case, if I may say so, sir.''

"Yes, well . . . these things happen, you know,'' Röttiger answered. "How the devil did you find out so quickly, eh?'' He cut Alvensleben short as the latter tried to find an answer that would not be too far from the truth. "Well, never mind about that. Tell me now, you disobeyed my order last night, did you?"

"Frankly, sir, yes."

"We'll settle that matter later. For now, I want you to stay where you are and to continue looking after the prisoners you have with you there. I've just had word that General Garibaldi has made contact with the partisans. Cooperate with him, and if you have any sense you'll listen to his advice at least fifty percent of the time. Is that clear? Stay where you are and cooperate with Garibaldi and his men. What's the situation with your friends of the SS?"

"I don't know, sir," Alvensleben answered. "They seem to be lying low, but I don't trust them. I think we can hold them off if they try anything, but I'm badly undermanned. I need reinforcements. One company would be enough."

"Who doesn't need reinforcements?" Röttiger muttered angrily. "Well, the war is as good as over, and a million men wouldn't pull us out of the hole we're in. I'll see if I can get some men to you. But the chances are that the Americans will reach your part of the world before any reinforcements I can send you. And when they do, you surrender your troops and the prisoners without a fight. Is that clear?"

"Yes, sir. But begging the general's pardon, sir, I was wondering if you could tell me, if I may be allowed the request, what happened with regard to General Scholtz?"

"Nothing very much," Röttiger answered merrily. "I simply had him and one or two of his boys arrested. General Vietinghoff is negotiating a general surrender of all the forces under his command with the Americans, and some Party hacks in Berlin tried to interfere. But the surrender will go through, probably in the next forty-eight hours."

"Yes, sir. Does that include the Waffen-SS forces in Italy?"

"Of course it does. Wolff is negotiating alongside General Vietinghoff."

"Then if I may, sir, might it be possible to have General Wolff, as commander of SS forces in Italy, order *Obersturmführer* Stiller— he's the SS man in charge here—to place his men under my command? That way we can be reasonably certain that he will not try to execute the Dachau prisoners."

"Good idea, Alvensleben. I will put through a call to Wolff at once, and I suggest you get hold of this fellow Stiller and have him call Wolff. Give me half an hour or so before you try reaching him. And Alvensleben, you're doing a good job. Good luck to you and your men. The Third Reich is *kaput*." With that, he hung up.

Alvensleben stared at the receiver for a minute or two before replacing it on its cradle. "Corporal!" he shouted, turning toward the doorway behind him.

The Italian general was standing in it, a broad grin on his face. He shrugged his shoulders. "All's fair in war, my friend. But I must admit you had me fooled there for a while. Very good! Very good!"

Abashed, Alvensleben ignored him and spoke to the corporal, who was standing discreetly behind the Italian. "Corporal. Go find the SS *Obersturmführer*—his name is Stiller—and tell him to come here at once. General Wolff has a personal message for him. Make sure you mention that—a *personal* message from General Wolff. I don't know where you can find him, perhaps in the inn down the road."

"No," Garibaldi said, turning to the corporal. "There's a house with big flower boxes in the window, next to the inn. That's where the SS men are staying now."

"Find him wherever you can," Alvensleben said, determined to have the last word. "And bring him back with you." The corporal saluted and left. Alvensleben noticed that the Italian made a point of returning the salute.

"General," he said. "I have been ordered by my commanding officer, General Röttiger, to enlist any partisan troops you have at your disposal under my command. That confirms what I said to you earlier. My orders are to stay here and to safeguard the lives of the Dachau prisoners until the Americans arrive. Stiller is going to be ordered to turn over command of his men to me by General Wolff, commander of the Waffen-SS forces in Italy."

"Good, good," the Italian said. "But before we discuss our plans, why don't we go and have that coffee which you so kindly ordered for us? It's getting cold next door."

"About a thousand meters above here," Garibaldi said as they sipped their coffee, "there's a very nice hotel. Pragser-Wildsee, it's called, I believe. A German hotel. I suggest that we commandeer it and lodge our people there."

"My orders are to stay here in Niederdorf, General," Alvensleben objected.

"The hotel is, strictly speaking, in this village. But it has the advantage of greater security. Down here, the prisoners are scattered in billets throughout the village, and it's more difficult to look after them. And the longer we stay down here, the more the villagers will resent us and therefore be likely to cooperate with the SS. I have already ordered my men to take over the hotel and secure its perimeter. So, if you have no objection—"

"What about communications? I can't just leave the telephone exchange for the SS to commandeer."

"Then let me suggest that the SS be our honored guests at the hotel, and that you leave some of your men and an armored car down here to guard this building."

It did not sound like a suggestion. It was more like an order, and with just a slight implication of threat to it. "I'm reluctant to disperse our forces, General," Alvensleben said candidly. "But if I can disarm Stiller's men, I'll be happy to agree to your suggestion. Otherwise, it's out of the question."

Later, when the call to Wolff went through, Alvensleben listened to the conversation on an extension phone. To the very end, the SS insisted on doing things their way. Instead of ordering Stiller to place his men under Alvensleben's command, Wolff instructed him to drive with them to Bolzano, where they were to surrender to American forces. He did add, however—though almost as an afterthought—that the hostages (as he called them) were to be left in Niederdorf under the protection of the Wehrmacht. They were not to be harmed.

There were no partisans in sight when they arrived at the Pragser-Wildsee Hotel. Garibaldi was nonplussed. "They'll be here soon enough," he reassured Alvensleben. Commandeering the hotel was no problem. The manager welcomed the presence of armed soldiers who shared his interest in keeping the hotel safe from the bands of partisans and deserters who were roaming the mountain forests. And when he learned that his guests were among the most distinguished in Europe, he could not have been more delighted. "It's like the old days!" he kept on repeating as he rushed around giving his small staff orders.

Alvensleben climbed up on the hood of the armored personnel carrier and leaned his weight gently against the windshield. He was exhausted. The way he was feeling, it should now be the end of the day rather than only early afternoon. He looked down at the silver tray beside him. He hadn't even asked for anything, and yet here it was—a plate with two chicken sandwiches, the bread crusts delicately trimmed off in the English manner. A large pot of coffee, with matching silverplate containers for cream and sugar. He smiled. This was quite a vacation spot.

He picked up one of the sandwiches and gazed out over the lake. The Pragser-Wildsee. Indeed, he thought, there is something wild, almost fearsome, about this spot. The towering mountains were manifestly menacing. The lake seemed too placid to be trusted, as if it were the discreet guardian of hidden, terrible secrets. Beautiful, yes; no one could deny that. But it was a beauty without charm that this place possessed, a beauty that placed you on your guard rather than one that invited you to relax and enjoy it. It seemed disturbing to him that this was a vacation spot. The hotel was grand, and very comfortable, to be sure. But he couldn't imagine wanting to spend any time there. He fancied for a moment it was the remote retreat of a mad old nobleman who carried out diabolical experiments on passing travelers who sought shelter on stormy nights. . . .

He forced himself out of his reverie and ate the sandwiches. He had seen Stiller and his men drive off in a truck toward Bolzano, as ordered. But how far had Stiller taken his men? It seemed improbable that he would surrender peaceably to the advancing American forces. Is this place making me paranoid? Alvensleben wondered, shivering with a sudden chill. He doubted it. Stiller *was* a fanatic, he reminded himself; and he, Alvensleben, was now among the foremost targets of his hatred.

There was no reason to relax his guard yet, Alvensleben told himself, just because they were at the hotel. He made some rapid calculations and figured that by stretching things he could probably have fourteen men posted on sentry duty around the clock. Not much of a force, but it would be sufficient until his reinforcements arrived: the Wehrmacht troops the general had promised him or Garibaldi's partisans, whom, at this point, he would be just as happy to see.

He drank a cup of black coffee. Would the reinforcements get here before Stiller returned? he asked himself. Possibly with his own SS reinforcements?

13. The Train at the Gate

Not a soul was in sight on the streets in the town of Dachau. It was a familiar enough sight to Colonel Robert Wiley. A pretty little town, old yet well preserved, neat and clean, the windows shuttered, and white sheets hanging from many of them as a token of surrender. It felt a bit like being on a film set, except that he had strayed onto the wrong one by mistake: turn left for the war movie.

The sounds of war were real enough, though at a distance and already somewhat to the south. For much of the morning they had been harassed by German 88s. But the resistance the Krauts were putting up really was no more than that—harassment—and the Air Force was taking out the German guns pretty effectively. K and L companies were pushing on to Munich, with the main body of the American advance, and Wiley was keeping in touch with them every few minutes by radio. His hunch that things would become stickier as they got closer to Munich had been correct. The two companies had taken some casualties in a couple of firefights already, and more could be expected by nightfall. He looked forward to completing his assignment at the concentration camp and bringing I Company up to reinforce the other two. But he was glad of his decision to stay with I Company through the day. No one seemed to know what lay ahead, and if any tricky situation developed he wanted to be there on the spot to handle it directly.

There had been one moment of tension a short while earlier when his right flank came under shelling from American artillery. An angry message to S-3 put an end to that after a couple of minutes, and luckily no one was hurt. But an incident like that unnerved men

160

and heightened the GI's good, democratic, American mistrust of higher-ups.

The tanks were halted when the bridge blew up. The charges had not been placed well, however, and enough of the structure was left to make it possible for the men to cross on foot. But Wiley decided to play it safe. He radioed S-3 for a pontoon bridge and was promised it in half an hour. It was worth the wait, he reckoned, to have the tank support. He ordered the tanks back from the exposed roadway leading up to the bridge. The GIs riding the tanks were dismounted, and a platoon was deployed to cover the approach to the bridge.

The radio crackled. "Sir," the operator told him a moment later, "the tanks report there's a bridge in upstream at seven-five-oh-six-eight-eight. That's just a couple of miles upstream from here."

"How've they managed to get there this quick?" Wiley demanded, quickly checking the grid reference.

"They haven't yet, sir," the operator answered after putting the question to the tank unit. "Seems they came across an old dame cycling like crazy to nowhere, and she just told them about the bridge. They want to know, should they move to it?"

Wiley told them to wait until they were joined by a squad of foot soldiers he was sending them. A short while later, the radio crackled again. "The bridge *is* in, sir," the operator reported. "The tanks have crossed it without opposition and have secured it."

Wiley ordered the tanks to proceed downstream until they reached the far side of the blown-up bridge, where he would rejoin them with the rest of I Company. "And then tell S-3 the bridge is in but that I shall want to have that steel bridge put in here." The operator radioed the messages.

It was 1532 hours when Wiley sent another message to S-3, the operations officer at the regimental command post. "I Company moving to concentration camp" was all it said.

At 1535, three minutes later, S-3 sent Wiley a message that greatly reassured him. "Concentration camp guarded only by *Volksturm*," it said, referring to the underequipped and untrained civilians hastily mobilized as part of Hitler's last-ditch effort: young boys and old men, for the most part, who would not be able to put up effective resistance.

It was the first intelligence report he had received about the camp. It was good to know that he wouldn't be dealing with the SS. And as if to answer his next question, S-3 reported on the situation in Munich. "Revolt in Munich was put down by SS troops and the Fifth SS Division Viking last night. No gun positions in town. All bridges Munich to Dachau were in, early this morning."

That too was good news. Very good news. There would not be a heavy fight for Munich, as there had been for Nuremberg. Did the departure of the SS division to the southeast mean that Hitler was indeed creating an Alpine redoubt, as rumor had it? It would be one hell of a fight digging the Krauts out from the mountains, if that's where they were going to make their last stand, Wiley thought. But he didn't pursue the idea. There were more pressing matters at hand to attend to. Let tomorrow bring what it would. And the day after that, too. Right now, he had to have only one thing in mind: capturing the concentration camp a couple of miles down that road.

Supported by the tanks, I Company moved on. The terrain was flat and quite open, with only a few small houses dotted alongside. Bad country in which to get caught in an enemy crossfire. But enemy resistance was so light now that Wiley felt easy enough about this. The clank of the tanks' treads on the cobbled road was a reassuring sound. Ahead lay a thick clump of trees, through which one or two buildings were just discernible. Wiley checked the map again and confirmed his guess that this was the concentration camp. It didn't look at all sinister.

Wiley felt extraordinarily alive as he moved forward with the unit. He was a soldier now, in a combat situation, his own life on the line. His instincts, his eyes and ears, were totally alert in service of the soldier's supreme imperative: kill or be killed. And yet at the same time he was not just a soldier but a commander, too, responsible for his men's lives and for the objective they had been assigned. Wiley did not glamorize war, but there was something tremendously exhilarating for him in this combination of roles.

Jackson came up to him. "I'm going to deploy the men into skirmish order," he said. "There's a stone wall up ahead. No sign of the enemy, but the lead scouts will go over first, on either side of the gate, and move over to secure the gate."

"Fine, Bill," Wiley replied. "I'll go over with the scouts and take a squad with me."

He saw Jackson's quizzical, slightly resentful expression.

"I don't know what kind of situation we're getting into here. Once we're inside that camp, I want to be on top of everything the moment it happens. And another thing, Bill. Don't have the scouts move over to the gate. I want them to remain ahead and at the flanks. Send in another squad on the other side and have them move in and meet me and my squad at the gate."

A sentry box at the gate seemed deserted. Wiley moved off with a small group of men to a point about fifty yards to the right of the gate. The wall was no more than eight feet high, and they scaled it without difficulty. Wiley was the third man over, and he sprawled out on his belly scanning the terrain ahead through his binoculars. In every direction lay pleasant, well-tended lawns . . . clumps of pine trees . . . elegant villas, and, in the distance, several larger buildings that resembled hotels or schools. "Geez, Colonel!" the man next to him whispered. "What a place! It looks like a resort!"

Wiley smiled briefly. The man was right. This was no hellhole. Fact was, it was probably the pleasantest, best-maintained spot he had seen since coming to Europe. For a moment he allowed his binoculars to play on beds of roses just coming into bloom in front of one of the villas. Obviously, these were the officers' quarters, and the larger buildings in the distance housed the enlisted men. *This* was the notorious concentration camp? It was difficult to believe that anything evil happened in a place that looked so pleasant.

"Do you see any sign of the Krauts?" he asked the men. No one did. Gingerly, they moved toward the gate, where they found the other group waiting for them. They too had not seen any trace of the enemy and were marveling at the splendor of the layout.

"Bet they put the wall up so's no one could see how well they live here!" Wiley heard one of the GIs joke. He ordered the gate opened and signaled Jackson and his men to come forward. After a moment's hesitation, he ordered the tanks deployed by the gate. They could secure his retreat if he found himself faced by overwhelming forces up ahead. And they could also make sure reinforcements entered the camp if he needed them.

Wiley entered the nearest villa and set up a temporary command post there while the men were flushing out any Krauts who might be hiding in the other buildings. The house was beautifully furnished. In the living room, Wiley plunked himself onto a deeply upholstered sofa for a moment, just to savor its luxury. A small toy truck and a teddy bear lay on the Persian rug—evidence that the occupants of this house had left in a hurry. About twenty-five minutes later, Jackson informed him that the search was completed. The buildings were vacant; there was no sign of the enemy. One of the men had brought back with him a large map of the camp, which at last made it possible for Wiley to determine its layout. "Here's where we have to get to," he said to Jackson, pointing to the large compound that lay some distance to the east. He drew a line on the map to indicate the route he wanted the men to take.

They were about to set out when a message came over the walkie-talkie from one of the lead scouts. The man at the other end insisted on speaking directly to Wiley. "Colonel, sir," he said in a voice that, even through the tinny, static-laden earpiece, sounded on the verge of tears. "You'd better come here right away. There's something you've got to see, sir. We're right by the railway tracks near a big archway that's got a Nazi eagle on top of it. Behind a U-shaped complex of barracks east of the main gate."

"What is it, man?" Wiley asked impatiently.

"I—" The man paused. "It's a train, sir. A train. Like no other you've ever seen."

"It's pretty late in the day for lunch," Plaga remarked jovially, "but who's complaining?" He brought Maas his bowl of soup and sat down beside him on the edge of the bunk. The two men drank down the lukewarm liquid greedily. Their tutored palates discerned a larger quantity of fat in the soup than was normal, and they nodded appreciatively to one another.

"Hey, there's a bit of potato in my bowl," Maas announced happily. He held up the chunk, which was perhaps two inches long. "Look at that—a real potato!" Carefully setting the bowl beside him, he broke the potato into two pieces and plunked one into Plaga's bowl.

"Thanks," his friend said quietly.

"You know something?" Maas said. "I'll bet you this is the last meal we have as prisoners. The next one, we'll be free. Do you hear the bullets whistling over the building? I can't figure out where they're firing from, or at whom, but that's small-arms fire, and it can't be coming from far away. The Americans will be here soon. I bet you anything."

"Well, I guess you're right," Plaga replied. "But you know there's been all that talk about how the Nazis are going to try to do us in before the Americans get here. . . . I'll only believe it, really, when I see them."

"There's no way they could pull anything on us now, Plaga; they have their hands full running away from the Americans. No, I'm sure. This is it. Give them another hour or so. That's all it'll be."

"We'll see," Plaga said cautiously. "It's strange," he added. "A short while ago, I was sure we were going to be liberated today and you were skeptical. I was all excited, but you weren't. Now *I'm* the one who's feeling scared—a bit depressed, actually. And you think we're about to be liberated. But even you don't seem very excited or happy. Have you noticed that?"

"Not until you pointed it out," Maas admitted. He paused reflectively. "You're right, though. It seems sort of matter-of-fact. And like everything else, it's something out of our own control. It's happening to us; it's not something *we* are doing. Do you know what I mean?"

"Of course. But is that any reason to be depressed?"

"I didn't say I was depressed. You said you were."

"I know. But you are depressed, aren't you?"

"Leave me alone, Plaga, for God's sake. What is all this crap about being depressed? If you feel unhappy because we're going to be liberated, that's your business. But don't try to make me unhappy, too." Angrily, Maas reached into his pocket and pulled out his diary.

> *1600. With Herman ate soup. Continuous*
> *machine-gun fire. Bullets fly over the*
> *camp. They are coming.*

He sat there for minutes, staring at the page. His entry seemed flat and unenthusiastic, as well as quite banal. But he couldn't think of anything else to write. Self-consciously, he changed the period at the end to an exclamation mark. It seemed to him, the moment after he had done so, a dishonest thing to do. "I'm sorry, Plaga," he said, turning to his faithful companion. "I'm sorry I snapped at you."

In the *Revier,* Connally allowed a brief smile to play across his face. "It seems obvious, gentlemen, that the Americans will be here within an hour or two. My guess is that they've already taken Dachau and are on the road to the camp. For all we know, they have already entered the camp and are on their way to the prison compound. We will not throw caution to the winds, but I think it's impossible that the Nazis will try anything against us at this point, with the Americans breathing down their necks. We'll leave it to the historians to try to figure out whatever happened to *Wolkenbrand.*"

"And I said from the beginning they would never do anything," the Russian general muttered in a surly tone just loud enough for the others to hear.

Connally ignored him. "There are two things that I suggest need to be done now. We must ensure absolute compliance with the curfew. No one is to leave his *Block* until the Americans are here and have taken over the camp. We just cannot afford to give—"

"And the second thing is?" the general asked.

"We just cannot afford to give the Germans an excuse to start shooting at us," Connally continued. "The second thing we have to do now is to find some way of detaining informers and collaborators. Once the Americans get here, there's going to be an incredible amount of confusion, and it will be all too easy for those swine to get away. They must be arrested and dealt with. We owe that to ourselves and to the dead."

"Dealt with?" someone asked. "How? By whom?"

"We'll kill the bastards, is what we'll do with them," someone else said.

"I suggest we settle that later," Connally cut in. "In any case, we may not be the ones to decide anything once the Americans take over the camp. All we can do is make sure these traitors are available for whatever is to be done with them."

There followed a brief discussion of how these men should be identified and prevented from escaping in the turmoil of the liberation. Someone hit on the idea of stripping them of their clothes. Even in Dachau that would make them conspicuous. The proposal engendered grim amusement among the men and was adopted.

Accompanied by Jackson and one of the lead platoons, Wiley marched through the "resort" area. The absence of German soldiers, and the delightful grounds through which they were moving, had put the men in a lighthearted mood. But Wiley knew that his battle-hardened veterans would not be any the less alert for the slightest sign of the enemy.

The thick stand of pines gave way abruptly to a gently curving road. It was a narrow road, no wider than two Jeeps. At one point it broadened to accommodate a row of gas pumps protected from the elements by a cast-concrete roof. It looked much like an American gas station. A railroad track, only slightly elevated on a bed of gravel, bounded the other side of the road. A long train, of at least forty cars, stood on the track.

In startling contrast to the well-trimmed grounds through which Wiley and his men had just marched, the train was messy-looking: an irregular assortment of open cattle cars, closed freight cars, and coaches variously painted gray, dark green, and dark brown. The big doors of the cattle cars and freight trucks were all open, many sticking forward from the track at different angles. In front of many of the cars messy piles of clothing lay on the ground. From a distance they looked like manure heaps.

Stepping out onto the road, Wiley was met by one of the lead scouts. The man looked directly into Wiley's face but said nothing. A heavy flow of tears was pouring down the stubble on his cheeks, and his body shook with sobs. He was not making the slightest effort to control himself, despite the colonel's presence.

Outraged, Wiley bellowed at the man, "Pull yourself together, soldier! What in tarnation is going on?" Jackson had joined them and was staring menacingly at the scout. The man's expression did not change. Turning his body slightly, he pointed at the train behind him with his right arm. The effort seemed to snap something inside him. To Wiley's astonishment, he sat on the ground and began blubbering like an infant.

Angrily, but also with an overpowering sense of curiosity,

Wiley stepped past the soldier and crossed the road to the train. He looked through the open door of a cattle car.

It was a mess, offending profoundly his ingrained military sense of order and neatness. Scraps of straw were scattered over the floor of the car, intermingled with a few rotting turnips. Empty metal mugs and bowls were strewn around, too. And everywhere those shabby, messy mounds of rags.

Rags?

Wiley had never before in his life experienced horror. Sheer, unadulterated horror. The kind that strikes you just like that proverbial kick in the stomach and makes you gasp for breath as your heart seems alternately to have stopped beating and to be racing away with you at a lunatic pace. Horror: the kind that confronts you with sights you know are real but that you also know could not possibly exist. Sights so fantastic that you feel, no less fantastically, that you possess the power to sweep them away. Horror: a feeling that, even more than fear itself, translates into the physical and captures your body, at one moment freezing it into immobility, at the next convulsing it with nausea.

Rags? There were rags there, Wiley saw; clothes and blankets. And under them were bodies. Human bodies.

Grayness permeated everything, as if suffocating vision. The cattle car into which Wiley was looking was painted gray inside as well as out. The straw, the turnips, the clothing, and the blankets— all were in shades of gray that camouflaged shapes, melting them into the gray skin of the emaciated bodies.

As the initial shock receded, Wiley found himself playing a game. Detect-a-limb. Spot-the-body. He stopped, appalled at the grisly entertainment he was providing himself. A thought entered his mind and clung tenaciously there: The bodies of human beings can seem to disappear right before your eyes. So inconsequential that they can scarcely be distinguished from dirty blankets and rotting turnips.

He stepped back, forcing himself to do something, even if only the simple movement he was now taking, to stem the wave of horror that was threatening to engulf him again. Check the situation, Wiley! he told himself angrily. Remember your training. Give your men instructions.

He set himself the task, first, of explaining the scene before him. A trainload of people. Horrendously emaciated. None of them could have weighed more than sixty or seventy pounds. Obviously, most of them had died in the train. Brought here from God knows where, but on a long journey whose purpose was probably to kill them. Some had survived, though. They had reached Dachau alive. They had walked or crawled out of the cars, or perhaps had been dragged out. And then shot. The lucky ones, that is. Some hadn't been so lucky. They'd had their brains beaten out, literally beaten out. By rifle butts, Wiley guessed. He saw a body lying underneath a freight car. It was difficult to see it at first—but he did see it—and gray matter was oozing out of the broken skull.

Railroad cars filled with the bodies of prisoners who had died en route to Dachau from another concentration camp.

He walked on. Another body under the train. This time ripped open in a way that could only have been done by an animal. A dog, he guessed. He vomited.

For God's sake, give the men something to do! a voice inside him barked. He looked for Jackson, tearing his eyes away from the grotesqueness all around. He couldn't find the lieutenant. The platoon had broken up into individual fragments, each staring silently at the carnage. Moving only like sleepwalkers to look into other cars, or under the trains. Some, then, like the scout, sat on the ground crying. Others were vomiting.

Where was Jackson, for Christ's sake? Wiley asked himself. He's lost control of the company. It struck him that the men were looking as empty, as ghostlike, as the corpses at which they were staring. Wiley's sole concern now was for the unit. Getting them back together. Forging them again into the superb fighting machine that they had been only a few moments earlier.

He found Jackson sitting on the road by himself, sobbing hysterically. "Get up, Jackson, and pull your company together," Wiley snapped. But Jackson ignored him and continued to sob. With a rapid, brutal gesture, Wiley reached down and, grabbing Jackson by the front of his tunic, pulled him to his feet. Twisting the cloth around in his fist, he created a vise that forced Jackson to pull himself together. "I'm taking over direct command of your company, Jackson. Assemble the men and have them fall in here. I'm giving you five minutes, and not a second more."

"Yes, sir," Jackson said limply. But his eyes stared hatefully into Wiley's as the colonel returned his salute. Wiley thanked heaven that he'd decided to come along on this assignment himself.

While the men were being assembled, Wiley strode back and forth over a short stretch of the road as if to wind up his spirits for the task ahead. But the horrors all around intruded at every moment. The bodies scattered helter-skelter. The faces with their sunken cheeks. He could not escape them. If he forced his eyes away from the train, they fell on the ground where more bodies lay—and these more hideously murdered than the ones in the train itself. How many bodies were there? he wondered. He had never seen so many piled up in one spot in his entire life—and he had not yet walked more than a fraction of the length of the train. A thousand was a modest estimate, he told himself. There could be as many as three thousand here. *Three thousand!* And killed in a way that defied comprehension. Not like soldiers shot or blown up on the battlefield. They were civilians simply—done away with.

It was frighteningly, hauntingly quiet. In the distance the noise of war reverberated. But here there was not a sound, except an occasional sob from one of his men. It occurred to Wiley that for the first time he really understood why they were fighting the Germans. The lectures they had been given—"orientation" sessions, as they were called—had seemed to him mere propaganda at the time, and he knew that most of the men felt that way too. And they *had* been propaganda. Not even the most anti-Nazi talk he had ever heard could match what he was seeing now. The war really was a struggle between good and evil. Evil such as no one, not even the indoctrination specialists, had been able to imagine.

The entire company was assembled. And a sorry sight it was. Wiley called over Jackson, Walker, his exec, and the platoon leaders. "Divide your men into teams of four," he ordered. "Send them through the entire train. I want every car searched, every body checked. And on the tracks as well. I want every body checked carefully. There may be one or two people left alive. We won't leave here until we know that for certain. And let me make one thing absolutely clear," he added, his voice steellike and cold. "When this has been done, I want a company of disciplined, fighting-mad men, not a bunch of slobbering wrecks!"

The ghastly task began. While the men were at work, Wiley strode up and down the road, needling the men in the way that a Marine Corps drill instructor might. "I didn't see you check that corner there, soldier!" he would say. "Well, then, check it again!" "How many bodies in this car, soldier? Are you sure you didn't count one body twice? Count 'em all again!" Gradually, discipline was restored. Even body counting became yet another dreary Army chore. But Wiley was under no illusions. His men's nerves were stretched tight. From now on, they weren't going to be taking many prisoners. They were out for blood.

An hour later, the job was finished. There were 2,310 people on the train, including 21 children and 83 women. Not a single person was alive on this train that had reached the gates of Dachau.

How many more trains like this were there? Wiley asked himself. And how many more bodies?

Like a voyeur who guiltily averts his eyes when, after an interminable wait, a naked woman at last steps into view, Berenson batted
his eyelids at just the wrong moment. For years afterward, he would
remember the precise sequence. He had been staring through the
skylight from his upper-bunk perch at the *Jourhaus* for hours, each of
which seemed like a day. Nothing stirred other than the white sheet
flapping from the flagpole on the *Jourhaus* roof. Not a person was
to be seen. The excited, tense bustle in the *Block* made the scene
outside seem alternately unreal and ominously calm. Then it happened.

He saw a movement at the right-hand side of the gate. A furtive

*Rows of corpses of Dachau prisoners viewed by American jour-
nalists on May 4, the week after the camp was liberated.*

but bulky movement. Even from this distance Berenson could tell that there was something unfamiliar about the figure, though he could not yet spot what it was. But he knew *what* that figure was, and he batted his eyelids. When the scene returned to focus—perhaps only two seconds later—the figure, which had been advancing toward the prison compound, had now turned its back and was retreating hastily.

That was all Berenson saw. He did not move, and he felt only a tingling numbness, the kind you feel a moment before vast emotions overpower you. He waited for them to come, to savor them before announcing the incredible news to the men below.

But before this could happen, a volley of machine-gun fire spurted from one of the guard towers.

For a second, and no more, the sound of the machine-gun burst mesmerized Wiley and his men. And then they sprang into action. Their training and experience in combat guided their every movement as the assembled company spread out into platoons and squads in response to the terse commands that came automatically to the lips of Wiley and his subordinates.

But the energy that infused their movements was not that of ordinary combat soliders, nor was the grim set of their faces. Nothing could stop these men. A demoniacal hatred seized them as they charged toward the sound of the gunfire. They were not out to take a position or to capture prisoners. They were out to kill.

Ahead, from a maze of low concrete buildings, bursts of ill-aimed rifle fire were directed at the advancing Americans. Their defenders didn't have a chance. Within a couple of minutes they were dead.

Sheltering momentarily in these sheds, which were workshops, the men looked through a row of trees onto a road and a moat. Behind the moat was a high barbed-wire electrified fence and line after line of long huts.

They had arrived.

Large concrete guard towers with white flags flying from them overlooked the moat. From these, the advancing Americans were greeted with long bursts of heavy machine-gun fire. Viciously, but skillfully, the GIs began to assault these positions.

The faithful Plaga was still at Piet Maas's side, helping him to his crutches. But Maas refused to move until he had recorded the moment in his diary. He scribbled hurriedly:

> *1715. Screaming from the Appellplatz.*
> *Rush to it.*

And then, teetering precariously on his crutches, he joined in the surge.

14. 1728 Hours: A Time to Remember

They poured out of their huts. Frenzied, starving, sick. Screaming like banshees. Bumping blindly into each other, tripping, picking themselves up, and rushing forward again. Impelled by unknown reservoirs of energy that had been filled, drop by drop, for just this occasion. Frantic to reach the fence. Conscious of no other purpose and not recognizing any meaning in this purpose. The heavy machine-gun fire from the towers and the answering staccato of American carbines did not drown out their insane shrieks but seemed to assist them. The chorus of thousands was unlike any heard before or since, a cacophony of anguish, rage, despair, joy, and hope that combined the wail of a funeral and the triumph of a football game and virtually every other sound known to man.

Hopman, in better physical condition than many of the other men, pushed through the throng at the same time that he ran along with it. But he was also big enough to delay, for just a split second, a sudden surge that tumbled hundreds of men to the ground of the *Appellplatz*. And as he fell, he saw what they were trying to duck—the spectacularly rapid advance of a line of angry eruptions on the ground as an SS soldier, in a last desperate affirmation of his faith, turned his heavy machine gun away from the advancing Americans and onto the hordes of prisoners rushing to meet them. The line of bullets sped directly toward him. Desperately, shocked not only by the sight but by the drastic return of reality, he pushed his falling body to one side. But it was too late.

It was as if a white-hot poker had been drawn across the top of

175

his skull. "Oh, God!" he shrieked. "Not now. Not now!" He fell over a body, which cushioned his fall. Incredulous despite the pain, he realized that he was not dead, and that the bullet had only grazed him. The others were on their feet again, resuming their rush across the *Appellplatz*. Hopman looked around. Fantastically, no one else seemed to have been hit—let alone killed—by that savage burst of machine-gun fire. Far from deterring the prisoners, the shots from the guard tower, after the one brief lull, renewed their bestial outpouring of sound and emotion, raising it to even greater intensity.

The Americans, too, had seen the machine gun on the tower open up on the prisoners. That unleashed the last restraints on their inhibitions. Light machine guns were brought up and within seconds had saturated the platforms on top of the guard towers with a deadly assault of lead. Now GIs stormed across the moat separating them from the towers. But even before they reached them their doors swung open and SS men came stumbling out. Their hands weren't exactly raised in surrender. Or perhaps they were. But everything happened too quickly to be sure, and, surrender or no, the Nazis were pulverized by fire from a score of rifles as they stepped out. Climbing over their corpses, the GIs rushed into the towers. More shots were heard. More Nazi corpses were thrown onto the piles outside.

The prisoners had reached the *Jourhaus* gate, and others were crowding up near the electrified fence. As each Nazi was shot, the mob let out a roar of jubilation that defied the impossible by making the incredible tumult out of which it arose seem like silence itself. Hopman, who had pushed his way against the wave of prisoners rushing toward the Americans, now stood up against a windowsill of the *Revier Block* while a Polish doctor divided his attention between the events unfolding close by and the more practical matter of stitching the wound in Hopman's head.

To their horror, the two men saw a sudden rush near the electrified fence and the brief—and to them, all too familiar—scream of a prisoner dying as the voltage surged through his body. Firing continued in several locations and did not, in fact, die down for about half an hour. But already, groups of soldiers, freed from combat in their immediate zones, were staring across the fence at the prisoners and digging in their pockets and packs for cigarettes, candy bars, and rations to throw over to them. But the savage fights that erupted as

Bodies of SS guards lie at the entrance to a guard tower where they were killed by rifle fire.

the prisoners tore at each other for these unheard-of luxuries dissuaded the GIs from continuing the handouts.

"Where's the powerhouse?" one of the Americans at the *Jourhaus* gate asked. A hundred prisoners volunteered to show the way. Cautiously, the Americans opened the gate and allowed two prisoners to step forward. They disappeared for about ten minutes. When they returned, the electricity in the wire had been disconnected.

The men milling behind the fence were the stronger and healthier prisoners. Nonetheless, from time to time their hysterical outpouring of emotion abated somewhat, from sheer exhaustion, and was transmuted into coherent expressions of joy and relief. Strangers and friends alike embraced each other. "We've made it! We've made it!" they exulted to each other in the scores of languages spoken in the camp. "Now everything will be OK." And they noticed for the first time the individual men who were their liberators. The general consensus was that the Americans were overfed, and that their helmets and asses were both far too large. Maas, hobbling up on his crutches, was distressed. He found the shooting of the SS men unnecessary, a violation of the laws of decency and war. But no less than any other man, he was overwhelmed with the desire to shake hands with an American soldier, to touch an American arm or shoulder, and to say anything, no matter how inconsequential, to an American. For this, however, he would have to wait several hours. But long afterward, the sheer magic of Americanness would remain with him.

Wiley was troubled by many cares. His men were fighting with deadly effectiveness, but they were once again close to the point where he could no longer control them. And how was he going to secure a perimeter of this size with the 150 unnerved men at his disposal? Soon another problem presented itself, one for which his military training and experience left him entirely unequipped.

While the shooting was still continuing in several zones, he was startled to see an American Jeep drive right up to the *Jourhaus* gate. A major general, whom he at once recognized as the commander of the division in the adjoining zone of combat, sat in the front seat next to the driver. In the rear seats were a lieutenant colonel and a

woman—a very attractive blonde—in the uniform of a war correspondent.

Wiley set off at a trot and arrived at the *Jourhaus* gate a moment
after the Jeep. He saw the woman correspondent get to her feet and
jump out of the vehicle even before it had braked to a stop. She
stumbled, caught herself, and then pushed past the two GIs standing
by the gate. They watched passively as she fumbled with its bolt and
swung the gate open.

"Shut that gate at once, for Christ's sake!" Wiley roared. All he
needed now were thousands of half-crazed prisoners running all over
the place. It was already too late. The woman, standing in the opened
gateway, was brushed aside by a throng of prisoners who swept past
her to freedom. Ludicrously, she tried to stop them. She wanted her
interview.

The threat of being overwhelmed by a flood of prisoners mobilized a group of GIs nearby. Without a direct command from Wiley,
they linked arms and formed a barrier across the narrow roadway
leading to the gate. Slowly, and with great effort, they forced the
prisoners back. Swearing and grunting, pushing as though they were
dealing with a horde of animals, they nevertheless kept their cool.
The problem now was to extricate the woman from this crowd. In
forcing the prisoners back behind the gate, the GIs had shoved her
into the compound with them.

"Get me outta here!" she shrieked, close to tears. The prisoners
ignored her, their eyes focused crazily on the spectacle of American
soldiers. They didn't prevent her from getting out, but they didn't
open a way for her, either. Now she began to feel desperate and
pushed her arms forward, as if doing a breaststroke through this
ocean of bodies in an effort to reach the gate. She was taller than
most of the men, and stronger, and before long had reached the metal
grilles.

Wiley stared down at her. His voice trembling with fury, he
said, "I should shoot you for this!" Maliciously, he let her be flattened against the gate for a few seconds. Then he opened it the few
inches necessary for her to pass. Leaning with all his weight to
prevent the prisoners from sweeping the gate open, and with his arm
stretched across the gap to prevent anyone from escaping, he banged

the grille shut again the moment she was through. He half hoped that it would graze her heel in closing, but her alacrity, and her desperation to get out, had her almost all the way back to the Jeep before Wiley had secured the heavy metal bar across the gate.

He stormed back toward her, determined to throw her out of his zone. By the time he was near her, however, she had recovered her composure and was staring up at him in a sexy, provocative fashion. "Thanks, Colonel!" She smiled, as though he had done nothing more than hold open a door for her.

"You get out of here, lady, and that's an order!" Wiley growled, turning on his heel and setting out down the road to check the situation at the guard towers.

A corporal from Philadelphia, Pennsylvania, distributes his last pack of cigarettes to the former prisoners behind the fence.

"Colonel!" It was the general speaking. Wiley had actually forgotten about him in the absurd little drama that had just taken place. He turned back and saluted. Slowly, arrogantly, the general got out of his Jeep. He returned Wiley's salute. "Colonel, this lady here's a correspondent, and I've okayed it for her to be here to interview the VIPs in this camp she wants to do a story about."

"What VIPs, sir?"

The general seemed uncertain, but the woman answered for him. "There's Schuschnigg and Léon Blum and some of the people involved in the bomb plot against Hitler last year, and all sorts of other people who the world thought died years ago. It's a great story, Colonel, and I'm sitting on top of it. So I've gotta go inside and get my story!"

"Sorry, lady. This is all the story you're getting for now," Wiley answered brusquely. "My orders are to let no one in and no one out of this compound. You can see how crazed the men in there are, and no one's going in until things settle down here and we get medics to check them out for contagious diseases and—"

"That's OK, Colonel," the general interrupted, winking at the woman. "I'm taking over command here, and you let me worry about those things."

For a moment, Wiley was speechless. "I'm sorry, sir, but with all respect I have my orders from General Collins, who is my commanding officer, and only he can change them. Until I hear from him, I'm running the show here." He couldn't resist taking a swipe at the headline-hunting general. "Lieutenant Colonel Robert Wiley, ma'am!" He smiled at the correspondent. "Now, if you'll kindly get back into your Jeep—"

"I'm taking over here, Wiley," the general roared, "and that's a direct order."

"I'm afraid that's impossible, sir," Wiley answered. He was suddenly very conscious of the scores of men pressing up against the gate only a few feet away from him. They were getting a fine impression of the United States Army in action, he thought bitterly, hoping that they could not hear or understand the exchange that was taking place.

"You can't talk to my general that way!" the colonel who had been sitting in the back of the Jeep warned Wiley.

"Oh, yeah?" Wiley answered. "And what are you going to do about it?"

"If there wasn't a lady here, I'd show you soon enough!" the gallant colonel responded.

Wiley ignored him. "Soldier!" He beckoned a GI over to the group. The man came up and saluted. "See this lady gets safely into the Jeep, will you?" The soldier gave him the slightest hint of a grin.

"This way, lady," he said, taking the woman's elbow and guiding her the two steps back to the Jeep.

The general's face flushed. "Take your hands off her," he ordered. And then, in the next second, he whipped him across the arm with the riding crop he carried in his hand, a hard, painful blow.

The group froze. The general flushed. The woman blushed. The soldier winced but did his utmost to hide the pain. Wiley's mind momentarily went blank. He became conscious again of the prisoners at the gate and realized that in their continuing frenzy they evidently hadn't so much as noticed what had just happened. But he was also conscious of the other soldiers standing around who *had* witnessed this extraordinary scene. Wiley sensed that unless he did something drastic, his own men would do it for him.

He broke the silence. Hardly bothering to disguise the gesture, he put his hand on his hip, just above the holster in which he carried his .45. "General," he said in a flat tone, but looking his superior officer directly in the eye, "I'm ordering you out of this camp. I want you out of this camp altogether, not just the prison area here but the whole camp. Either you get out now or I'll have you thrown out. And take that lady with you!"

The general forced an expression of outrage onto his face. "I'm gonna get your hide for this," he snarled at Wiley.

Like hell you think you are, Wiley thought to himself, noticing how the general was unable to bring himself to confront him eye to eye. You're going to be hoping and praying that I don't get yours. Even in Patton's army you're not going to get away with horsewhipping a GI!

The general and his party left. Wiley took out a pack of chewing gum, helped himself to a stick, and passed the rest around. Secure the perimeter! he told himself. You've got to secure the perimeter. Keep the Krauts from getting in and the prisoners from getting out!

Through the gateway he could see that the prisoners were still as excited and out of control as before. He would have to pacify them, get them organized. But later. Right now, it would be impossible to do that. And he would need Stock around to translate for him. He sent a soldier to find Stock.

"The towers are all out, Colonel," Jackson said as he came up to join him. "One of our boys got grazed in the arm, but that's the only casualty. The men are fanning out to search for Krauts hidden in the buildings. Some have already surrendered. But we understand there's more. Those sure weren't no *Volksturm* guys, Colonel. Real fanatics."

He's right, Wiley thought to himself, remembering the false intelligence report that the SS had vacated the camp. "So much for G-2," he said aloud.

Jackson smiled. "Yeah. And if that woman correspondent knew there are VIPs in the camp, how come G-2 didn't?" he added.

"I want the area behind that wall there set up for Kraut prisoners," Wiley said, pointing to a concrete wall about ten feet high that stretched across an area about fifty yards away. "Take a squad with you to guard them, and a machine gun. Leave a platoon here with me to secure the perimeter, and send the rest of the boys off to look for more Krauts."

Already a group of about twenty Germans, guarded only by three GIs, was coming down the road toward them. Surrendering Germans had become a familiar enough sight to Wiley in recent weeks. But he felt different about these men. He remembered the corpses piled outside the guard towers. Too bad they didn't get it, too, he thought to himself. The road down which the Germans, a shabby, dispirited-looking group, were walking paralleled the moat behind which the howling, shrieking mob of prisoners was still engulfed in frenzied exultation. For a brief but identifiable and distinct moment the sight of the captured Germans being paraded past them robbed the mob of its voice. An awesome, and awed, hush gripped the crowd. Dead Germans, shot out of this life in front of their eyes, was one thing for the prisoners, yet another variant of the pervasive encounter with death that they had been having for years. But this: live German soldiers, Nazi SS men, in abject, helpless surrender! This was a far more astonishing and persuasive spectacle.

But the prisoners' astonishment lasted only a moment. Their silence gave way almost at once to a vast paroxysm of jeering, hooting, derisive hatred. Even some GIs joined in, adding their catcalls to the hubbub and shaking their fists at the Nazis. Altogether a terrible sound. The Germans looked as though they would gladly have escaped from it into the jaws of hell itself. They shuffled their feet more rapidly in a desperate endeavor to block their ears to the tumult. But it was at least five minutes before they came to the end of the road and were led off behind the wall to await their captors' pleasure.

Brigadier General "Pop" Crashaw rechecked the map coordinates. There was no mistake about it. The town of Dachau, and the area to its east, lay in the next division's zone. Dachau. Crashaw was familiar with that name. Unlike many of his fellow officers, he kept closely informed about world events, and in fact had done so well in his modern history courses at West Point that he had once even toyed with the idea of an academic career. But he was an Army brat (as, in fact, his father and both his grandfathers had been before him—he was the fourth generation of soldiers in his family), and that wasn't something he could shrug off just like that. So he had remained in the Army and was now acting commander of the regiment.

He had been congratulating himself on his good luck. If the line had been drawn only a couple of miles to the east, he realized when looking at the map in the morning, Dachau would have been in his zone of action. And God knows, he thought to himself, what *that* would have meant! His job was fighting, and it had never been so enjoyable a task as now. You could almost spit into Munich, it was so close by. And that would be the big one, and the last one. They'd had some pretty good battles, and now he wanted the triumph and glory of victory. He wanted it, and he knew that it was just beyond his reach—hours, and certainly not more than a day, away. It was a fantastically good feeling, and as things now stood there was an excellent chance that his would be the first regiment into Munich. That would cap it all! He thanked his lucky star again that he was out of the Dachau area. Liberating a concentration camp was a fine thing to do, sure. But he didn't want to be the one to do it. His job was fighting, not carrying out missions of mercy. Dachau was a mission of mercy. Munich was fighting. Dachau was the other division's baby. Let them worry about it.

Then the message came. The general was in Dachau. Not just in Dachau, but at the concentration camp. And he wanted Crashaw over there at once, top priority. What the hell was the general doing there? he asked himself. It wasn't his zone, so why the hell was he ordering Crashaw over? But the message was unequivocal: Meet me at the entrance gate to the concentration camp in fifteen minutes.

He took a squad along with him in Jeeps and got to the general in twenty minutes. Crashaw detested the general, and never more so than now, since his intuition had already told him what was going on. He saw the general was in one of his famous rages. "There's some son of a bitch lieutenant colonel from the next division in there, Crashaw," he growled, pointing to the large, parklike enclosure behind him with his riding crop, "and he thinks he can handle the situation with his one lousy company of men. I want you to bring up another company—two if you can spare 'em—and take over security of the entire camp."

"But, General—" Crashaw began.

"Don't give me any of that, Crashaw," the general said fiercely. "I'm in no mood for a debate. You bring your boys in here and take over the camp. No one to go in or come out. Seal off the entire area until further notice. Except for correspondents." He paused, nodding in the direction of his female companion. "Make sure you give them every opportunity to report on what they see."

"The—uh—colonel, sir," Crashaw began tentatively. "What do I do about him? We're in his zone of combat, sir. Does he know we're taking over from him?"

"He's gonna know soon enough. You get your boys up here, and by the time they've arrived you'll have orders that'll set him straight." Even as he finished talking he tapped his driver on the leg with the riding crop, and the Jeep sped off.

"Shit," Crashaw shouted emphatically when the general was a safe distance away.

He thought for a moment and then ordered his radio operator, "Get Colonel Frazer. Tell him I want him here in fifteen minutes."

Wiley walked down the road alongside the moat. He noticed with grim satisfaction the bodies of two SS men floating face downward on the water. Across the moat, the howling crowds were still caught up in their frenzy. For the first time, Wiley looked closely at their faces. He shuddered. They were horribly distorted. In their baldness. In their starvation. The hollow cheeks and bulging eyes. And in the contortions into which their emotions were forcing them. It seemed scarcely credible to him that bodies as frail as theirs were capable of so much, and such sustained, noise. And their emaciation was heightened, in a sense confirmed, by other sights. One body lay, dangling by the elbows, impaled in a horrible crucifixion on the electrified fence. Looking past the men crowded on the other side, Wiley could see, between the endless rows of drab barracks buildings, naked corpses lying on the muddy ground. They were so thin it was almost impossible to believe they had once been human beings. Again there rose up in him that feeling of indescribable sadness and rage. How could anyone have done this to other human beings? He fought back the tears. A fierce determination formed itself in his mind. He had to do something—*something!*—for these people. For his own sake as well as for theirs. He reached into his pocket for a candy bar and felt sickened, a moment later, by the insulting futility of his intention. A candy bar to atone for years of suffering. He couldn't bring himself to throw it over to the men on the other side of the wire.

Although still numb and shocked, his mind was gradually adjusting to the ghoulish situation. Recalling the mad scenes he had witnessed a few minutes earlier when the prisoners fought wildly with each other for the gifts the GIs were throwing at them, he decided to issue an order putting an end to that.

He had gone about fifty yards down the road from the *Jourhaus* when a burst of machine-gun fire erupted a short distance away. For some reason, he knew at once what it signified. Without a second's hesitation, he turned in his tracks and sprinted off in the direction of the gunfire as fast as his feet had ever carried him.

Images danced in Jackson's mind. Emaciated bodies spread out in the contortions of painful death pirouetting frantically around invisible axes. Stick figures tumbling endlessly out of their cattle cars, skulls plowed open by rifle butts. Scenes made all the madder by the silence in which they were performed. Made all the more inevitable by the movielike slow motion of their fatal gymnastics. Dead, they came to life again as jumping, screaming skeletons in striped uniforms stampeding behind a barbed-wire fence. Those little, little, helpless bodies. So little. Poor, little, helpless bodies. His anguish for them was authentic, but it also merged with deep racial memories. This, he felt sure, though without articulating the thought to himself, is what it must have been like for his Indian ancestors. This is what they must have looked like. Driven off their hunting grounds, mercilessly tracked down and exterminated by the white man. Starved and battered to death.

Wiley had taken away his command. Left him with a squad to do guard duty. He looked at the Kraut prisoners. They were being brought in in small groups, ten or fifteen at a time. Small enough groups to make out the individual faces and to sense the fear and humiliation that each man felt. He had them line up against the high concrete wall facing the machine gun on its tripod. He stood next to the gun. His men fanned out to either side of him, their rifles pointing menacingly at the Nazi prisoners.

A fresh group of Nazis was brought in. Only five men this time, but one of them was a tall, blond-haired officer in an immaculate black uniform, peaked cap, shiny boots, and all. "This here guy says he's the commander, sir," Hardwick called out. "He wants to speak to you." Jackson walked over and looked the man up and down.

Skodzensky gave a military salute, which Jackson ignored. "I am the commanding officer of the guard in the camp," he said in fluent, British-accented English. "And I herewith surrender the camp to your forces." He looked down at Jackson, perfectly at ease, it seemed, as if waiting for Jackson to thank him for his courtesy.

"Line this piece of shit up with the rest of 'em over there," Jackson said to Hardwick in a quivering voice. "And I want to see his hands higher than anyone else's." He turned and strolled back to the machine gun.

Skodzensky's arrival had an extraordinary effect on the GIs. The previous batches of Nazis had been men of all ages, but uniformly shabby and despondent-looking. Skodzensky, on the other hand, looked—and behaved—as though he were on a parade ground. There was nothing dejected or servile about his appearance, and his manner was just a little too cocky. Lined up against the wall with his men, he conveyed some of his arrogant assurance to them. Almost imperceptibly, their bearing changed, and this change did not go unnoticed by either Jackson or his men.

Up to now, the GIs had stood guard in tense silence, each man lost in his own thoughts, coping in his own way with the shock of the past couple of hours. Now, however, as though responding to the Nazis' provocative self-assurance, the men began swearing threats at their prisoners. At first they only muttered them, scarcely audibly, under their breaths. Rapidly their curses escalated—in volume as well as in intensity, fusing into a chorus whose backdrop was the distinctly audible howls and screams from the prison compound not far away.

Jackson understood that his men were going berserk with murderous rage and that there was nothing he could do about it. Not only because he had lost control of them, but because he was feeling everything they were and was losing control over himself, too.

"They're vermin, sir," Smitty, looking up from the machine gun, said to him. Tears were rolling down his cheeks. "They don't deserve to live another minute. But there's no death that's bad enough for them."

"I'd like to kill 'em with my bare hands," Jackson agreed.

"Kill 'em!" someone echoed. "Kill 'em! Kill 'em!" Others took up the cry until it seemed that the whole squad was chanting the same refrain: "Kill 'em!"

Screaming the words now, his body convulsed with sobs, Smitty let off a burst of fire from his machine gun. Noiselessly, ten or twelve Nazis slipped to the ground, dead. The spectacle did not propitiate any of the men. Without even pausing, they continued to scream. "More, more! Kill 'em all!" they yelled. Again Smitty pulled the trigger, and again Nazis fell to the ground—this time about thirty of them. Skodzensky was in this batch. But his death did not appease the GIs, either. Smitty took his time. The seconds ticked by until the suspense became unbearable. Again he opened fire, in a long, raking action that felled thirty, forty, fifty, and finally nearly eighty Nazis. Now only three remained standing, miraculously unscathed by the spray of lead. Two had their hands dutifully in the air, as they had been ordered, while a third, whether out of defiance or despair, crossed his arms in front of him and awaited his fate. Smitty, however, noticing that some of the men on the ground were wounded rather than dead, temporarily ignored the three still on their feet and directed the gun at the pile of bodies on the ground. They soon stopped twitching. Now he turned his attention to the three survivors.

"Stop that crazy bastard!" The shout rang out loud and clear despite the murderous chanting of the GIs. Seemingly out of nowhere, Wiley came charging into the scene, his holster and canteen flapping crazily at his waist. He was no more than ten or fifteen feet away when Smitty loosed off the final burst. In frustration, or because the momentum of his charge could not be broken in time, Wiley continued his dash forward and, leaping in the air, kicked Smitty with enormous force in his head. His helmet prevented the kick from shattering the soldier's skull. But the blow sent him sprawling onto the muddy ground in a daze. Even then he continued muttering, "Kill 'em, kill 'em."

But there were no more to kill. One hundred and twenty-two Nazis lay dead in a neat row along the base of the wall.

"I don't know exactly what's in there, Jim," Crashaw said to Frazer, one of his battalion commanders, "except there's a company from the division next door guarding a part of it. But I guess it's gonna be a pretty weird sight. I want your men carefully briefed before they go in. Keep tight control of them. Now, which company can you spare? A rifle company?"

"Able Company, Pop," Frazer said immediately. "It's my reserve company. They're a fine bunch."

"OK. Then get them over here at once. Priority. But remember what I said: you're gonna have to keep 'em in tight control. There's a prison camp in there. My guess is there's twenty thousand men behind the wire. Don't let 'em out. Don't go inside unless you have to. They've probably got every disease under the sun in there. But keep tight control. That's what matters more than anything in this situation." He got into his Jeep. "And now *I've* got to go and fight a war," he said with a grin.

"What do I do about that colonel in there? Does he know we're coming?"

"I'll have orders for you about that pretty soon. And Jim, I want a report on the whole camp situation tonight. I'll let you know where my CP is. You come and see me there and fill me in on what's going on there, what you need for the prisoners, that kind of thing."

"Hey, Pop," Frazer called out. "How long are we going to be here? We've got a war to fight, too!"

"This is part of your war, friend." Crashaw smiled. "But I'll see if I can't get you back into the front line tomorrow."

Crashaw and his squad drove off down the long straight road back to Dachau. Frazer was left alone with Schuler, his driver, and Roth, the radio operator. "Get me Red Five on the hooter," he told Roth. It took a moment to make contact. "Furnace Red Five, this is Furnace Red Six," he said into the speaker. "Listen, Bud," he said

Three SS guards remain standing against the wall after the second volley of gunfire.

when Fussell acknowledged the greeting. "I want you to beg, borrow, or steal any truck and Jeep you can lay your hands on and get Able Company up here as soon as possible. There's a big gate at the end of the road. Have 'em meet me there."

"Hey, Colonel!" Schuler said. "You hear that noise?"

For the first time, Frazer became aware of a muffled but powerful roar of human voices. It was so distinct that he wondered how he had missed it before. It came from somewhere to the east, behind the gates. The sound reminded him of the cheers of a crowd at a football stadium heard from outside. "Let's go in and check this place out a bit," he said to the two men. They drove into the camp.

Wiley established his command post in an office on the ground floor of the *Jourhaus,* a sparse, orderly room messed up only by the shattered fragments of two large framed portraits of Hitler and Himmler which had hung on the wall behind a desk.

He felt drained. This day was unlike any in his life, and now there was passing through him a feeling unlike any he had ever felt. Or perhaps he had felt it once or twice in his life, long ago, when he was a small kid. Still, a very unfamiliar feeling, but one that he had no trouble identifying. Self-pity. Why the hell did *he* have to be subjected to all this in one day? He sighed deeply. With a vast effort of the will, he pulled himself together. The prisoners' howling continued unabated, reaching through the thick walls of the *Jourhaus* to haunt his soul. He searched for a way of calming himself. If he could get the prisoners to settle down, his own men might ease up, too, and discipline could be restored. But how to do that? He toyed with the idea of ordering the prisoners back into their barracks. But he recognized that there was nothing he could do to force them if, as seemed probable, they disobeyed the order. And in that case he would only complicate matters still further in terms of restoring discipline. Besides, the thought of ordering the prisoners into their huts was distasteful. He didn't want them to think of him as a Nazi.

And as for his own men . . . he would have to do something about Jackson and that GI at the machine gun. A court-martial, probably. Not probably, he corrected himself, but certainly. They had massacred 122 Nazis in cold blood, and that was not the kind of thing that could be tolerated in the United States Army. Cold blood? Well, hardly. He shivered, recognizing how easily he could have done the same thing. But that was no excuse. And talking of court-martials, what was he going to do about that dumb-ass general? There were probably about five separate charges that could be filed against him.

"Geez!" he muttered out loud, glad that he was alone in the room and that his men couldn't see his face right now. It's going to take a miracle to get things here straightened out, he thought to himself.

Stock came excitedly into the room, a smile breaking out on his haggard face as he said, "I was just thinking that what we need most to settle ourselves down is a real good prayer, and no sooner did I think that than this chaplain appeared out of the blue, said he'd heard we'd liberated Dachau, and wanted to come over right away to see if there was anything he could do to help. I don't know what unit he's with, sir, but he'd like to see you."

Even without seeing the chaplain, Wiley felt a great weight removed from his mind. He broke into a smile. "Show him in!" he ordered Stock.

Wiley never learned the chaplain's name. Or his denomination. "Padre," he said, when the young man was ushered in, "what we need now is just what Stock says. A real good prayer. For us. For the prisoners. For the dead."

The chaplain nodded. Without a further word, Wiley took him by the elbow to a staircase that led up to a large, turretlike structure on top of the *Jourhaus*. The landing on which they stood faced the crowded *Appellplatz* but commanded a view of the entire compound. Stock followed them a couple of seconds later, bringing with him a bullhorn that he had managed to find somewhere. He gave it to the chaplain.

For some moments, the chaplain stood facing the *Appellplatz*, his arms spread out as though he were crucified. Wiley, standing behind him, could not see his face, but he sensed the tension that held the chaplain's body rigid. Slowly, the men below saw the clergyman and began to fall silent. It was as if little pockets of calm surfaced at different points in the crowd and then rippled through it until every person on the *Appellplatz* was standing peacefully, his eyes lifted up to the crucifix on top of the *Jourhaus*. Christian eyes. Jewish eyes. Communist eyes. Agnostic eyes. It did not seem to matter to any of the prisoners who the clergyman was, what his denomination was. For each man this was a moment of mournful thanksgiving, a moment of sublime recognition.

He spoke first in English. It was, Wiley suddenly realized, the first time he'd heard the chaplain's voice. It was clear and healthy, and gave just the right quality of reassurance to his words. "Comfort ye, comfort ye my people, saith the Lord your God." His voice faltered, and he paused to regain his composure. "Comfort ye my people," he repeated. "We thank you, O God, for preserving us to this moment of deliverance. We pray that you return us speedily to our homes and to the embrace of our loved ones."

He lowered the bullhorn and gave it to Stock, who now stepped forward and translated the prayer into German, first, and then into French. When he was finished, the chaplain turned toward Wiley. Tears were rolling down both men's faces. Wordlessly, they shook hands, and the chaplain disappeared down the steps. Wiley never saw him again.

Wiley stepped forward for a clearer view of the *Appellplatz,* taking care not to intrude on the privacy of Stock's thoughts and feelings. A profound calm had settled on the crowd. Hardly a man stirred, though some turned to their neighbors and embraced each other. Some men were shaking in what appeared to Wiley to be deep, if silent, sobs. The calm settled on Wiley's mind, too. But he had never known such sadness as he now felt. "Comfort ye my people." The words echoed in his ears. For him they were associated with *The Messiah,* and thus with Christmas, and thus with warm and innocent happiness. Comfort! Where would these people find that? he wondered bitterly.

He and Stock stayed up there for many minutes after the chaplain had left, each man lost in his own thoughts and watching the crowd below slowly disperse to different parts of the compound. A soldier came up to find Wiley. He handed him a message that had just come in from division headquarters.

For Wiley it was the second miracle of the afternoon. Units of the neighboring division were coming to take over control of the prison compound, the message informed him, and would be arriving within the hour. Wiley's men were to remain at Dachau overnight, but would be responsible for security only in the part of the camp that contained the SS quarters and the workshops. Tomorrow morning, Wiley's job at Dachau would be done and he would rejoin the attack on Munich.

"Well, bless that dumb-ass general!" Wiley said to himself with a smile.

Already the first frenzied outpouring of emotions had passed, sealed off by the soothing balm of the chaplain's prayer from the *Jourhaus* tower. Now was the time to try to collect one's thoughts, to catch up with the fantastic sequence of events that had occurred during the past forty-five minutes. Deeply ingrained instincts prompted Piet Maas to leave the *Appellplatz,* that field of danger, but he was too drained to gather up the energy to hobble off back to his *Block.* A shed stood on a nearby corner of the *Appellplatz,* just in front of the *Wirtschaftsgebäude,* and he made his way slowly to it. He sat down, his back leaning heavily against the wall.

To catch his thoughts. To put some recognizable framework on what had transpired, and on his feelings. A single phrase repeated itself in his mind, either because he would not allow anything else into his consciousness or because there was nothing else, in these moments, that was possible for it. *Himmelhoch jauchzend, zum Tode betrübt.* "Divinely happy, depressed to death." It seemed inappropriate to have a German phrase in his mind at this time. Was it Goethe? he wondered, but he couldn't identify the line for sure. What does that matter? he asked himself impatiently, recognizing the appropriateness, to him, of these words—German or no. He forced himself to reach for his diary and to record the momentous happenings that had just taken place. But even with the pencil in his hand he could not begin to write. Almost idly, he turned the pages of the little book to the end. He looked down at the list of names, neatly inscribed in double columns on each page. Nearly five pages were filled with these names. Over 230 Dutchmen he had known who had not lived to see this day. Softly, he read them out as his private memorial service to his dead comrades.

His pencil was a two-colored one, black lead at one end, and red at the other. This entry, he decided, definitely called for red. He began writing:

*1728. First American comes through the
entrance. Dachau free!!! Indescribable
happiness. Insane howling.*

He paused, uncertain of how to continue. Howling didn't seem to go
with happiness; but then, as he recognized, *Himmelhoch jauchzend*
didn't go with *zum Tode betrübt,* either, but that was how things
were.

He tried to continue the entry; there seemed so much to record—
the things he had seen, his feelings. But words would not come. He
began recalling incidents and found that doing so at last enabled him
to put some words down on paper. Briefly, he jotted them down.
How the first men to reach the *Jourhaus* broke through the door
reserved for SS personnel and, climbing to the second floor, threw
portraits of Hitler and Himmler out of the window to the crowd gathering below. He recorded that, and the surrender of the first German
soldiers. "Indescribable" was the only word he could find for the
sight of them marching forward with their hands in the air. Although
he had not been able to get close to the fence, he had succeeded,
somehow, in catching one of the cigarettes that the GIs threw over
the wire to them. It was, he noticed, a Camel. He smoked it then and
there, delighting in the luxurious indifference he felt to the great
value it had in the prison's barter economy. He recorded the Camel in
his diary too.

He paused again. It all seemed so trivial. Trivial? It suddenly
occurred to him that to find such things trivial you had to be alive and
free—and he was alive and free! He had made it through, and he was
alive! "It's happened," he told himself. "I've survived. It's over,
and I'm alive!" He began crying.

Minutes later, he realized that the faithful Plaga had found him
and was sitting on the ground next to him. "Up we get again, Piet,"
Plaga said presently. He laughed. "I seem to have said that ten times
to you today. But look—the Americans are entering the compound!"

Maas looked up and dried his eyes. By the *Jourhaus* gate a mob
of two or three hundred men was once again milling around excitedly. A big cheer went up from the crowd, and a moment later a GI
was lifted up into the air and balanced precariously on the thin
shoulders of some of the prisoners. Arms reached up to touch him.

Even from this distance Maas could detect the man's discomfort and embarrassment. He saw the soldier self-consciously wave his arms to acknowledge the prisoners' greetings. The gesture displaced his weight in a way that almost caused him to topple over backward, but he was caught by other prisoners and let gently down onto his feet. Rather brusquely, now, he pushed some of the men aside and shook himself free. Prisoners struggled to reach him, hungering to shake his hand, even just to touch his uniform. The GI looked bewildered and a bit frightened. Soon, however, other Americans came in to join him, and there were enough American hands for the crowd to shake. Shortly after, Maas and Plaga saw Connally step out of the crowd, flanked by two Americans and followed by three more. Since neither of the two in front carried rifles or submachine guns, Maas guessed that they were officers. They headed down the *Appellplatz* toward the *Lagerstrasse*.

Wiley wondered who this man Connally was. What a story *he* must have to tell, he thought to himself. He was quite certain, though, that he did not want to hear it now. He looked across at Frazer. He seemed like a good man, he decided, and he'd kept his unit together pretty well. Better than I did, he thought bitterly.

"I warned my men at the front gate that they'd never seen anything like they were about to see," Frazer said to Wiley. "But when they saw that train back there, I thought they'd go berserk. I'm glad you had to shoot it out with the Krauts, Wiley, because I'm telling you, I don't think my boys would have taken one of them alive!" His voice trembled with emotion.

My boys didn't take one of them alive, Wiley was about to say, but checked himself. Instead, he said, "I know what you mean."

"There have been lots of trains like that in the last few months," Connally broke in. "They've come from all over, sometimes weeks on the way. I don't think there's been one in which as many as half of the people arrived alive."

"Are there likely to be more Krauts around?" Frazer asked.

"I'd guess there are dozens of them here. Some are hiding inside the *Lager* as prisoners. Others, we think, are still in the administrative buildings. And there are also a number of prisoners who collaborated with the SS. Many of them are as guilty as the SS."

"Well, you just tell us who they are and we'll round 'em up,'' Frazer said with enthusiasm.

There was a long pause. Halfway across the *Appellplatz* Connally turned to face Frazer. "I'm not sure, Colonel,'' he said ironically, "how many of them will be alive until we are able to point them out to you.''

Just then a hideous shriek rang out, almost instantly to be engulfed in an angry roar from the direction of the *Lagerstrasse*.

"This way, if you please, gentlemen,'' Connally said quietly.

15. A Camp Tour

A shot rang out, and the screams ended abruptly. The three men, accompanied by Frazer's GIs, hurried over to the crowd that was milling around excitedly inside the *Lagerstrasse*. Connally pushed a way through for the two American officers. A burly man in his mid-thirties lay on the ground naked. And dead. Blood was still trickling out from a hole in the center of his forehead and across one of his open eyes. His torso bore the livid signs of merciless assault: long, shallow gashes that seemingly had been inflicted by a hundred knives. But little blood flowed from these, for around each of them had been sprinkled generous quantities of salt to heighten the man's agony. Wiley and Frazer watched, aghast, as the prisoners took turns kicking the corpse, once, twice, before moving on to allow others the same privilege. "Meansarrian," Connally said, looking down at the mangled body with hate-filled eyes. "He was one of the *Kapos* who outdid even the SS in his brutality." After a moment's hesitation he turned around and pushed his way out of the crowd.

The prisoners who had followed the American officers from the *Jourhaus* were drawn into the circle around Meansarrian's body. Those who had already seen and reviled it now became aware of the presence in their midst of the American soldiers. They tried to approach them. A confused melee began to develop as one group tried to enter the ring around the *Kapo*'s body and the other tried to leave it to throng around the American officers. Frazer ordered his men to try to form a fence between the two groups. But the GIs were, at the least, confused about what to do. They didn't want to get rough with the prisoners—"crazy, starved rag dolls" is how they appeared to one of them, Ed Campbell, a farmer's son from northern Wisconsin—but they also felt menaced by them. "Filthy, diseased-looking people," another Wisconsin GI, Bob Jensen, thought they were. He didn't want to be touched by them, not knowing how they might contaminate him but certain that there was something contagious about them. Jensen held out his carbine as a barrier to keep the milling prisoners at a distance, and others followed his example. But this only heightened the confusion, for the onward rush of prisoners, halted by the GIs at one point, was merely redirected to the end wall of a *Block* where those nearest to the building were in imminent danger of being crushed to death.

Connally saved the day. In a sharp tone he barked out a series of orders in French and German that were instantly obeyed by a group of prisoners near at hand. They cut their way through the throng and, seizing Meansarrian's body, dragged it out of the *Lagerstrasse* and onto the *Appellplatz*. Their effort was hindered by the kicks that the men nearby directed at the corpse as it was pulled past them, but presently they were clear of the crowd and halfway across the *Appellplatz*. Incredulous, Wiley and Frazer watched the men who had acted on Connally's orders force other prisoners into some semblance of a line, which now began to file slowly past Meansarrian's corpse. Each man kicked it as he passed by. Many spat on it as well.

The prisoners left on the *Lagerstrasse* had become calmer. Each man wanted to shake hands with the American liberators. Some asked for autographs on pathetic scraps of paper that they handed to the soldiers. One or two managed to come close enough to the Americans to throw their matchstick arms around the burly men and hug them. They cheered and applauded, and their faces were wreathed in grotesque, toothless smiles of welcome and thanks. The Americans felt touched, embarrassed, sad, and, in different measures, repelled by their ghostlike escorts.

Connally took them down one of the alleyways between two barracks. Here Wiley saw close at hand the corpses that he had first seen from across the moat; Frazer now saw them for the first time. Both men blanched. "Typhus, mainly, but also TB," Connally remarked. "They've been the main killers here for the past few weeks.

These"—he pointed at the twenty corpses in view—"these are probably the ones who died last night. There's a work detail that picks
them up and takes them off to the crematorium every day. Perhaps
we'll try to get it started again tomorrow."

"Why are they naked?" Wiley asked, trying to avoid looking at
the corpses. He noticed that men starved to death are not entirely
emaciated. Their heads retain their normal size, and so do their geni-
tals, which thus stand out as grotesquely large.

"We didn't have enough clothing here for the living," Connally
replied. "So it made sense to take it from the dead."

In a choked voice Frazer asked, "Did they know we were coming? Did they know that before they died?"

"Maybe some of them did," Connally replied tersely. "Would
it make you feel better if they did?" The Americans both picked up
the hostility in Connally's question, and neither of them said anything. "There'll be many more tomorrow morning, and for days to
come. *They* at least will know they were liberated before they
died. . . ."

During this time, wave after wave of well-wishers approached
the Americans. At the entrance to one of the barracks, however, they
dispersed, so that when Connally and the Americans stepped inside,
they were by themselves. The excited bustle and noise in the alley-
way made the stillness inside the *Block* all the more gloomy. The
stench was overpowering, and although the rooms were not dark, the
sheer volume of men and bunks within was so great that it absorbed
much of the light that came in through the windows and gave an
eerie, gloomy tinge to everything. At first, Frazer thought the room
was empty. In fact, as he rapidly realized, there were probably two
hundred men in it. Row after row of three-tiered bunks ran down the
length of the room, and although the beds were narrow, two and
often three men occupied a single bed. The appearance of the Americans in the doorway prompted a light, scurrying movement that
spread down the length of the room as the men turned their bodies
painfully and awkwardly at right angles to their beds, the better to
face their visitors. And so it was that, walking down the aisles, Wiley
felt that he was moving along a three-tiered wall of skulls: shaven or
bald heads out of whose deep sockets haunted eyes stared only half-

seeingly out at their liberators. The Americans moved past as though in a trance, their vigorous bodies feeling almost like a badge of shame mocked by the toothless grins on some of the faces. Wiley, though, had the presence of mind to stop every few feet, gently patting some of the men on their backs or shaking the occasional outstretched hand. "I'm pleased to meet you," he said to a few men before switching to the more appropriate, "We're going to take good care of you now. You're safe now." He knew that probably none of

The Dachau crematorium, where the bodies of many thousands of prisoners were burned each year.

An American flag made by prisoners to honor their liberators.

them understood English, but he felt foolish, nonetheless, for having come across at first like a Presidential candidate.

A fluttering sound broke out around the Americans, and Wiley realized that he and his party were being cheered by the prisoners; some were even clapping. The noise reminded Wiley all too uncomfortably of the death rattle.

They left the *Block* and inspected several more. On the *Lagerstrasse,* groups of prisoners were still milling around, pouncing on the Americans each time they appeared, to shake hands and get their autographs. On many buildings crude handmade flags were now flying. Russian flags seemed the most numerous, but Free French and Polish banners also stood out. Here and there, in honor of the liberators, the Stars and Stripes fluttered in the early evening breeze.

Coming out of one *Block,* Frazer saw a group of men beating someone to death with shovels. They were working with a quiet, passionless deliberation that contrasted with the last, unconscious convulsions of their victim. Frazer looked away, and did not know whether Wiley had seen the execution.

At the end of the prison compound they turned left and crossed the moat to a group of sheds, from the roof of one of which rose a tall chimney. In the open space at one end of the complex, huge mounds, perhaps eight feet high, twenty feet long, and fifteen feet wide, were arranged at neat intervals. "This is the crematorium," Connally explained. "Those are clothes," he said, pointing at the mounds. "They haven't been sorted out yet."

They entered a shed, one of whose walls was open to the outside. Three large ovens almost filled the space, and although their doors were shut, a terrible smell that made the Americans come close to retching hung in the air. "Over there"—Connally pointed— "those piles there are where the ashes from these ovens were dumped."

He led the way into an adjacent building. The only light inside came through the doorway in which they were standing. The room measured about forty feet by twenty. It was stacked from floor to ceiling with naked bodies that looked, if anything, even more emaciated than the ones the Americans had seen on the train. "Geez!" Frazer whispered to Wiley. "They look like cordwood."

"Fuel ran low, and although you may not believe it, the ovens were too small to deal with our death rate. This is about four days' accumulation of corpses here," Connally explained. They walked over to a spot behind the crematorium where tightly packed bodies were laid out on the ground.

From there they went to the kennels nearby. In each of about forty wire-mesh enclosures a dog lay dead. Most of them were Dobermans; some were German shepherds. All had been shot by the first wave of American troops. It was easy to come to terms with these relatively innocuous deaths. Frazer vomited.

Dead prisoners piled high against the bloodstained walls of a crematory room in which the bodies were kept before cremation.

A large Army truck drove slowly through the *Jourhaus* gate and headed across the *Appellplatz*. It halted not far from Meansarrian's broken body. Two GIs stepped out from the cab, rifles in hand, and walked to the tailgate. A crowd of prisoners watched as three SS men in shirt-sleeves jumped to the ground from the back of the truck and began unloading large cardboard cartons. The crowd began moving menacingly toward the Germans, who worked frantically, as though their lives depended on unloading the truck. They did. The cartons contained huge loaves of bread, still warm from the ovens. Next came enormous pots, filled almost to the brim with a rich stew. Finally, more cartons were unloaded: khaki cases filled with K-rations. The prisoners' attention was easily deflected from the three cowering Germans to the food. But they helped themselves to the meal in an orderly fashion, hurrying back to their barracks to bring food to their companions and to fetch bowls for the stew.

Lieutenant Bill Jackson got out of the cab and checked that the truck had been unloaded. Finding supplies in the SS kitchens had made him feel incredibly good. At last he was able to *do* something for the prisoners. And as for the K-rations, well, he wasn't going to tell *anyone* how he'd managed to get hold of them.

The Germans had been only too happy to cook for their former wards. Now, however, they looked at Jackson, their eyes silently pleading with him not to abandon them in the middle of the *Appellplatz*. "Let's go back and get the next load," he said to the two GIs.

"What about them Krauts?" Harvey asked.

"We've got more in the kitchen. Leave them here," Jackson ordered.

The truck turned slowly across the *Appellplatz* and passed back through the *Jourhaus* gate.

16. Evening

"I'm still wondering how you managed to dig up such good chow," Frazer said appreciatively. "To tell you the truth, it's the best meal I've had in quite a few months!"

He felt uncomfortable. The International Committee members seemed to be in much better shape than the other prisoners. Were they collaborators? The thought crossed his mind once or twice, but he decided against it. The other prisoners would have turned against them now, as they had against Meansarrian and others whom they had done to death. He had seen two collaborators killed. Reports from his men indicated that at least forty or fifty other executions had taken place in the past few hours. So the Committee people were not collaborators, he decided, but officers, who always have an easier time of things. It reassured him, in a way, to conclude that even in this hellhole of a concentration camp there were top dogs who managed to get themselves privileges and make things a little better for themselves. Apparently the other prisoners accepted that. Not only did they *not* turn against the Committee, they actually obeyed orders from it, as though it were the official government of the camp.

Veal cutlets, roast potatoes, and garden peas—all graced with more than one bottle of wine. "It seems to me all wrong that you're sharing your good food with me, gentlemen," Frazer continued, "but seeing as how you wouldn't allow me to do the honors, I'm mighty grateful to you."

"It's courtesy of the SS," one man replied.

Frazer thought it just as well not to pursue the matter. He

reached down to a pack that hung over the back of his chair. "And now, gentlemen, before we get down to business, let's have some of the good stuff to help with the digestion!" He pulled out two bottles of brandy and set them on the table. Then a can of Prince Albert tobacco and fistfuls of Hershey bars. "Well, then, gentlemen. I have to report to my commanding officer in forty-five minutes at his CP in town. I need to know two things and settle another. First, what is the situation in the camp? How many people are there here, and what is their condition? Second, what supplies and services are needed, and what is the priority for them? Third, I want to be as sure as I can be that discipline will be preserved among the former prisoners. My unit pulls out tomorrow morning, and rear-echelon types will be moving in to take over from me. But my orders are to see to it that the situation remains stable, to set up the machinery for keeping the camp in order."

It struck Hopman that the American was more concerned with keeping discipline in the camp than in bringing relief to the prisoners—the former prisoners, as they now were. Hopman relished the phrase.

"It's going to be awhile before we are able to move people out of here and get them sent back home," Frazer continued on the same theme. "Europe's a mess, transportation is a big problem, and top priority goes to fighting the war, of course. So while I know all of you want nothing more than to get out of here right away—and I sure can understand that—and while the United States Army is going to send you home the quickest we can, you've got to recognize that it's going to take time."

"How much time?" Parra, the Spaniard, demanded, after Frazer's remarks had been translated into German for the benefit of those who couldn't understand English.

"There's no way to tell that now. I don't want to sound like a Nazi, gentlemen," Frazer said with an apologetic smile, "but discipline must come first. I've had reports that some of the former prisoners are armed. All weapons must be surrendered first thing tomorrow morning. Lynching collaborators and SS men must stop, and there's no exception to that one. Any Nazi found hiding in the camp is to be turned over to the guard at the *Jourhaus,* and we'll handle things from there. Next, we're responsible for your safety, and we can't look after you if you're wandering all over the place. There's a war going on outside, and I guess there's a pretty hostile population just down the road. So no former prisoner will leave the camp except with a written pass to be obtained from the CP at the *Jourhaus* here. Your Committee will, I hope, see to it that these orders are known to all the men here. You can have the loudspeaker facilities for that purpose if that's how you want to handle it. We confirm your authority within the camp on the understanding that you play by the rules.''

"Agreed," Connally said brusquely, without waiting for the others to speak.

"And now, Commander, I need to give my general a rundown on the situation here, and the priorities.''

"It's quite simple, Colonel," Connally answered. "We have thirty thousand prisoners here and perhaps as many as eight thousand corpses. Our death rate is about four hundred a day. We can expect it to climb. Many people died today from overeating. Some died from the sheer excitement of the day. This situation will continue for some time. But over and beyond that, there are thousands dying from typhus and from TB. I predict that for a week or more we are going to have five hundred deaths a day. Disposing of the bodies is a problem. We need fuel for the crematorium and people to operate it. As of now, the entire United States Army couldn't force a single one of our people to work the crematorium, though I think we might be able to get them to remove bodies from within the prison compound. I don't know exactly how to handle this problem, but if I had my way—and you may want to think about this—I would get the good people from down the road, the citizens of Dachau, for that job. They're going to spend the next weeks and months and for all I know the next years telling anyone who'll listen that they never knew anything about what happened here. So perhaps they'll get a chance to learn now. . . .

"We have enough food in the camp for two days," he continued, "so that's not an immediate problem. What we need above all is medical help. Doctors, nurses, drugs. And a disinfectant that works against the typhus louse. Almost as important, we need to do something about morale. Today the men are very happy, and crazy, but tomorrow and thereafter they're going to be anxious and depressed and care only about getting home. I suggest that priority be given to finding some ways in which we can get messages home to our families. And get news from home. Nothing will do our people here more good than that.''

For Ed Campbell and his buddy Bob Jensen, the two Wisconsin boys, the sights and experiences of this day were too baffling to digest, let alone comprehend. Off duty now, they wandered around the area in which the SS men and officers had lived. With considerably less ardor than usual, they looked for souvenirs, but the fear of stumbling unexpectedly on still further horrors kept them pretty much to the beaten track. Like many men this evening, they felt a strong need just to walk and to be more or less on their own—or, at the most, with a trusted pal. Campbell and Jensen had fought side by side for over a year now, and they had stuck close together during some of the roughest battles of the war. There was almost nothing that either would not do for the other. They talked frequently of buying a gas station somewhere in northern Wisconsin after the war was over. They'd operate it together as partners.

Tonight, though, they had little to say to each other. ''Geez, this place gives me the creeps!'' ''Could you believe all those bodies stacked like a pile of cordwood?'' ''I can't get over seeing the old man cry!'' ''I sure could kill a whole bunch of Krauts right here and now!'' ''I wonder what those people did to deserve being treated that way?'' These and similar remarks were made because something *had* to be said to ease the horror and perplexity that each man felt. Neither expected or received a reply from the other. In fact, they kept their faces pointed determinedly ahead to avoid each other's gaze.

Turning a corner, they saw a large building ahead, three floors high, with a steeply pitched roof. It was about 150 feet long and looked like a dormitory building. Bright lights shone through a row of windows on the ground floor. Unmindful of the risk—indeed, without even unslinging their carbines from their shoulders—the two men entered the building and found their way to the room in which the light was shining. It was a dining room, with four long rows of well-scrubbed tables flanked by benches. In the near corner, just to the right of the door, a German soldier sat slumped over a bowl of what looked like bean soup. A spoon was still in his hand, but he was quite dead, and the congealed blood on the table indicated that he had finished his last meal several hours before.

At the other end of the room, facing each other across the table, sat two prisoners in their striped uniforms. They were very much alive and were slowly sipping from large ceramic mugs. It did not occur to Campbell or Jensen to wonder what these men were doing outside the prison compound or, in particular, how they had gotten into the building and cooked themselves whatever it was they were drinking. Seeing the two Americans, they jumped gingerly to their feet and, with broad smiles that reminded Jensen and Campbell of so many scenes from earlier in the day, beckoned them over with rapid waving of their hands. *"Kaffee! Kaffee!"* one of them called out.

"What the hell, I guess that means coffee," Jensen said. "Let's get ourselves some."

It was real coffee; and the cream with it was real, and so was the sugar. The young Americans sat across from one another, each next to one of the prisoners, and drank the hot liquid.

"SS," one man said, pointing to the mugs. *"SS Kaffee. SS kaput!"* He laughed hideously and then lapsed into silence. His companion said nothing and moved only to bring the mug up to his lips.

"I'm Ed," Campbell said, holding out his hand, "and this here's my buddy, Bob Jensen. We're both from Wisconsin." Jensen didn't hold out his hand, but smiled uncomfortably.

"SS kaput!" the man said again, shaking Campbell's hand and beaming broadly. His companion didn't move or look up. Campbell thought that he might be deaf.

Campbell began to get nervous as it also occurred to him that the other man, the one who kept repeating *"SS kaput!,"* might be mad. He looked closely into his face, as if hoping thereby to confirm the diagnosis. But there appeared to be nothing distinctive about it. Nothing distinctive, that is, as compared with all the other frightening-looking faces he had seen during the day. The thought struck him that perhaps the man kept repeating *"SS kaput!"* because the defeat of the SS was so incredible to him. But beyond that, Campbell had little curiosity about the man; and Jensen seemed to have none. Both of them continued drinking their coffee out of a sense of politeness. Otherwise, they would have hightailed it out of there minutes before.

The loquacious prisoner changed his line. "Abramowitz," he said, pointing to himself. The Americans gathered that that was his name, and that the indecipherable sounds that followed formed the name of his hometown. They beamed acknowledgment of the message.

Abramowitz got to his feet, helped his companion to rise, and beckoned the two Americans to follow. A mixture of politeness and curiosity led them to do so. They went out of a nearby door, crossed a hall in which the light was also shining, and then entered what proved to be a large bathroom. Six huge tubs lined one tiled wall; a row of washbasins stood in front of mirrors against the opposite wall.

Evidently quite familiar with the place, Abramowitz turned on the taps in two of the tubs and went to a wall closet, from which he took a bar of soap and a long-handled back scrubber. The streams of water from the faucets were hot and powerful, and it took only a few minutes to fill the large tubs. Abramowitz checked the temperature of the water and nodded his satisfaction.

He stood in front of the tubs, beaming expectantly at the two Americans. They looked back at him, utterly baffled by what he had in mind. Soon, however, his purpose became clear. Speaking excitedly in a language that the two men could not identify, let alone understand, he mimed the act of undressing, interspersing his gestures by pointing at the soldiers and at the bathtubs.

"Geez, Ed!" Jensen said. "The guy wants us to have a bath. Tell him he needs one more than we do, and let's get the hell outta here!"

"You're crazy," Campbell replied. "There's nothing I'd like more than a bath." Without waiting for his friend's approval he passed his carbine over, stripped naked, and plunged into the bath. "Hey, this is fantastic!" he called out gleefully. "When did you last have a bath, huh?"

And so, with Abramowitz grinning happily, his companion staring vacantly ahead, and Jensen looking on disapprovingly, Campbell lay back in the hot water and shut his eyes. "This *is* the life, Bob! How do you think you're going to get one of those Munich fräuleins if you go on smelling like a dog?"

His eyes were still shut when he felt bony hands closing on his ankles and lifting them to the edge of the tub. A couple of seconds later, he felt the tough thistles of the scrubbing brush working over the soles of his feet until they were sore and as pink as the day he was born. He opened his eyes and smiled gratefully at Abramowitz, who, satisfied that the job had been well done, now walked over and, beckoning him to sit up in the tub, vigorously scrubbed his back, too. Then he handed Campbell the bar of soap and disappeared into an adjacent room. He returned a moment later with a large white towel draped over his arm.

Campbell was in no hurry to get out of the tub. He lay back in the water again, shut his eyes, and hummed an indecipherable tune. "What are you scared of, Jensen?" he asked his friend good-humoredly. "You don't know what you're missing!"

"For Chrissake," Jensen grumbled. "Get the hell outta there. We gotta get back and have some sleep."

Eventually Campbell got out of the tub. Abramowitz handed him the towel and then revealed what he had hidden under it. Two pairs of brand-new woolen socks. Decidedly nonregulation. Decidedly Nazi. And decidedly a thing any footsore soldier who hadn't changed his clothing in over two weeks would give his right arm for. "Hey, Jensen, get a load of this!" he shouted in delight. "Clean socks!"

Abramowitz understood that his gift was appreciated, and with a little smile nodded his head humbly. He watched happily as Campbell put on the socks and did a little jig in them on the tiled floor. Aware of Jensen's disapproval, Abramowitz timidly handed him the other pair of socks. No less shyly, Jensen reached out for them, stuffed them into a pocket, and politely said, "Thank you."

Campbell was now fully dressed again and took his carbine back from Jensen. "Thank you very much, sir," he said to Abramowitz. "And good luck to you!"

Abramowitz's eyes filled with tears of gratitude. *"Amerika gut,"* he said in a trembling voice. *"Amerika sehr gut."* He continued repeating these words as the two soldiers left the room. *"Amerika sehr gut!"*

Piet Maas had been careful not to overeat, but what with the food provided by the Americans and the cake that Hans Linden, a fellow Dutchman, had mysteriously "organized" from nowhere, his stomach felt painfully bloated. He also felt exhausted and, for the first time in months, sleepy. He checked in his pocket to make sure that the day's souvenir was still there. It was: a trigger from one of the machine guns thrown out of a guard tower by jubilant prisoners. He wondered how many men that trigger had helped kill.

A light from the *Lagerstrasse* shone through the window onto his bunk. For the last time this day, he reached into his pocket and pulled out his diary. He wrote in English:

2245. The end of a perfect day.

Only a few minutes later, he was fast asleep.

17. "Proclaim Freedom"

The two rifle companies left Dachau early in the morning of April 30 and a few hours later took part in the capture of Munich, Nazism's birthplace. Far to the north, in a shelter buried deep under the ground of Berlin's Chancellery, Adolf Hitler committed suicide. And in Dachau, seemingly endless columns of hospital units, Red Cross officials, journalists, chaplains, and staff officers rode down the Niebelungenstrasse into the concentration camp. A census of the camp's population was taken, and lists were prepared identifying the survivors by their country of origin. These would be distributed to next of kin by the Red Cross. Huge quantities of DDT were brought in to spray every part of the camp—and every person in it—to halt the epidemic of typhus. Squads of GIs were sent into the town to round up civilians to dig mass graves so that the thousands of corpses strewn around the camp could be buried safely and decently. Teams of intelligence officers moved in and began the vast task of accumulating evidence for war crimes trials. A Signal Corps detachment recorded the horrors of Dachau on film before any progress had been made in tidying up the camp. The SS barracks were converted into hospitals, into which over four thousand patients were at once admitted. The quartermasters outdid themselves in scouring the countryside, and their own stockpiles, to rush abundant supplies of wholesome food to the starving prisoners.

An inmate wearing a shabby dark-blue overcoat over his striped uniform walked slowly to the *Jourhaus* gate. The two GIs on guard there were already familiar with the prisoners' custom, singly or in

214

small groups, of walking up and staring at them, a disbelieving expression in their eyes. Sometimes they said nothing and shuffled off again after a few minutes. Others engaged the GIs in simple conversation and were rewarded by a cigarette or a candy bar.

The man approaching the gate now, however, was walking more purposefully than most; and while he had the same gray complexion and hollow expression as most of his fellows, he was better built and preserved than the average prisoner. That, and his overcoat, gave him an air of authority in the eyes of the guards. In a thin, dignified voice, he addressed them. "I am Kurt von Schuschnigg, once chancellor of Austria." He searched for words. "Please to tell your officer!" he commanded.

The GIs had never heard of Kurt von anyone, and didn't know what a "chancellor of Austria" was, but they assumed that he must be someone important and went off to fetch the lieutenant. He arrived, and although he was no less ignorant of these particulars than his men, he was not disposed to reveal that. Moreover, he had heard that there were many VIPs in the camp. This man, he decided, must be one of them.

With considerable ceremony, he ordered the guards to open the gate and ushered the prisoner into an office on the ground floor of the *Jourhaus*. A mug of cocoa was produced, and the prisoner drank it greedily. A Hershey bar came next, but the prisoner was sated and, with a smile, accepted the gift and placed it in his overcoat pocket.

Speaking slowly and rather too loudly, the lieutenant said, "I am going to notify headquarters that the chancellor of Austria is here. I'm sure they'll want to know, and I guess they'll be sending a staff car to pick you up right away, sir!" He saluted.

"Please." The prisoner hesitated, again looking for words. "I go for little walk. Freedom." He smiled apologetically, pointing to the world that stretched away from the prison compound.

"Yes, sir. Of course, sir," the lieutenant answered warmly. "I sure can understand your desire for that. I sure can." Without a moment's hesitation he reached for a pad and scribbled some words on it. "Here's a pass, sir, so that my men will let you come and go freely. But can you please try to be back here in half an hour or so for our people from headquarters?"

"Yes," the man replied. The lieutenant held the door open for him. Clutching the pass in his hand and infinitely grateful for the bit of English he had once learned, Ernst Kroll stepped out, a free man.

It was slightly overcast, but warm for the time of the year. Kroll knew exactly where he was headed. Avoiding the main roads as much as possible, he headed west toward the town of Dachau. Nearly an hour later, he arrived at his first destination, the gentle, winding banks of the Amper River.

He sat under a tree and gazed at the softly flowing current. Soon, the water seemed to flow through his very soul, washing away the terrible accretions of twelve years' agony. He reached for the

Former prisoners of Dachau cheer the U.S. Army on April 30, the day after they were liberated.

chocolate bar and nibbled it slowly until it was finished. It gave him a great infusion of energy. Jumping to his feet, he tore off all his clothes and dove headfirst into the river. The cold sharpness of the water pumped life into every core of his being. He swam underwater for two strokes, lovingly experiencing once more the blur on his eyes before surfacing. The effort exhausted him, but he was not yet willing to climb back to dry land. He turned over on his back and, kicking occasionally in order not to get carried downstream, floated on the water for a few minutes. The sun broke briefly through the clouds. He felt better than he ever had in his life.

Presently, he climbed out of the river and fell, exhausted, on the ground some yards away from his clothes. His body tingled, but he knew that soon he would be shivering from the cold. With great effort, he crawled back to his clothes and wiped himself dry with one of the two shirts he had worn. He got dressed. He thought that perhaps he should take a little nap before continuing on his way, but he decided that his happiness and excitement would give him enough vigor to get where he was going. It was only another kilometer or two to his comrades' house.

Rabbi David Eichhorn, a chaplain with the Fifteenth Corps, arrived in Dachau on April 30 and the next day drove with his friend Meyer Levin, the novelist and, at the time, a war correspondent, to the satellite concentration camp at Allach, five miles away from the main camp. There was a large Jewish population at Allach—proportionately much larger than at Dachau itself—and conditions were, if anything, even worse than at the main camp. Eichhorn spent two days at Allach, comforting the dying and attempting to instill fresh hope among the survivors. On the evening of his first day there, a service was held at which he presented a Torah scroll to the Jews of Allach. The entire congregation was in tears as a cantor from Warsaw sang the beautiful old prayer of praise and mourning, *"El Maleh Rechamim."* After the service, hundreds of Jews crowded around Eichhorn, kissing his hand in thanks and asking for his autograph. It was a humiliating experience for him, for he felt that he should be honoring them for what they had suffered and surmounted.

The next morning, Eichhorn witnessed a scene that was, if any-

When the camp was liberated, many prisoners stole potatoes from the warehouses and cooked them in the alleys, as shown here during a snowstorm on May 1, two days after liberation.

thing, even more moving. Gerhard Schmidt was the prototype of Hitler's Aryan beast: tall, blond, and handsome. A pilot in the Luftwaffe, he had been shot down and wounded and then was forced into the SS. In the spring of 1944 he was sent to Allach as *Blockführer,* or section leader, of the Jewish inmates.

He did everything he could to protect his Jewish wards and to sustain their morale. When he learned that certain individuals had been marked for execution, he hid them until the danger was past. When a prisoner contracted typhus, which was often the same thing as being sentenced to death, Schmidt would smuggle him out of the camp in a hay cart, take him to his home in Dachau, where his wife would nurse him back to health, and then smuggle him back into the camp in the same way. Every evening for months he listened to BBC newscasts and reported to the inmates the latest details of the Allied advance. Three days before the liberation, Schmidt smuggled two machine guns and a large supply of ammunition into the Jewish section. The SS, he warned, had plans to exterminate the entire population of the camp. If they attempted that, he said, he would stay and fight with his Jewish brethren to the last bullet.

In the event, the SS fled and the massacre was averted. Three days after the liberation, Schmidt, in civilian clothes, arrived at the main gate at Allach with his wife. He described himself as a former guard in the camp and was promptly arrested and taken to the office of Lieutenant Schreiber, the American administrator of the camp, for interrogation. He told the skeptical Schreiber that he and his wife had come back to Allach to see if they could be of any help to the prisoners, and that they were, moreover, afraid of reprisals from their neighbors, who somehow had gotten wind of the Schmidts' efforts in behalf of the Jews.

Schreiber had the leaders of the Jewish community in the camp brought to his office; Eichhorn went along with them. When the prisoners saw their former *Blockführer* they broke out into exclamations of delight and shook his hand enthusiastically. None of them had met Frau Schmidt before, but they had all heard stories of her heroism and compassion. They now greeted her warmly and with many expressions of gratitude. Schreiber and Eichhorn, who only a short while earlier had bitterly agreed with each other that the only good

German was a dead German, looked at each other in astonishment, and Schreiber readily agreed to let the Schmidts work in the camp and stay there for a few days in the Jewish committee's headquarters. With the Jewish leaders, Eichhorn accompanied the two Germans back to the Jewish compound. It was the homecoming of a hero. The Jews crowded around their beloved *Blockführer,* hugging him, kissing his face, his hands, his feet. The big man broke down and cried like a baby. So did his wife. And so did Eichhorn.

Eichhorn returned to the main camp on May 3. The next day was a Friday. In the morning, two very young women approached him and shyly told him that they represented 225 Jewish girls who had been brought to Dachau only a week before the liberation. They came mainly from Hungary, Greece, and Italy and had been working in factories in the Munich area. "That's why we're physically in better shape than most of the people here," one girl said, addressing herself to Eichhorn's unspoken fear that they had also been employed in SS brothels. They begged Eichhorn, if he had time free from his other duties, to hold a special prayer service for them that afternoon.

Eichhorn at once agreed, and the service began at five thirty in the women's *Block.* At the end of the service a lieutenant colonel who had been standing at the back of the room came up to Eichhorn. Tears were streaming down his cheeks. "My name is George Stevens," he said, holding out his hand. "I'm in charge of the Signal Corps detachment that is taking the official Army pictures of Dachau. When are you going to hold another service? I want to get a film of it for the historical record." Eichhorn recognized the famous director of *Talk of the Town, A Place in the Sun,* and other Hollywood movies and appreciated his modesty in describing himself so simply as commander of the Signal Corps unit. He told him that a camp-wide service was to be held on the *Appellplatz* the next morning and that he was welcome to film it if he wished.

The service was scheduled for ten o'clock. The International Committee had undertaken to decorate the platform on the *Appellplatz* with flags of every nation represented in the camp, and every nation was to send a delegation to attend the service as a token of its brotherly sympathy for the Jewish people. Eichhorn arrived at the *Appellplatz* at nine that morning, an hour before the service was to begin, to make sure that everything was in readiness. To his astonishment, he saw that no preparations of any kind had been made.

Anxiously, he sent for Charles Baum, the young Belgian who represented the Jewish community on the International Committee. Why, the chaplain demanded, had the arrangements for the service not been made?

Baum was terribly embarrassed. There were problems, he said, which went back a long, long time. They had to do with the Poles, who hated Jews almost as much as the Nazis themselves did. The Polish prisoners, he went on to say, had informed the International Committee the previous evening that they would not tolerate a Jewish service on the *Appellplatz* and that they would break it up by force if the Jews nevertheless went ahead and held it.

Eichhorn was astonished. "Don't all the men here feel solidarity for each other, after all they've been through?" he asked.

Sadly, Baum shrugged his shoulders. On the few occasions that parcels had arrived at Dachau from the Polish Red Cross, he told Eichhorn, they had been distributed on the basis of one for every Polish Gentile and one for every two Polish Jews. "That's the kind of thing we've gotten used to expecting from the Poles," he said.

Baum reported, too, that the Jewish community, unwilling to cause a disturbance, had decided to cancel the service on the *Appellplatz* and hold it instead in the camp laundry.

"How many people can fit in there?" Eichhorn asked.

"We figure about eighty," Baum replied.

The chaplain decided not to argue. The Jewish inmates, he figured, were more knowledgeable about matters in the camp than he was and should be allowed to do what they considered best.

The service began. The room was jam-packed, and hundreds of Jews crowded outside the doorway and windows to hear the ancient prayers. While the service was in progress, Colonel Stevens elbowed his way through the throng to Eichhorn's side.

"What's going on, Rabbi?" he demanded. "My camera crews are all set up and ready to go. What are you doing in here? Why aren't you holding the service on the *Appellplatz?*"

"I'll tell you after the service," Eichhorn whispered.

Stevens was waiting outside when Eichhorn emerged from the

laundry room. In a few words, he summed up the situation. Stevens's face flushed angrily as he heard the story. "Come with me, Rabbi!" he said, striding rapidly to what proved to be the office of the American commander of the camp.

Stevens saluted perfunctorily and said, "Sir, I didn't give up a good job in Hollywood and risk my life in combat for many months to help free the world from fascism only to stand by while a bunch of hooligans gets away with behaving like Fascists right under my very nose!"

The commander, a burly, good-natured former police commissioner from Boston, jovially agreed with Stevens's statement of principle. "But what's been going on?" he asked.

"The Jews were going to have a prayer service in the big square in the camp, led by the chaplain here," Stevens said. "The Polish inmates threatened to break up the service if it was held in public!"

"They did *what?*" the commander roared. Stevens repeated the facts. Even before he had finished talking, the commander turned to Eichhorn. "Chaplain," he ordered, "you're going to hold the service tomorrow on the *Appellplatz* at ten A.M. Every nationality is going to have its delegation there. And just so those Polacks get the right idea, I'm going to have two platoons of my boys out there with you. Call it an honor guard."

They left the commander's office with uplifted spirits. To show that he still had a touch of Hollywood in him, Stevens asked Eichhorn if he would teach some of the Jewish girls to sing "God Bless America" in time to perform it at the service. Eichhorn said he would try.

That Saturday night, Eichhorn sequestered a part of the women's barracks and rehearsed fifteen Hungarian girls in the Irving Berlin song. Some GIs had helped write out copies of the lyrics, and between Eichhorn and the two hundred women in the *Block* there was enough Yiddish to convey to the choir the meaning of the words they were singing. Everyone had great fun, and after two hours' hard work the girls were able to come up with a more than passable rendition of the song.

The next morning, a crowd gathered around the festooned platform on the *Appellplatz*. Every Jew able to be there—some twelve

An emaciated Dachau inmate photographed in front of a bar-rack wall, the day after liberation.

hundred in number—attended, and delegations from each of the thirty-odd nationalities in the camp turned up. Ringing the crowd, but with their backs to the stage, was a line of GIs with loaded rifles and fixed bayonets—the "honor guard," which, in the event, did not perform any other duties since the Poles stayed away from the ceremony.

The service began with a few words from Ali Kuci, the former Albanian minister of propaganda and a member of the International Committee. All the inmates were very aware, he said, of the exceptional intensity of the suffering that had been endured by the Jews under the Third Reich. Along with all free men, he rejoiced that the Jews of Dachau were at last able to resume their religious life without hindrance.

Rabbi Eichhorn stepped forward and opened the Torah ark. He recited the ancient benediction *shehechiyanu:* "Blessed art thou, O Lord our God, King of the Universe, who gave us life and established us and brought us to this time." Loud sobs from the crowd punctuated the holy words. After further prayers, a lovely young Jewish girl presented Eichhorn with a bouquet of flowers on behalf of Dachau Jewry. Other girls came up and gave him small American and Zionist flags that they had sewn the previous night out of old clothes. The crowd was cheering wildly now, and Eichhorn held up his hands for silence. Reluctantly, the people quieted down and listened to the rabbi's words. He spoke in English, pausing every few minutes to allow them to be translated into Yiddish. This is what he said:

My Jewish Brethren of Dachau:

In the portion we read yesterday in our holy Torah we found these words: "Proclaim freedom throughout the world to all the inhabitants thereof; a day of celebration shall this be for you, a day when every man shall return to his family, and to his rightful place in society.

In the United States of America, in the city of Philadelphia, upon the exact spot where one hundred and sixty-nine years ago a group of brave Americans met and decided to fight for American independence, there stands a marker upon which is written these very same words: "Proclaim freedom throughout the world to all the inhabitants thereof." From the beginning of their existence as a liberty-loving and independent people, the citizens of America understood that not until all the peoples of the world were free would they be truly free, that not until tyranny and oppression had been erased from the hearts of all men and all nations would there be lasting peace and happiness for themselves. Thus it has been that, throughout our entire history, whenever and wherever men have been enslaved, Americans have fought to set them free; whenever and wherever dictators have endeavored to destroy democracy and justice and truth, Americans have not rested content until these despots have been overthrown.

Today I come to you in a dual capacity—as a soldier in the American Army and as a representative of the Jewish community of America. As an American soldier, I say to you that we are proud, very proud, to be here, to know that we have had a share in the destruction of the most cruel tyranny of all time. As an American soldier, I say to you that we are proud, very proud, to be your comrades-in-arms, to greet you and salute you as the bravest of the brave. We know your tragedy. We know your sorrows. We know that upon you was centered the venomous hatred of power-crazed madmen, that your annihilation was decreed and planned systematically and ruthlessly. We know too that you refused to be destroyed, that you fought back with every weapon at your command, that you fought with your bodies, your minds, and your spirit. Your faith and our faith in God and in humanity have been sustained. Our enemies lie prostrate before us. The way of life which together we have defended still lives, and it will live so that all men everywhere may have freedom and happiness and peace.

I speak to you also as a Jew, as a rabbi in Israel, as a teacher of that religious philosophy which is dearer to all of us than life itself. What message of comfort and strength can I bring to you from your fellow Jews? What can I say that will compare in depth or in intensity to that which you have suffered and overcome? Full well do I know and humbly do I confess the emptiness of mere words in this hour of mingled sadness and joy. Words will not bring back the dead to life nor right the wrongs of the past ten years. This is no time for words, you will say, and rightfully so. This is a time for deeds, deeds of justice, deeds of love. . . . Justice will be done. We have seen with our own eyes and we have heard with our own ears and we shall not forget. As long as there are Jews in the world "Dachau" will be a term of horror and shame. Those who have labored here for their evil master will be hunted down and destroyed as systematically and as ruthlessly as they sought your destruction. . . . And there will be deeds of love. It is the recognized duty of all religious people to bestir themselves immediately to assist you to regain your health, comfort, and some measure of happiness as speedily as possible. This must be done. This can be done. This will be done. You are not and you will not be forgotten men, my brothers. In every country where the lamps of religion and decency and kindness still burn, Jews and non-Jews alike will expend as much time and energy and money as is needful to make good the pledge which is written in our holy Torah and inscribed on that marker in Philadelphia, the city of Brotherly Love.

We know that abstractions embodied in proclamations and celebrations must be followed by more concrete, more helpful, fulfillments. We do not intend to brush aside the second part of the Divine promise. Every man who has been oppressed must and will be restored to his family and to his rightful place in society. This is a promise and a pledge which I bring you from your American comrades-in-arms and your Jewish brethren across the seas:

> You shall go out with joy, and be led forth in peace.
> The mountains and the hills shall break forth before you in singing;
> And all the trees of the field shall clap their hands.
> Instead of the thorn shall come up the cypress,
> And instead of brambles myrtles shall spring forth;
> And God's name will be glorified;
> This will be remembered forever.
> This will not be forgotten. Amen.

And then, with Stevens's cameras still whirring, the Hungarian girls sang "God Bless America."

18. Survival

In the prison cellar in Munich, before she was sent to Dachau, Natalie Walter had a dream. She was in an apple orchard, in late summer, and the branches were bent under the weight of their fruit. Lush grass grew on the ground, its green interspersed with clumps of wild flowers. It was a bright, cloudless day. A delicious aroma wafted into her nostrils. Investigating, she strolled through the trees until she came to a clearing, where a cow was being roasted on a spit. Three strapping young farmers were tending the fire. They offered her a flagon of cider and asked her to stay until the meat was ready.

When she woke, two women were cooking something on a stove. Seeing that she was awake, one of them turned to her and said, with great delight, "We got a cat! Wait a minute and we'll give you a piece!"

A lonely old woman now, Natalie remembers that dream—and waking from it—very often. Her survival is something of a miracle to her, but not necessarily a welcome one. The dream was better than what followed. She isn't sure how she has managed to stay alive for these past thirty years. She says she's never attempted suicide, but she is under more or less constant sedation for chronic anxiety and depression. "I would do it all again for those people," she says with unexpected ferocity. "They were good, brave, selfless people. And in the camps I had many friends, and we looked after each other and cared for each other. But today . . . the young people today, I wouldn't lift my finger for. They are rude and threaten you in the street, and all they care about is having a good time and getting drunk."

She feels the Dutch government is more interested in currying favor with the West Germans than in remembering the past; the ordeals she and thousands of others suffered are something of an embarrassment and preferably are not recalled. Meanwhile, the circle of survivors diminishes each year. Their annual gathering has become an occasion for mourning lost friends rather than for recalling the closeness that bound them together in their suffering. The handkerchief with the names of her comrades—and later of U.S. Army personnel—embroidered on it, which she had treasured as a lifeline to the past, she gave to me, on an impulse, and I accepted it with tears in my eyes. I remain uncertain whether it was given to me as a memento for the future or because it was a talisman that had lost its magic.

Today, Ernst Kroll looks like a sprightly old man, which is a paradox, for although he has a vigor that belies the appearance of his age, that appearance gives the impression of someone who could be twenty years older than Kroll in fact is. He retains his belief in the coming of a classless society. Exposing and thus helping to resolve contradictions in capitalist economies, he intones solemnly, the Third Reich speeded up the historical process that will inevitably lead to Communism. Does this conviction make it any easier for him to accept the terrible sufferings he endured for twelve years? he is asked. "I have neighbors who were wounded fighting for Hitler," he replies. "One man lost an arm and a leg and has terrible scars on his face. And all that for Hitler! Soldiers have to accept suffering. But my suffering was for victory, theirs was for defeat."

"What about people in Soviet concentration camps?" he is asked, perhaps unkindly. "What is *their* suffering for?"

A bit impishly, and with an explanatory wave of the arm around the elegant room in the Vierjahreszeiten Hotel in Munich in which he is being interviewed, he answers, "That's just bourgeois propaganda."

His eyes cloud over, however, when he is asked about his return home. "Some of the neighbors gave me a hard time," he replies tersely. "Their children even threw stones at me, said I was a criminal, a traitor." But, he adds, "the comrades" sorted things out, and the harassment stopped. And what of Katerina, the woman who was waiting for him? "She was married and had two children by the time I got back. I never saw her again. I heard the other day she's living near Frankfurt and is a grandmother."

Yaakov Kovner heard distant mumblings, vaguely familiar through the static that encrusted them: *"El moleh rochomim shochen bomromim elah slichot chonun verochum erech opoyim verov chesed."* "O Lord, who art full of compassion, who dwellest on high, God of forgiveness, who art merciful, slow to anger, and abounding in loving-kindness . . ."

Without knowing at quite what point he did so, Yaakov too began to mouth these words of the ancient prayer of mourning. There was a sudden startled cry and then a frantic jostling movement that ended when strong hands seized him under the arms and gently carried him to a stretcher. *"Boruch ato adonai elohaynu melech ho'olom shehechiyonu vekimonu vehigiyonu lazmon hozeh,"* a voice was now chanting fervently. And as if in a dream, Yaakov whispered the same words: "Blessed art thou, O Lord our God, King of the Universe, who gave us life and established us and brought us to this time!"

Later, Yaakov learned that he was the only survivor of the more than thirty-four hundred people on the train, which was found, some hours after American troops entered Dachau, about ten miles away from the camp. A prayer for the dead had saved his life; this is how he understands his rescue. After his recovery, he met and married a survivor from Mauthausen in a Displaced Persons camp near Munich. Their two children have grown up and left home. One is a teacher in the Chicago public school system; the other, a boy, is a television engineer in Philadelphia. Yaakov and his wife still operate their small dry-goods store in the Bronx. But the neighborhood has deteriorated, and the terrible experiences of their past do not shield them from fears of muggers and arsonists. Soon, they hope, they will be able to sell their store and move down to Florida.

For nearly three years, Yaakov, in defiance of custom, said the mourner's Kaddish every evening. Rabbis pointed out to him that the daily recitation of the prayer was permitted only for one year. Angrily, he turned away and told them not to talk about what they could not understand. It was only when Leah gave birth to their first child, Chavah, whose name means "life," that Yaakov abandoned the daily ritual. In accordance with custom, he now says Kaddish once a year on the date—the fourteenth of Ab, in the Hebrew calendar—which, more or less arbitrarily, he assigns as the day of the deaths of his parents, his wife, and his three children:

> Magnified and sanctified be His great Name in the world which He hath created according to His will. May He establish His kingdom during your lifetime, and during your days, and during the life of all the house of Israel, even speedily and at a near time, and say ye Amen. . . . Blessed, praised and glorified, exalted, extolled and honored, magnified and lauded be the Name of the Holy One, blessed be He; though He be high above all the blessings and hymns, praises and consolations which are uttered in the world; and say ye Amen. May there be abundant peace from heaven, and life for us and for all Israel, and say ye Amen. He who maketh peace in His high places, may He make peace for us and for all Israel, and say ye Amen.

Of the members of the International Committee, Jim Connally was the first to return home. It soon became general knowledge that the Irish sailor was in fact a Belgian Army doctor and one of the great undercover agents of the war. The British government awarded him the George Cross, the highest medal for valor it could give to a foreigner. After the war he abandoned spying and returned to his post as a military officer; he rose to the rank of major general before retiring.

George Pallavicini, the dashing Hungarian marquis, returned to Budapest and involved himself in bizarre political intrigues, which—as though the Potsdam Conference signing over Eastern Europe to the Russians had never taken place!—seem to have included efforts to restore the Hapsburg monarchy. Word reached him that the NKVD, the Russian secret police, had issued a warrant for his arrest. His mother pleaded with him to escape from Budapest. He dismissed the idea. "If I did," he argued, "the Russians would think I had something to hide." And he added, "I'm not afraid, Mother. You have a grotesque idea of the Russians. They're not monsters, and they're not bogeymen. They fought on our side, they were with me at Dachau, and they'll never do a thing to one of their fellow deportees."

Pallavicini was arrested on August 11, 1946. Early in December, his mother was allowed to visit him at the secret police prison at Conti Utca. The handsome young man looked like a skeleton; his spirit, too, was broken. "Mother," he told her, "there is only one thing I want and that is to be shot right away. Dachau was a paradise compared to what it is like here!" She never heard from him again. But in 1956 word reached her that her son had died in the Siberian concentration camp of Taishad-Lak in 1948.

Less certain is the fate of the more than three thousand Russian officers and men who were prisoners in Dachau on the day of its liberation. The Soviet government demanded their repatriation. The Russians themselves, having learned through the grapevine that Stalin regarded captured soldiers as traitors and had decreed a dire fate for them, were less than enthusiastic about the prospect of their return to Mother Russia. A demonstration was staged in which hundreds of Russian internees demanded to be allowed to remain in the West. The demonstrators got out of hand, smashed furniture, broke windows, and eventually were shipped back to the U.S.S.R., courtesy of the United States government. It is known that large numbers of them were transferred posthaste to Stalin's version of Dachau. Very many of them died cruel deaths in those concentration camps.

Among them may have been the three young boys who had adopted Pierre Martin. Martin survived, despite Igor's "great news" that he would not. By mid-June he was healthy enough to return to the small town near Marseilles where his wife, Marie, and their two sons, Claude and Jean, had continued to run their little inn, which today boasts one star in the *Guide Michelin*. Here he worries about inflation and the quality of this year's vintage. German tourists frequently stop at the inn. It is understood that Pierre will never speak to a German, and so they are served by either Marie or Claude, their younger son, who lives nearby with his own family but continues to help run the restaurant.

God, Martin says in a direct and unapologetic tone, guided and preserved him in the camp. It was God's will that he survive and return to his family, and to bear testimony to His mercy. He is asked whether it was also God's will that Dachau should have been created, and the Third Reich. "It must have been," he replies, "but it's not for us to question His wisdom." Despite his faith, Pierre regards as the most memorable moment of his life the time he opened his eyes and saw with astonishment that an American soldier was looking down at him as he lay, semicomatose, in the *Revier*. Momentarily, his fever vanished. *"Je suis libre!"* he whispered incredulously. *"Oui!"* the soldier replied tenderly. *"Vous êtes libre!"* He vanished. Pierre, to his knowledge, never saw him again. "He was an angel in khaki!" he says, still with wonder in his voice. "With a big helmet and a rifle slung over his shoulder. I think of him so often!"

From that moment, Pierre has felt free. "It's not a complicated thing, freedom," he says, hunching his shoulders and tucking in his chin in that inimitably Gallic way. "If I want to go for a walk. If I want to go to sleep or get up. If I want a cup of coffee with a croissant or a glass of wine. If I want to put on this shirt or this sweater. If I want to read a newspaper or say that our government is selling out France to the Arabs. That's freedom. And that's what I have." But he admits to bouts of depression and anxiety that seem to come over him from nowhere. And occasionally his heart feels as if it were breaking when he thinks of Igor and his two little companions.

It was something smaller that brought home to Piet Maas the fact that he was free. The hysterical mood of the day of liberation blanketed any real recognition. But the following day, it dawned on him.

When he first arrived in Natzweiler, his personal effects were taken away from him. He remembered, in particular, his wedding ring and signet ring and—his comb. The latter seemed the most immediate deprivation; it upset him to know that he would no longer be able to comb his hair. Ten minutes later, though, his head was shaved, and that put an end to this particular deprivation.

On April 30, the day after Dachau's liberation, word spread among the prisoners that the International Committee had opened the huge storage room in the *Wirtschaftsgebäude* in which the prisoners' personal effects were kept. Maas did not expect to find anything belonging to him there. After all, he had been evacuated at the very last moment from Natzweiler and shipped to Dachau in a way in which one might hesitate to transport a dead cat. Yet he went to the storage room and to his amazement discovered that his two rings were there.

He still marvels at what this reveals of the German character. "They decide to exterminate a man, having first amputated his legs without anesthesia. But they can't kill him in time because the Americans are coming. So they ship him off to Dachau in a cattle car. If the journey doesn't kill him, they figure, he'll be finished off one way or another in Dachau. But he survives and is liberated. And what does he find has followed him across Europe and through the most unimaginable horrors? His rings, with his name and number neatly printed on a tag!"

The rings gave him back his past—his family and his identity. Slipping them on his shrunken fingers was like erecting a barrier between himself and the gruesome surroundings of the camp.

But for him this was only the first, though an important, step. "The word 'free,' " he says, "is something people will never be able to understand unless they have been for a considerable time not free. For me the simple fact that I could be outside a particular place if I felt like it, that I could leave and go somewhere else, was something so incredible that it only slowly dawned on me that I was now 'free' again. Bit by bit. I had been in prison for four years. Before that, I was a pilot flying what was then the longest route in the world—from Amsterdam to Jakarta. To be confined and immobile when you have earlier been flying on such a route is an overwhelming experience. I could only allow my world to expand again a little bit at a time. Even now it sometimes strikes me spontaneously as incredible that I can go next door and visit my neighbor if I want to do that! That 'can' of freedom—and that *is* what it's all about—is too amazing if you've been without it for a long time, to take in all at once. And then you expand in other directions. The day after liberation, I began to write to my wife, and this was another fantastic thing for me. It implied that I still had a future, don't you see? Is she still there? Are the boys still alive? I'd been thinking of her, and them, a lot in the past four years, of course, but not in the sense of something real, in the sense of 'I'm going to be seeing them soon.' That kind of thought was for later on. Now it was dawning on me that this 'later on' was at hand.''

He has never discussed his experiences at Dachau in any detail except with his wife. He wants his sons to know about them now, though, and he asks that a copy of my tape-recorded interview be sent to him so that he can give it to them. It is through this medium that he will tell them about his years of agony.

In general, people are, he thinks, indifferent to freedom. ''It's so tremendous to be free that sometimes what frustrates me is all these people in the West who have been free all their lives and don't bother to think what it means to be free. To be free—it's the grandest thing on earth. Nothing is more devastating than not to be free. That you have no choices to make about anything important that affects you. And with that, in our cases, was the uncertainty. Nowadays, people commit a terrible crime, and they go to jail for four years, and that's that. For me that would be nothing, since I would know that my lack of freedom is going to come to an end in x number of years. But we didn't have that knowledge, and that was, if anything, more terrible than not having our freedom itself. It meant that the future did not exist. There's no way you can know what that's like unless you have experienced it. Compared to that hopeless assurance that your unfreedom will continue forever—compared to that, death is nothing. Hell has no fury for me anymore insofar as death is concerned. I've seen and experienced, physically and mentally, everything that it is possible for a person to do without going mad or dropping dead. Life without freedom—that's far worse than death. And people don't seem to want to know that.''

I was lighting my pipe. ''That match you've just blown out,'' Piet Maas remarked. ''To me that's a beautiful thing, fire. The Nazis put out lives with less care than you put out a match. One Christmas Day, they made us all stand in the snow and watch some people being hanged. They hanged them in such a way that their toes could just touch the ground, which prolonged the execution. We had to stand there for about fifteen minutes watching them die. You feel a murderous rage when you see something like that, though of course you can't show it. But for me, seeing something like that has taught me, not in an intellectual manner, but as a very deep and spontaneous feeling, the value and beauty of everything that lives. Whether it is a match or a human being. That is something I would never have known with such intensity if I had not been in the concentration camps. And there's another thing. If I had not lost my legs, I would have gone back to flying the day after I got home. As it was, I had to search for other things to do, develop strengths in myself so that I would not be a burden to my family, and perhaps also to excel in ways I could not have thought possible for me before so that people would never say of me, 'Poor Piet, after all he's been through, he deserves this job,' or whatever. So you see, in strange ways I've come out of all this a much richer person than I would have been." Maas has been talking fluently and rapidly. Now he falters. "Yet . . . there are so many things I saw which will haunt me for the rest of my life."

Joop Weinsma still prides himself on his military bearing, which he casts in an old-fashioned, aristocratic mold. "I dream of naked women," he says, when asked if his experiences in Dachau linger on. And it is more or less in the spirit of masculine after-dinner conversation that he tells the following anecdote of a camp in which he was imprisoned before being sent to Dachau. The food there consisted of the usual watery "soup" with a few scraps of vegetable peel floating in it. A group of prisoners, desperate with hunger, killed one of the guard dogs and roasted it in their *Block* stove. The terrible reprisal that they feared would be exacted by the SS failed to materialize. Indeed, on the following day, all the prisoners received an unusually rich and nourishing soup. The next morning at *Appell* they were addressed by the camp commandant. "Some prisoners," he declared, "murdered one of my dogs in order, as I believe, to eat it. If you have been wondering why your soup last night tasted so good, let me tell you. Following the example set by some of your comrades, I took one of *you* dogs and made him into your soup."

Only on two subjects does Weinsma betray any emotion. While other prisoners were chafing to be returned home, he managed to obtain a forged pass and, dressed in an odd assortment of GI cap and shirt, Norwegian Army pants, and Italian boots, he hitchhiked through Germany all the way back to his home near The Hague. "I could not walk very well. I knew nothing—was anyone alive, what had happened to my family, and so on. The Jeep dropped me off at the entrance to the lane. I saw the house was still standing. As I walked toward it, my old battery dog came out of the house. If the dog is still alive, I figured, some people must be living there. Our old maid came out after the dog. She hugged me and sobbed hysterically. 'Quickly,' I said, 'Tell me who all are dead.' She replied that no one was dead—oh, yes, my old grandmother had died. 'Where is the missus, my wife?' I asked. 'She's out in the back field, eating potatoes.' 'And my son?' 'He's there with her.' I saw my old bicycle leaning up against a shed, and I raced down a little path to where my wife and son were. And it was . . . a very moving experience."

Later, Weinsma helped organize a column of trucks, buses, and ambulances, and drove with it to Dachau to bring the Dutchmen there home. "They said I was mad to go back there," he reports, "but I said it was my duty."

Since that return trip to Dachau at the end of May 1945, he has not been back to Germany except to testify at the Nuremberg trials. With sudden and seemingly uncharacteristic intensity, he explains, "What I learned from the camps was above all that you must never trust a German. When I'm asked why I never go to Germany on business, I say, 'When I want to visit an undeveloped country, I prefer to go to one with a warmer climate.' "

Seventeen operations were required to repair Joachim Berenson's face. The surgeons worked with such skill that it is now almost impossible to detect any scars. From his manner, which is pleasant and friendly, one would never guess at the experiences he has passed through; he seems confident and purposeful in his work as an electrical engineer. "Just to be alive was a wonderful thing," he says of the day of liberation. "And the Americans were fantastic. What we owe them, we can never repay. And we don't even try to. Instead, we hate them and flirt with the Russians." He casts his arm over the prim, dreary Parisian suburb where he now lives, a bachelor. "Hard times are coming for Europe again, I can feel it. And no one seems to care. When there are elections, fifty percent of the people turn out to vote. The rest want to sleep late instead. And you know what? I hope that when it happens—the hard times, I mean—that for once the Americans don't come over to help us. Let the people look to Moscow for help. And let them see what kind of help Moscow gives them.''

He weeps unabashedly when he recalls his first fleeting glimpse of American soldiers in the *Jourhaus* gate. ''I can't tell you what that felt like,'' he says. And he laughs with delight, like a child with a new toy, when he describes the execution of SS guards and collaborators. ''Very few people will tell you this,'' he says, ''but the fact is that the prisoners killed scores of them, on the day of liberation and on the next two days.''

''It's a lovely day today,'' he answers when asked if he himself killed any of them.

''My face is rebuilt,'' he says, cheerily slapping his cheeks, ''but we all lost something in Dachau. I think we closed off a certain portion of our lives, and we got instead something that we did not want. We lost enthusiasm for the task of attaining what cannot be attained. . . . There is a vacuum inside us somewhere, perhaps the part which makes life worth living. Though I shouldn't say it quite like that, because I still have the feeling of wonder, simply at the fact that I am alive. But there is that vacuum. And what did we get instead? Amazement that such things are possible. You would rather live without it, but you can't lose it. It makes you rather sad. And you look at the world today, with a brute like Idi Amin, and the way they're all trying to kick Israel around, and you ask yourself: Is *this* what we fought for? Just after the liberation we thought that now everything will be OK. But there are still so many reasons to be amazed. People seem to have learned more from the Nazis than from their victims. Isn't *that* something to be amazed about?''

The VIPs at Niederdorf were rescued on May 4 by a detachment of the United States Army. Most were taken to Capri for rest and recovery—and were, in effect, held there until the Allies could make up their minds what to do with them. Hjalmar Schacht, the economist who had once been Hitler's darling, was sent back to Germany, where, despite his ardent protestations of democratic zeal, he was placed on trial with the major Nazi war criminals at Nuremberg. The real Kurt von Schuschnigg was barred from returning to his native Austria and eventually found a job teaching history at Washington University in St. Louis, Missouri. A number of the British prisoners wrote accounts of their ordeals, in almost all of which the author appears as the mastermind of plans to foil the SS plot to assassinate the entire group. Stiller—and Alvensleben—disappeared from sight.

Sturmbannführer Weiter, the last SS commandant of the camp, was hunted down by his fanatic erstwhile subordinate, Ruppert. A bullet in the back of the head was the form in which Ruppert extracted whatever outstanding payment Weiter owed him; the precise nature of Ruppert's grudge remains unclear. According to reports, Weiter's body was found clutching a portrait of his beloved Führer. Ruppert himself was one of forty men, including the physicians responsible for the infamous "medical" experiments, who were brought to trial by the United States Army for crimes committed in Dachau. The trial, which lasted from November 2 to December 14, 1945, was held in the concentration camp. Thirty-six men, Ruppert among them, were condemned to death by the court. One man was sentenced to life imprisonment, three others to ten-year terms. Three death sentences were commuted to prison terms. The remaining death sentences were carried out in May 1946, in the nearby prison of Landsberg, where, twenty-three years earlier, Adolf Hitler had been imprisoned, and where he wrote *Mein Kampf*.

Neither the Dachau trials nor historical research have produced convincing explanations of why *Wolkenbrand*—code name for the plan to murder all prisoners in Dachau before the arrival of American forces—was never carried out. It seems clear that some of the less than totally fanatic Nazis sought to save their own hides by evading the order or getting others to carry it out. But it also appears that there were men who were determined to implement the order, and that on April 29 a huge quantity of poison was sent from Munich laboratories to Dachau—possibly to poison the prisoners' midday meal. It also seems that the poison never arrived. The vehicle or vehicles carrying it may have been wiped out by Allied fire. The two batches of prisoners who were sent out of Dachau, by train and on foot respectively, as the first large-scale implementation of *Wolkenbrand* were rescued in the days after Dachau's liberation. About half the people in these convoys perished.

Two courts-martial were never held. Charges against Jackson and Smitty filed by the division commander were dropped, according to reports, because of the embarrassment that it was thought the trial would cause the Allies while they were engaged in prosecuting the major Nazi war criminals, not far to the north, in Nuremberg. Colonel Robert Wiley's charges against the general were also dropped, again according to reports, as a result of General George Patton's intervention. For obvious reasons, the prospect of court-martialing a general who had slapped a GI did not sit well with the great commander. Unit after-action reports for the day were prettied up to conceal the massacre of the surrendered SS guards and to enable each division to claim that *its* units had been the first to liberate Dachau.

Rabbi David Eichhorn returned to the United States and to a distinguished career in the Reform rabbinate; he is now living in Florida. The flags given to him during the Sunday memorial service were among his most treasured possessions, though he has recently given them to the Institute of Holocaust Studies in Brooklyn. While that Sunday service was in progress, a wagonload (the famous *Moorexpress*) of naked corpses came past the assembly on the way to the crematorium. Colonel Stevens ordered the cameras turned on the wagon and recorded this backdrop to the prayer service. Several years later, Rabbi Eichhorn was invited to the Army Pictorial Center at Astoria, New York, to view a showing of the Dachau service. The "staged" singing of "God Bless America" was included in the film, but the shots of the *Moorexpress* carrying corpses to the crematorium were deleted. "We had to take those out," the movie people explained to the rabbi. "It seemed so improbable that a viewing audience would suspect that the scene was 'staged'!"

Colonel James Frazer, now retired from the Army and living on his pension in the South, is an unabashed patriot. America, in his view, is the bastion of freedom and democracy in a world threatened by Communist totalitarianism. The liberation of Dachau epitomizes the role America plays and ought to play in the world. What Frazer saw at Dachau remains indelibly in his mind as a warning of what will happen again if America abandons its global responsibilities. In particular, Frazer is passionately committed to the survival of Israel, a haven of democracy, as he puts it, and the home of the Jewish people. He would gladly volunteer to fight for Israel, he says, if his services were needed. A tough, blunt, no-nonsense man, he seems somewhat perplexed—and hurt—that more attention is not paid to his views and, in particular, to his role as liberator of Dachau. "I suppose that people just don't want to be reminded," he says with the understanding and regret of an old soldier.

The other liberator of Dachau, Colonel Robert Wiley, reached the rank of brigadier general before retiring from the Army. Today he heads a resources planning board in a state in the Southwest. His air of competence is what one would expect from a distinguished military man. The indignation with which he still speaks of the publicity-seeking incursion of the rival division's general into his territory suggests that perhaps his heart is still rooted in the loyalties and rivalries of service life.

April 29, 1945, he says, is a day that was "pretty well etched into my memory, one of the days of the war that really stands out." Even now, tears flow out of his eyes as he recalls the sights that he saw in Dachau that day, and he ceases talking for a few moments until he has regained his composure. Of many American soldiers interviewed, he is the only one to react in this way, more than thirty years later. He also is the only one to volunteer that on that day he asked himself: "Could *I* ever treat people in this way?"

For days after, Wiley made inquiries about the condition of the prisoners at Dachau. How many were in the camp? he wanted to know. What was their condition? What steps were being taken to feed them? He asked for and received a list of the troop hospitals to which some of the sick had been transferred. He kept the company commanders informed as best he could and told them to pass on the information to their men. But in the immediate aftermath of the liberation, and since that time, he has seldom spoken about the events and sights of that day. "It was like a bad dream," he reports. "Everybody tried to erase it from their minds." He asked me to accept a large collection of snapshots taken in Dachau by some of his men. "You hold on to a bad dream despite yourself," he explained, almost apologetically. "But there comes a time when you have to let yourself let it go."

Bill Jackson now lives with his grown-up grandchildren on an impoverished, dusty reservation in the West. He has prepared a careful description of the day's events and recites it as though it were a well-rehearsed speech; he pauses from time to time to point to a simple but wildly inaccurate map of the camp that he drew the day before in anticipation of the interview. Surly and suspicious, he will allow the interview to be tape-recorded only on condition that I have no objection to his making an additional recording on his own machine. His narrative makes no mention of the massacre of the SS guards. "I hoped you wouldn't be asking me about that," he says in a crestfallen tone. "Who told you about it?" He is guarded and terse in answering questions about the slaughter. "They called killing the SS a war crime!" he declares bitterly and disbelievingly. Soon his answers and comments become almost monosyllabic. He does not volunteer any additional information but seems overcome by resentment and despair at the turn his life took thirty years ago when, for a few seconds, he apparently lost control of his men.

Brigadier General "Pop" Crashaw, although now a weak old man, has never given much thought to the role he played in liberating Dachau. "It doesn't loom particularly large in my life," he says. Taking pains not to imply disloyalty toward his former commanding officer, he nevertheless makes it clear that it was entirely irregular of the general to move into another division's zone. His own primary concern was to get to Munich. In the days after the liberation, a lot of his men went to visit Dachau, out of what Crashaw considered to be morbid curiosity, which he tried to discourage. "A year later," he recalls, "there was a reunion of prisoners and GIs, but I didn't go. I had too much paperwork to do as a liaison officer in Salzburg, and I didn't want to come back to two days' accumulation of it."

Bob Jensen and Ed Campbell never did get around to buying their own gas station. Jensen, now gray-haired and rotund, is the manager of a luxurious conference center—which just happens to give the appearance of being a hunting lodge—in South Dakota. As if abashed by his feelings of revulsion toward the emaciated inmates, he says, "I'd have liked to stay there just to see how they got those people out, and what happened to them—how they were brought back to life, if you know what I mean. But I never did find out," he adds, without real curiosity. Did he learn anything from what he saw? "I never gave any thought to that. But it was a day I'll never forget. There must be some lesson to all of that, now you mention it. I guess it would be: Don't ever let anything like that get started again. Never."

Ed Campbell remembers trying to sort out his impressions of Dachau in the days after the liberation. Dachau was an unspeakable thing, it seemed to him, and this was the reason we were in the war: to free oppressed people. He remembers a lingering feeling of frustration at wanting to do something for the inmates but not knowing what to do beyond giving them cigarettes and candy. "There was not much conversation about Dachau later on," he recalls, "so much as private thinking—why could such things happen, that kind of thing—but we'd exchange just enough words to let each other know that we were thinking along the same lines. And we didn't roughhouse as we normally did in off-hours. The next few days, the last days of the war, we shot prisoners, which we wouldn't even have thought of doing before.

"I never told my wife about what we saw in Dachau," he added. "I couldn't bring myself to describe such things to someone I love."

Epilogue:
Dachau—Visiting Hours Nine to Five

Some of them *do* look like beasts—bearing the outward form of human beings, it is true, but with eyes, mouth, forehead, posture that set them apart from our species and suggest a capacity—even eagerness—to perform deeds of unimaginable horror.

For the most part, however, the Nazi men and women who preyed on Germany, first, and then on the rest of Europe in the years from 1933 to 1945 do not at all resemble the roles they played. They seem ordinary. Or jovial. Or sensitive and introspective. We look at their photographs perplexedly—and perhaps a little disappointed that the devil has no horns and fangs.

And as these people look benign, so too do the places they haunted. These places, whose soil was not long ago drenched with the blood of millions, whose air was rent by their screams of pain and fear; these places whose names still strike terror in us and evoke a sadness almost beyond bearing—they are not at all the landscapes of evil, valleys of the shadow of death, for which the imagination of Renaissance artists and Hollywood set designers has prepared us. They look pretty much like any other ravine in Russia or forest in Poland might. Or like any other small town in the south of Germany.

In countless such small towns you might climb cobbled streets lined with picturesque little houses to an ancient inn on the top of the hill and there, on a hot day, sit on a terrace drinking a stein or two of delicious Bavarian lager and enjoying the ample view of the gentle countryside that stretches off into the distance. Nothing seems to suggest the proximity—less than half an hour's drive to the south—of

243

Munich, city of infamous beer halls, pacts, and Olympiads, but a charming and vital metropolis withal. Indeed, as you gaze over the landscape there is little to suggest the twentieth century itself other than a flock of gliders floating lazily and sensually along tides of warm air before surrendering to the enticements of Mother Earth. Distinctive, too, are somewhat indecipherable structures, and an open space that might almost be a parade ground, that lie a mile or two to the northeast. But since they are largely obscured by a dense pine forest, you are unlikely to pay attention to them.

Unless, that is, they are the reason that you have come to this little Bavarian town. Unless, that is, you are drinking the beer not only to slake a summer's thirst but to postpone, for just a few more minutes, confrontation with an awful reality.

Reality?

You leave the inn, descend the hill, and soon after crossing the Amper River find yourself driving down the Niebelungenstrasse, surely one of the least tactfully named roads in the world. It leads straight into a pleasantly wooded area, but a barrier guarded by a sentry box blocks the way and forces you to take a detour of perhaps half a mile. The parking lot is large, and crowded with automobiles and tourist buses from nearly every country in Western Europe. Here and there is a vehicle with a German license. You point out the disparity to your guide, a graduate student from the University of Munich. She disputes the impression. Empiricism wins out; a count is made. One in seven or eight vehicles is registered in the Federal Republic.

At one end of the parking lot, a prettily crafted sign beckons. You go over to read the inscription, which is in English. "Visit Dachau," it says, somewhat superfluously, since you are already there, "the 1200-years-old artists' center with its castle and surrounding park offering a splendid view over the country."

Reality?

You enter the camp, and tears well up in your eyes at the thought of the desperate pain which had been here. The brutality. The starvation. The torture. The murder.

The first building you see is a huge U-shaped structure, solidly built, well lit with large windows and with a rather charming high-pitched roof that makes it appear like an enlarged version of the quaint houses you might find in any of the neighboring villages and small towns. Once the home of kitchens, showers, barbershops, and other amenities for the prisoners, it is now the Dachau Concentration Camp Museum. You move on to see the camp itself, not a museum about it. You cross the large assembly ground in front of it—the *Appellplatz*—on the other side of which are two long gray barrack buildings that seem to be made of some kind of asbestos and concrete mixture. Your guide gives you their precise measurements, ninety meters by ten, and explains that these are not the original barracks in which the prisoners were housed, but reproductions. The two rows of seventeen barracks each were torn down some years ago, she says, for reasons that no one now seems able to ascertain. But, she adds, the two that now stand here are authentic replicas and convey an accurate impression of how the prisoners lived.

Perhaps with too surly a tone, perhaps a little self-righteously, you say that you doubt whether anything can convey an accurate impression of how they lived. And died. You walk past the sites of the other thirty-two barracks, now razed and covered with a bed of gravel. A harsh, cruel covering. Given the prettying-up all around, you feel a bit surprised that they didn't lay down lawns, instead, and plant lots of flowers on them. At the far end stand imposing monuments. Socialist-realist megaliths. Jet-age modernist contrivances. To Polish priests who were killed here. To Jews who were killed here. To . . . There is even a little convent of nuns atoning. You notice that all of these are privately funded structures. The Federal German government and the Bavarian state government have stayed away from this Disneyland of remorse and remembrance. Not so much as a small "We're sorry, folks" plaque.

You turn left, guided by a sign that says: *Krematorium Geöffnet 9:00–17:00*. Your guide's sensibilities suddenly blossom. " 'Crematorium Open.' They could have worded that differently," she remarks with indignation. You stop, fascinated by the challenge.

"Well," you say, "what might one put instead?"

"Crematorium. Visiting hours nine to five," she suggests.

"Crematorium. Open to tourists who need have no fear of incineration, nine to five," you counter.

Finally you agree that the least ambiguous seems to be: "The inoperative crematorium may be seen from nine to five."

Actually, there are two crematoria: the little one and the bigger one, which they built later. This one has meat hooks attached to the rafters from which prisoners could be hanged for the greater convenience of almost all concerned. Fantastic but true, your guide says, but if you put your head into the oven you can still smell something. Skeptically, and only out of curiosity, you do so. The smell is like very rotten cauliflower, and quite distinct. You don't even have to sniff hard to smell it. You go from oven to oven sniffing each one, with the same result. You feel ashamed of this activity, all the more so when in one oven you see an empty and wholly uncharred Marlboro pack. But it is too late. Other tourists are following your example, and soon small lines have formed of those waiting their turn to sniff an oven.

The meat hooks aren't the only signs of efficient planning. Adjoining the crematorium—the other end of the disassembly line—is the gas chamber. As you expect, it is a large, windowless, cement-lined room, walls now emblazoned with tourists' signatures. At either end, heavy steel doors painted gray are swung back against the outside to facilitate the easy flow of tourists, as once they facilitated the easy flow from life to death.

A sign in the gas chamber identifies it as such and explains that it was never used. Your guide repeats this. But you have done your research, and remember photographs of the doors before they got their new coat of gray. On them—the outer side—were once stenciled a skull and crossbones and the words *Vorsicht! Gas! Lebensgefahr! Nicht öffnen!* "Caution! Gas! Mortal Danger! Do not open!" Above, in large letters, was another inscription: *Gaszeit: Zu   Uhr; Auf   Uhr*. Chalked in the blank spaces were the times when the doors were shut—at 7:36—and when they might safely be opened, that is to say, without "mortal danger"—10 something, the minutes of the hour being obscured by the helmet of the GI looking at the inscription.

Reality?

In the anteroom to the gas chamber is a window that looks out on a pleasantly grassed area, not very large and enclosed on the opposite side by a high hedge. A tree stands here, and underneath it you see the back of a nun. Her body is bent forward from the waist, and she is quite immobile. You prepare to join your own prayer to hers.

The doors to the gas chambers, conveniently located near the crematory, are examined by an American soldier whose helmet obscures the chalked-in time when it was safe to open them.

But then she turns slightly and you realize that she has been bending over not in humble supplication to her Creator but to prevent the orange she is eating from dripping its juice on her nice clean habit.

Walking behind the crematorium and gas chamber—in the garden where the nun was—you see a large new garbage can glistening in the sun. One side of it actually rests up against the outer wall of the crematorium. On the shiny aluminum of this garbage can, a small sign is affixed. *Keine heisse Asche einfüllen,* it says. "Not for hot ashes." Your guide explains that this is a common enough inscription on garbage cans in Germany.

The hedge behind this little garden is tall and thick, but not thick enough to block out the view of a row of pleasant houses—the kind you might expect to find in any suburb—whose lawns slope right up to the other side of the hedge. On the lawn nearest you a family is entertaining guests at lunch. They're having a cookout, and while the grown-ups sit on deck chairs drinking beer and waiting for the steaks to be done, the young children are playing on a swing or splashing in one of those little inflatable plastic baths. The smell of the steak reaches you, and you suddenly realize that you are hungry.

Reality?

You retrace your steps. Without thinking about it, you know where the main building lies—the one that houses the museum—and where the barracks used to be. From there, it requires only the slightest calculation to figure out the location of the *Jourhaus,* once the main entrance to the prison compound, its gate emblazoned with the infamous inscription, *Arbeit Macht Frei.* With a start, you realize that you have already become familiar with the layout of the camp. It's not quite that you are feeling at home in Dachau, but that the place *has* so rapidly become familiar. It seems to contain no surprises; it is predictable and unmysterious. It occurs to you that the water running peacefully in the moat alongside the prison compound, with trees growing gracefully alongside it, runs like any ordinary stream. That the sun shines here as it might anywhere else, and casts shadows in just the way bright sun always does. You feel you ought to be surprised by these facts, but you cannot conjure that up. The laws of nature have not been suspended at Dachau.

You inspect the *Jourhaus* and walk quickly through the museum. You return to the car, hungry for the sandwiches you left there. You drive back to the Niebelungenstrasse and turn toward the sentry box. Policemen armed with submachine guns ask you your business. You say you're a writer working on a book about Dachau and would like to view the part of the camp that has been sealed off. The sentries ask you to park the car some ten or fifteen yards away from their post and then phone their superior. You are astonished to recognize the order about the car for what it is: a precaution in case it's packed with explosives. The policemen tell you that an officer is on his way, and you ask what lies beyond. They explain that the part of the camp sealed off from the public was formerly the living quarters of the SS officers and enlisted men who ran the camp, as well as a railroad station and a number of small factories. The area is now used as the training school of the Bavarian State Special Police. And what is the Bavarian State Special Police? you ask. Oh, they reply, riot control, antiterrorist work, dealing with subversive elements in general.

The officer arrives in a small khaki Volkswagen. A young, tanned man in civilian clothes, he is humorless but anonymous in his manner, rather than unpleasant. You explain your request again. He asks for your passport and scrutinizes it carefully. Satisfied, he invites you into the Volkswagen and drives off at breakneck speed. He promises you a tour of the other half of the camp. You pass a railroad siding and a number of derelict factory buildings. "Nothing to see here," he remarks and swings off to the left, through a heavily wooded area. Presently you reach a large quadrangle, open on one side and lined on the others by high buildings, perhaps five stories in all, and capped by a steeply pitched roof. The buildings are of a cheerful orange-red stucco and enclose a large flat lawn on which, the officer explains, the men play soccer. The structures resemble a large resort hotel, except for one small detail. Over the entrance to the center building, the largest of the three, a vast Nazi eagle, the swastika in its talons, spreads its wings. You notice that it is freshly painted black and white. You ask your escort about it. "It's concrete," he explains, "and it would be a big job to remove it."

"Really?" you ask.

"Yes," he replies, "though I must agree it's a bit embarrassing."

Not so embarrassing that he refrains, a few moments later, from driving you past a heavy concrete arch raised gratuitously over a side road. It too has a large Nazi eagle, swastika and all, above the keystone. It too is freshly painted.

Soon after, you are driving down a road through an area it would be easy to mistake for an exclusive suburb. Fine old trees provide shade from the burning sun, but without subduing the fresh, glistening paint of a succession of spacious and elegant villas. Here, you are told, the senior SS officers lived with their families. That house over there belonged to the camp commandant. The Bavarian State Special Police officer hastens to assure you (although you haven't asked) that the houses are unoccupied now. But more than one of them has a car parked in the driveway, and the area looks so well maintained that you simply do not believe him. You debate with yourself whether there is any point in challenging him on this score. But before you can resolve the matter, you are back at the sentry box. The whole tour has lasted about five minutes. Without waiting to be thanked, the officer drives away as quickly as he came.

You feel you cannot just leave the place. You try chatting with the two young policemen on duty. They are not unfriendly, but evidently conversation is not in their line. And they seem suspicious. Or perhaps it is you who are. You ask them what their feelings are about living and working in this particular place. You are surprised by the readiness of their replies.

"Terrible things happened here," one of the men says, "but what can I do about it?"

The other nods, and in a Bavarian accent so thick that your guide must translate it for you, he adds, "All that was nothing to do with me. It's something the previous generation did, not I."

Glossary of German Terms

Appell: Roll call.
Appellplatz: Assembly ground.
Block: Barrack building in the prison compound.
Blockführer: SS rank, section leader.
Bock: Stocks.
Hauptmann: German Army rank, equivalent to U.S. Army captain.
Hauptsturmführer: SS rank, equivalent to U.S. Army captain.
Jourhaus: Guardhouse controlling entry into prison compound.
Kapo: Trusty prisoner.
Kommando: Prisoner work squad.
Lager: Prison compound within the concentration camp.
Lagerführer: Officer in charge of the prison compound.
Lagerstrasse ("Camp Street"): name of street running down the center of the *Lager.*
Moorexpress: Hand-drawn horse cart on which corpses were carried to the crematorium.
Nacht und Nebel ("Night and Fog"): Nazi decree ordering the deportation of political prisoners to concentration camps without notification to their next of kin. The prisoners would disappear into the "night and fog."
Oberscharführer: SS rank, equivalent to Army sergeant.
Obersturmbannführer: SS rank, equivalent to Army lieutenant colonel.
Obersturmführer: SS rank, equivalent to Army lieutenant.
Pfahl: Stake.

251

Plantage: Commercial plant and herb nursery tended by prisoners.

Reichsführer-SS: Head of the SS, a position held only by Heinrich Himmler.

Revier: Hospital barrack within the *Lager.*

Scharführer: SS rank equivalent to Army corporal.

Sturmbannführer: SS rank, equivalent to Army major.

Unterscharführer: SS rank, equivalent to Army lance-corporal.

Volksturm: Underequipped German troops consisting mostly of young boys and old men mobilized at the end of the war.

Wirtschaftsgebäude: Large building on southern side of *Appellplatz* containing cookhouses, showers, storage rooms for prisoners' personal effects, and so on.

Selected Bibliography

Berben, Paul. *Dachau 1933–45*. London: Comité International de Dachau, 1975.

Best, Sigismund P. *The Venlo Incident*. London and New York: Hutchinson, 1951.

Brome, Vincent. *The Way Back*. London: Cassell, 1957.

Cahnman, Werner. "In the Dachau Concentration Camp." *Chicago Jewish Forum*, Fall, 1964.

Churchill, Peter. *The Spirit in the Cage*. London: Hodder and Stoughton, 1954.

Dachau Concentration Camp and Town. PWB Section, CIC Section, Seventh Army, 1945.

Gun, Nerin E. *The Day of the Americans*. New York: Fleet, 1966.

Smith, Marcus J. *The Harrowing of Hell*. Albuquerque, N.M.: New Mexico University Press, 1972.

Steinbock, Johann. *Das Ende von Dachau*. Vienna: Oesterreichischer Kulturverlag, 1948.

Trial of German Major War Criminals, Proceedings of the International Military Tribunal, 42 volumes. London: His Majesty's Stationery Office, 1946.